DOS: A SHORT COURSE

FOR MS-DOS VERSIONS 5.0, 6.0/6.2
IBM PC-DOS VERSION 6.1

L. JOYCE ARNTSON

Irvine Valley College

BARBARA F. STOCKLER

Coastline College

Wadsworth Publishing Company
Belmont, California
A Division of Wadsworth, Inc.

Publisher: Kathy Shields
Assistant Editor: Tamara Huggins
Production Editor: Karen Garrison
Print Buyer: Barbara Britton
Managing Designer: Andrew Ogus
Cover Design: Craig Hanson
Printer: Malloy Lithographing

 This book is printed on acid-free recycled paper.

I(T)P

International Thompson Publishing
The trademark ITP is used under license.

Printed in the United States of America

1 2 3 4 5 6 7 8 9 10—99 98 97 96 95

Library of Congress Cataloging in Publication Data

Arntson, L. Joyce.
DOS: a short course for MS-DOS versions 5.0, 6.0/6.2; and IBM PC-DOS version 6.1 / L. Joyce Arntson, Barbara F. Stockler.
    p.   cm.
    Includes index.
    ISBN 0-534-23406-2 (alk. paper)
    1. MS-DOS (Computer file) I. Stockler, Barbara F. II. Title.
QA76.76.063A762 1994
005.4'469—dc20   94-6673

Preface

MS-DOS Versions 5.0, 6.0/6.2 and IBM PC-DOS Version 6.1: A Short Course has been written for the computer novice as well as the computer application wizard who has never taken the time to learn the Disk Operating System (DOS). Although this text assumes no prior computer experience or DOS knowledge and is directed to the novice, it can be used successfully by any individual who would like to brush up on his or her DOS skills. It is designed to help you learn the basics of DOS using versions 5.0, 6.0, 6.1, and 6.2 quickly and easily. Even though it was written specifically for versions 5.0, 6.0, 6.1, and 6.2, you will find the commands and operations to be largely compatible with all earlier versions. This book covers the important commands and operations of DOS to be covered in an introductory or short DOS course.

Learning DOS will prove to be invaluable as you work with software. Having DOS as your assistant can help you avoid traps and correct mistakes as you make them. Knowing DOS is a valuable tool as you work with the computer. It will provide the ability to perform numerous tasks from installing software and configuring the computer to disk and file management.

Because most computer users today have computers with hard disks, this text has been written with hard disk management in mind. Working with subdirectories and the DOS-based utilities will prove very useful in managing the hard disk.

Organization of the Text

This book is divided into ten chapters. Each chapter is written to facilitate learning with a read and do approach. The chapters begin with a list of objectives to prepare you for what is to be covered. For each new concept covered, you will find a reading assignment to explain the command or operation. Because nothing substitutes for hands-on practical application, each concept will be practiced after reading about it. All exercises are performance-based and have been written based on common usage by computer users in business and industry. To reinforce the lessons and so that you will be able to determine the abilities you will have mastered at their completion, each chapter ends with a Self-Check Quiz for reviewing the chapter and testing your understanding of the material. Having a perfect score is not as important as finding out what you do not understand about the concepts and operations. Always check your answers with those of your instructor and be sure to ask questions if you do not understand the answers.

You will find an assignment for each chapter which will challenge you to apply your new knowledge. These are designed to demonstrate how you can put DOS to work solving real-life practical problems.

We believe you will find DOS commands and operations worth the effort. With this knowledge you can take command of your computer and make it do your bidding. Be quick to ask questions so that you can gain a complete understanding of the concepts you are studying.

This book has been written for a short course in DOS. If you need more complete information, we suggest you consult the book <u>MS/PC-DOS:</u> <u>Concepts, Exercises, and Applications</u> written by the same authors.

Much apprciation goes to Trudy Gift of Hagerstown Jr. College and Floyd Winters, Manatee Community College. A great deal of the accuracy for this text may be attributed to the skills of the technical editor, Maria Tate, who tested all exercises and assignments many times.

Best wishes for success in learning and using DOS!

L. Joyce Arntson and Barbara F. Stockler

Contents

Chapter 1.   An Introduction to the Microcomputer System

Objectives 1
Using this Textbook...1
The Disk Operating System..2
The Computer System 2
Software 11
Working with DOS 12
Self-Check Quiz 19
Assignment 20

Chapter 2.   Basic DOS Commands

Objectives 21
Things to Remember When Using DOS 21
DOS Commands—Internal vs External 23
Clearing the Screen...24
Print Using Print Screen 24
Filenames and Extensions 25
Program Extensions and Device Names......................................26
The DIRECTORY 27
Wildcards...32
The Version (VER) Command 34
Asking for Help 35
Self-Check Quiz 36
Assignment 37

Chapter 3.   Disk and File Preparation

Objectives 38
Floppy Diskettes..38
More on Internal versus External Commands 40
Setting the Search Path to the DOS Command Files...............40
Aborting DOS Commands..41
Preparing Disks for Use...42
The Volume (VOL) Command 50
Specifying Disk Drives in Commands 50
Changing Default Drives 51
Using DOSKEY 52
Working with Text Files 53
Printing Files...57
Self-Check Quiz 59
Assignment 60

Chapter 4. File-Handling Commands

Objectives 62
Structure for File-Handling Commands 62
Copying Files 63
Comparing Files 74
Renaming Files with RENAME 76
DOS MOVE Command 78
DOS Editing Keys 79
Self-Check Quiz 82
Assignment 84

Chapter 5. Managing Files and Disks

Objectives 86
Deleting Files 86
The UNDELETE Command 87
Using MIRROR with DOS 5.0 to Undelete Files 89
UNDELETE using MS DOS 6.0/6.2 91
UNDELETE using IBM PC-DOS 6.1 93
UNFORMATTING Diskettes 95
Copying Disks 96
The DISKCOPY Command 96
Comparing Disks using the DISKCOMP Command 99
COPY *.* Compared to DISKCOPY 101
Checking a Disk with CHKDSK 103
SCANDISK (DOS 6.2) 105
The DEFRAG Command in PC-DOS 6.1 and MS-DOS 6.2 106
Self-Check Quiz 107
Assignment 109

Chapter 6. Creating and Using Subdirectories

Objectives 111
Introduction to Subdirectories 111
Creating a Subdirectory Structure 113
Specifying the PATH to a Directory 114
Changing the Current (Default) Directory 116
Printing Directory Listings 122
Searching for Files in a Tree Structure 122
Self-Check Quiz 124
Assignment 126

Chapter 7.   Working with a Tree Structure

Objectives 127
Directory and File Management 127
Adding Subdirectories to Create a Third Level...129
Using the CD Command with Another Drive 130
Using Subdirectory Markers..131
Removing a Directory 132
Using the TREE Command to Display the Tree Structure.........................134
DOS 6.0 DELTREE Command 135
Renaming Directories...136
Using the XCOPY Command...137
Self-Check Quiz 140
Assignment 142

Chapter 8.   An Introduction to EDLIN, the DOS Text Editor

Objectives 144
DOS Editing Techniques 144
Uses for EDLIN..145
Creating a Text File with EDLIN 145
Editing a Text File with EDLIN 150
The DOS Editing Keys for Editing in EDLIN 156
Self-Check Quiz 161
Assignment 163

Chapter 9.   An Introduction to EDIT, The DOS Text Editor

Objectives 165
The DOS Editor 165
Installing the Mouse 166
Using EDIT..166
Using the Mouse 167
Selecting, Copying, Cutting, and Pasting Text...171
Printing a File 175
Using the Search Menu..175
Using HELP...177
Self-Check Quiz 178
Assignment 179

Chapter 10. An Introduction to BATCH Files

Objectives 181
Creating Simple Batch Files 181
Batch File Commands: REM, Pause, and ECHO...185
The AUTOEXEC.BAT File...188
CONFIG.SYS 190
Custom Menus 191
Self-Check Quiz 195
Assignment 196

Index 198

CHAPTER **1**

AN INTRODUCTION TO THE MICROCOMPUTER SYSTEM

OBJECTIVES

When you have completed the activities and assignment in this chapter, you will be able to:

1. Explain basic concepts of microcomputer operation.

2. List and discuss the hardware components of a personal computer system.

3. Identify the parts of a floppy diskette and use the correct procedures for handling and storing floppy diskettes.

4. Describe features of the microcomputer system you will be using to learn DOS.

5. Load DOS starting with the computer off and on.

6. Recognize the DOS prompt.

7. Check and set the date and time in the computer's clock.

8. Set the prompt to display the current directory.

USING THIS TEXTBOOK

This textbook will be your guide and workbook for learning about DOS. To become thoroughly familiar with the operating system, we suggest you read the concepts in each chapter, complete the practice activities on the computer, and complete the quiz and assignment at the end of each chapter.

In this textbook, [Enter] denotes pressing the key marked Enter. (Do not key the [ ] or the word Enter.) Where commands to be keyed are shown, the letters in boldface indicate what should be keyed. You will see a bullet (■) preceding any required input. In the following example, you would key the letters DATE and then press the key marked Enter.

■ C>**DATE**   [Enter]

DOS commands are shown in uppercase letters throughout this text. However, you can key them in upper- or lowercase on the computer.

THE DISK OPERATING SYSTEM

DOS is an acronym for Disk Operating System, a program designed to manage the flow of information, programs, and resources of IBM and IBM-compatible computers.

This system was developed by Microsoft Corporation as MS-DOS. It was later sold to IBM to market under their name of PC-DOS. There is very little difference between the two. Your capabilities in MS-DOS will translate to PC-DOS. There have been many previous versions of DOS with each version offering more capabilities than the previous ones. Although this book focuses on DOS versions 5.0, 6.0, 6.1, and 6.2, the main commands and operations are compatible with earlier versions. For example, a command, DIR (for directory to show a list of the files on the disk), will work the same with identical results beginning with DOS version 1.0 and going through 6.2. Some commands in DOS 5.0, 6.0, 6.1, and 6.2 are not available in earlier versions; however, it is important to know about the newer functions even if your DOS version does not include them.

DOS is the software tool that enables you to control the personal computer hardware, to manipulate data in the computer's memory and in disk files, and to utilize other software programs. The disk operating system software manages the flow of information within the microcomputer. With instructions from you, DOS directs disk drive operations, the use of memory, and the central processing unit (CPU), as well as the flow of information to and from devices such as the keyboard, monitor, and printer.

> **Note:** Technology with DOS-based computers continues to evolve. There are both MS-DOS and IBM PC-DOS, both of which have several recent versions. Most MS-DOS and IBM PC-DOS commands and operations are interchangeable. While this textbook focuses on MS-DOS versions 5.0, 6.0, and 6.2 and IBM PC-DOS version 6.1, most commands and operations are compatible with earlier versions.

THE COMPUTER SYSTEM

To begin working with DOS, you will need to know the basics about the components of the microcomputer. A microcomputer is a device that can process and manipulate numbers very quickly. By representing characters and graphic elements as numbers, a microcomputer can also process text and

graphics. As a user, you do not need to understand the technical details of
how a computer operates; however, understanding some of the basics will make
learning to use the computer easier. The components of the microcomputer are
the system unit, the keyboard or mouse, the monitor, the disk drives, and the
printer. As represented in Figure 1-1:

1. The **system unit** houses the computer's main electronic elements. These
   elements include a **system board** or **motherboard** on which are found the
   microprocessor (also called CPU or Central Processing Unit), **memory**,
   and **math co-processor chip**. Also, **adapter cards** which connect the other
   devices such as the monitor and printer are in the system unit. These
   adapter cards are inserted into the **expansion slots** located on the system
   board.

   The system unit also houses the power supply that powers the computer as
   well as a small speaker unit which is responsible for the beep you may hear
   when you make an error.

   On the back of the system unit are **ports** and **connectors** into which
   printers, monitors, the keyboard, and other peripheral devices may be
   plugged. It will be important to learn to recognize the connection points in
   order to connect and disconnect computer components.

2. Input devices such as the keyboard, mouse, and pen allow you to
   communicate with the computer. The **keyboard** is the most commonly
   used device. You might also use a **mouse** as an input device. Pens are
   now available with 386 or higher computers.

3. The **monitor** or screen allows the computer to communicate with you by
   displaying the program screens, keyboard or mouse input, and the results of
   your computer operations.

4. The **disk drives** located in the system unit house the hard or floppy
   diskettes that permanently store programs and data files on fixed or
   removable disks. The drives are connected to the power supply and, by
   ribbon cables, to the **disk drive controller card(s)**. These controller cards
   fit into expansion slots on the motherboard and manage the transfer of data
   to and from the disk drives.

5. A **printer** allows you to make paper copies of your work.

These five components of any basic microcomputer system are found in a
variety of configurations. Other optional components or peripherals, such as
scanners, tape drives, and modems for telephone communications, are often
added to the basic system. It is important for you to examine the special
features of the system that you are using.

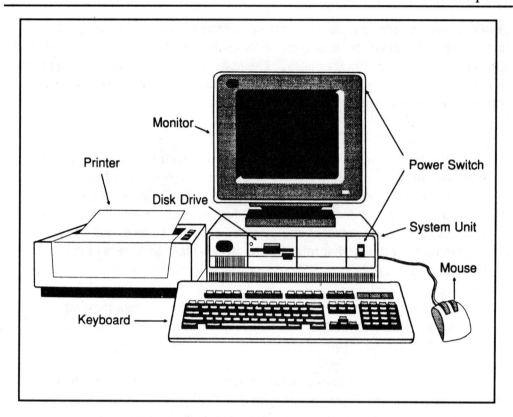

Figure 1-1. Components of a microcomputer system.

The System Unit

In each system unit, there is a **system board** or **motherboard**, which houses among other things the **microprocessor** chip, often thought of as the "brain" of the computer. It is the device that performs the calculations. It takes information in, manipulates it, and sends it out in a modified form. This in-and-out flow is called input and output. Intel Corporation manufactures the microprocessor chips. The first microprocessor chip used in the IBM personal computer was called the 8088 chip. It was replaced in the IBM PC-AT models by the 80286 chip. Today's computers use the 80386 and 80486. In a very short time the newest chip, the Pentium chip, will be commonly used.

On the system board or on special adapter cards are placed memory chips for processing and storing information. Part of the computer's memory is set aside as a keyboard "buffer" to remember the keys you have pressed. When you press a key, a numeric code defining that key is placed in memory in the keyboard buffer.

Memory Chips On the system board there are two kinds of memory chips. The system contains memory chips that have information permanently recorded on them. This information controls the computer's internal operations and its basic input/output system. This memory is called **read only memory**, or

ROM. ROM is used to store instructions that do not change and that the system requires for operation. You do not have access to read only memory.

The second kind of memory chips are called **random access memory** or **RAM**. You have access to RAM and will change its contents as you load application software programs and key data. Random access memory can be thought of as an electronic work space where you can place instructions and data for manipulations by the computer. For example, in this work space you can temporarily store the instructions of a word processing program and the document files you create with the program.

Pressing the Return or [Enter] key completes the input and sends the numeric character codes in the keyboard buffer to the microprocessor for action. This is **input** to the microprocessor. The microprocessor may then produce **output** that will be displayed on the screen and be stored in memory until further instructions tell the microprocessor what to do next.

The Keyboard

The keyboard is the primary means for communicating with the computer. Keyboards are manufactured by many companies, and although there are standard features, there are also differences. Most keyboards used in the United States have the alphanumeric keys (letters and numbers) arranged in a typewriter layout. To this basic keypad are added several special keys that you must learn to use to communicate effectively with your computer. See Figure 1-2.

Two of the special keys are the Control key and the Alternate key. The Control key is usually labeled CTRL or Ctrl. The Alternate key is labeled ALT or Alt. These two keys give different meanings to keys that are pressed simultaneously with either or both of them. In this way, the Ctrl and Alt keys give additional functions to the other keys.

When you press the Ctrl key, you are telling the computer that the next key or keys pressed will be sending control codes that should not be interpreted as characters. The Ctrl key functions this way in application software and in DOS. Some keyboards have several keys labeled with two names indicating that they have two functions, one activated when pressed alone and the other function activated when used with the Ctrl key.

The keyboard also has a numeric keypad, and it may have a separate group of cursor control keys and other data entry keys. The Number Lock (Num Lock) key switches the numeric keypad from numeric keys to "arrow" or cursor control keys. In the numeric mode, these keys are used for entering numbers. In the cursor control mode, the keys marked with arrows are used to move the

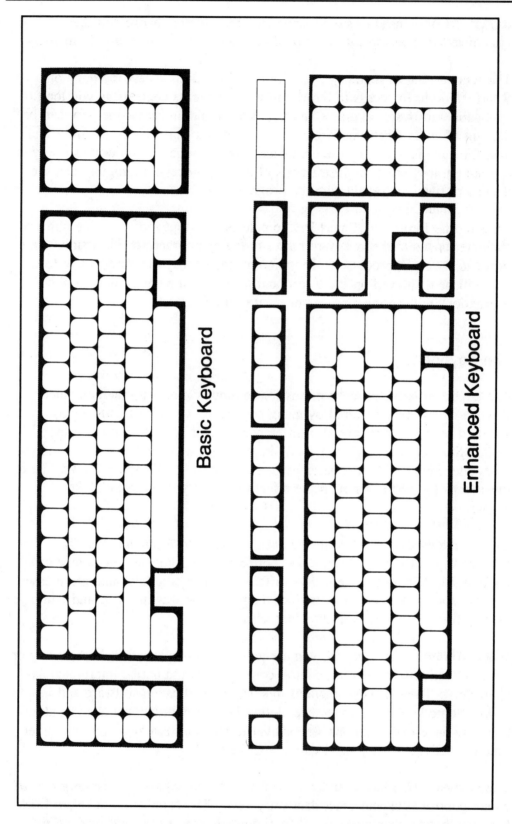

Figure 1-2. Keyboard layouts. Label the diagram that is most like your keyboard. Modify the drawing as necessary.

cursor, the blinking underscore or block on the screen that tells you where the next character you key will appear.

The keys on the computer keyboard are "typematic." That is, they will repeat when you hold them down. A quick tap is all that is necessary. The keys marked Home, Page Up (PgUp), Page Down (PgDn), and End are used by application software programs.

Two other special keys on the computer keyboard that are used in DOS are the Insert (Ins) and Delete (Del) keys. As you might suspect, these keys allow you to insert characters in an existing line or to delete characters from a line.

Perhaps the most unique keys on the computer keyboard are the function keys (F1, F2, etc.). This group of ten to twelve keys may be arranged in two vertical rows on the left side of the keyboard or in a single row across the top of the keyboard. The function keys work differently depending on the software being used. You should always check the software manuals to learn how the function keys are used by a particular program.

Take the time now to examine your keyboard setup and to identify the location of function keys and other important keys such as Ctrl and Alt.

The Monitor

The monitor is the primary device that the computer uses to communicate with you. It is also called the display, cathode ray tube (CRT) screen, or terminal. You will hear monitors described as CGA, MCGA, VGA, and Super VGA. This list represents an increasingly high quality of monitors based on the number of picture elements (pixels). Monitor technology continually brings bigger and better monitors to the marketplace. The sharpness and resolution of both monochrome and color monitors is constantly improving.

Disk Drives

Disk drives provide a means for storing and accessing information on magnetic disks. Understanding some technical details of how disk drives operate is essential for effectively using a microcomputer.

Disk drives are described first by the type of disks they house: floppy or hard. Floppy disks are made of Mylar coated with a metallic oxide. The diskette is flexible and rotates inside a protective jacket. The jacket for 5 1/4-inch disks is a strong, lightweight plastic. The 3 1/2-inch disk is enclosed in a thicker, more rigid plastic jacket. Hard drives contain rigid metal disks. Examples of common drive configurations are shown in Figure 1-3. On most computers, the upper or left floppy disk drive is called drive A; the lower or right disk drive is called drive B. When floppy diskette drives are in use, depending on the type of drive, the drive door must be closed, the latch must be engaged, or the diskette must be inserted so that it is lodged.

If your system has a hard disk drive, it is called drive C. Most systems come equipped with hard disks which commonly range in size from 10 megabytes (MB) up to several gigabytes (GB). The front plate of the hard drive does not have an opening like a floppy drive, as the disk is permanently sealed in its compartment behind the plate. If a second hard disk drive exists, it is usually called drive D. A very large hard drive may be divided into several "logical" drives named drive C, D, E, F, and so on.

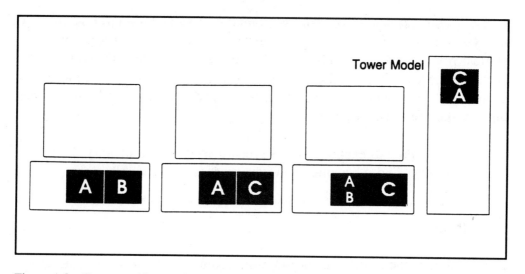

Figure 1-3. Common drive configurations. A and B are floppy drives; C is a hard drive. Tower models are available in many configurations.

The primary operational differences between floppy and hard disks are their storage capacity and speed. The 5 1/4-inch floppy disks in common use store 360 kilobytes (360K), or 1.2 megabytes (1.2MB), of data. The 3 1/2-inch floppy disks store 720K, or 1.44MB, of data. The 1.2MB and 1.44MB disks are called high-density (HD) disks and must be used in high-density drives designed to read and write information on them. The low-density 360K and 720K disks can also be used in high-density drives. Hard disks typically store 100MB or more, making it possible to store on hard disks large application programs and data that would not fit onto a floppy diskette.

An advantage of the hard disk is speed. Hard disk drives spin continuously when the computer is turned on. With internally installed fixed disk drives the disk is turning whenever the computer is on. Floppy drives rotate the diskette only when information is being written to it or read from it. Each time the computer accesses a floppy disk to read or write data, the drive's rotating mechanism must start and come up to operating speed. The hard drive is normally at operating speed.

Networked computers use other drives as well; in fact, drives named with all 26 letters of the alphabet may be used. The network drive names usually start with the letters immediately following the DOS drive names. For example, if DOS uses drives A–E, the network drives will begin with F. Your instructor will tell you about any special drive configurations in the system you are using.

Permanent Data Storage

Many people confuse computer memory and disk storage. It is important to differentiate between the two. Because you will use a computer for work that requires permanent records, the data stored temporarily in the RAM chips must be transferred to some form of permanent storage before the computer is turned off. Disks and tapes coated with a magnetic surface are used for permanent storage of the computer-generated programs and data.

Disks and tapes provide reliable, permanent storage for data, but not in a form that you can read. Printers are output devices that produce readable copies of computer program output. The microprocessor sends information to the printer in a form that can be translated into characters on paper.

Disk Maintenance

Care of your disks is very important. The most important practice to follow with both hard disks and floppy diskettes is to back up or copy data regularly in the event of a mishap. Then when the "impossible" happens, you will be able to restore your files. Examples of backup medium are other floppy diskettes, a tape drive, and another hard drive.

Hard drives require little maintenance. Some systems require manually parking the hard disk. Some disk drives are self-parking. Parking the hard disk ensures that the read/write heads do not cause data damage. Software is available for this task. Parking the hard drive heads is especially important before moving or shipping the computer. Your instructor will tell you whether or not parking is needed for the school computers.

One last type of hard disk maintenance may be necessary when the performance is slow when accessing files or displaying lists of files. This slow performance occurs when files become scattered over the disk surface as they are written, revised, and rewritten in new locations, creating "fragmented" files. You will learn later in this book some ways to remedy this situation with DOS; there are also other utilities which can work with file fragmentation.

There are some important maintenance tips to follow with floppy diskettes also. Observe the following precautions when handling your diskettes:

- DO NOT touch the exposed magnetic surfaces.

- DO NOT expose disks to excessive heat.

- DO NOT spill liquids or food on them.

- DO NOT expose disks to cigarette smoke, ashes, or dust.

- DO NOT bend disks or stack books or other items on them.

- DO NOT expose disks to magnetism.

Short-Term Data Storage: Memory

Computer memory is measured in **bytes**. A byte is eight **bits** of information. Each bit is actually an electronic switch that can be off or on. These two states are presented by the digits 0 and 1. Computers manipulate data using only these two digits in a "binary" numbering system. Using only 0's and 1's, eight bits can be arranged in 256 different orders to make up 256 different numbers, 0 to 255, representing each alpha character (upper- and lowercase), number, special character, and control code, such as a backspace or tab.

A standardized number coding system called **ASCII** (American Standard Code for Information Interchange) is used in most personal computers to provide a common computer language. The important thing to remember is that one byte represents one ASCII character; therefore, the computer's available memory and disk space measured in bytes can be an indication of how many characters are stored.

With the byte as the basic unit of measurement, computer memory and disk storage are expressed in **kilobytes** (K or KB), **megabytes** (MB), and also **gigabytes** (GB). In the binary numbering system, a kilobyte is 1,024 bytes, or 2^{10}. When we speak of a personal computer as having 640K of memory, we mean that its memory capacity is approximately 640,000 bytes. The actual memory size of a 640K computer is 640 x 1,024, or 655,360 bytes. A megabyte is 1,000 x 1,024, or over 1 million bytes. A gigabyte is 1,000,000 x 1,024, or over 1 billion bytes.

Memory capacity is the size of the computer's electronic work space. The memory size of most personal computers without memory expansion chips on the system board or special adapter boards is 640K or 1MB. However, many personal computers sold today are equipped with additional memory, perhaps 2, 4, 8, or 16MB. With special adapter boards to serve as memory expansion boards, personal computers can contain up to 64 or more megabytes of usable memory. Early versions of DOS are able to manage 640K of memory. In order to utilize additional memory, DOS requires the assistance of special memory-managing utilities such as those provided with DOS 4.0 and later; memory expansion boards; and software such as Microsoft Windows 3.1. The 80386 and 80486 microprocessors could manage 4GB of memory if the computer could hold the chips.

You will hear memory described as conventional, traditional, low, high, upper, expanded, and extended. As computer software continues to grow in sophistication, the need for additional memory increases. You need to understand memory and storage limitations when investigating software packages.

Printers

The printer produces a "hard copy" of your work on paper. Computer printers are varied in design, function, and cost; however, they can be divided into two basic types: impact and non-impact. Impact printers produce an image by striking the paper through a ribbon. They include daisy wheel and dot matrix printers. Non-impact printers include inkjet printers, plotters, and laser printers.

Printers can also be divided into two groups depending on the way they communicate with the computer. Some printers are connected to a parallel port and use parallel data transmission. Others are connected to a serial port and use serial data transmission.

Examine the printer you will be using. Is it impact or non-impact? Is it serial or parallel? Does the printer serve one or more computers? Look for the following switches or buttons:

On-line: Press this to put the printer on-line for printing or to take it off-line.
Line-feed: Press this to advance the paper one line. (It may be necessary to take the printer off-line to operate this feature.)
Form-feed: Press this to advance the paper one page or to the next form. (Again, it may be necessary to take the printer off-line to operate this feature.)

SOFTWARE

Software is loadable into a computer because of DOS. DOS takes care of the disk and file management tasks. Learning about software is as important as learning about hardware. Software like DOS or a word processing application program can be thought of as instructions used to control the computer's work.

WORKING WITH DOS

Now that you are familiar with the system components, let's jump right into working with the disk operating system (DOS). The startup procedure for MS/PC-DOS computers involves a sequence of steps. The process of turning on the computer or resetting it is called "booting" or "powering up." There are instructions stored in a ROM chip for doing this. When the power is turned on, the system follows these instructions to perform a check of the computer memory chips and other hardware.

Loading DOS

The first step in using the computer is to load or **boot** DOS. We will presume that you have used the normal procedure to install DOS. Therefore, your DOS files are probably in a subdirectory named DOS on the hard disk, drive C. If you have any other configuration, change the commands to adjust for the difference.

You will use two different methods for loading DOS or booting the system: one when the computer is off, and the other when it is on. If the computer is off, you will be starting it from a "cold" condition; therefore, this startup procedure is called a **cold boot**. If the computer is already on, the procedure used for booting or powering up is called a **warm boot**. Try both of these procedures now. First, read all the instructions for the *hardware configuration you will be using*. Then perform each step as you read through the instructions a second time.

Practice: Booting the System

Cold Boot—from Hard Disk

■ Make sure that drive A is empty or that the drive door is open. Turn on:

   a. *The printer*, if one is available.

   b. *The monitor screen.* Some monitors have an ON/OFF switch; some are automatically turned on when the computer is powered up.

   c. *The system unit.* The power switch is usually on the right side near the back, at the far right on the front panel, or near the top of the tower front panel.

Soon you will see a blinking dash (the cursor) near the top left corner of the screen. Wait while the system performs a check of memory and other internal components and loads the necessary files.

Warm Boot—from Hard or Floppy Disk

Now that you have loaded DOS starting with the computer off or cold, you can practice booting DOS with the computer already on. This is called a warm boot or "resetting" the computer. Warm booting is faster and less demanding on the hardware, so you should use this procedure whenever possible.

To boot from the hard disk system, the door of drive A must be open or the drive empty.

■ Three keys are necessary to perform the warm boot. Hold down the Ctrl and Alt keys, then lightly tap the Del key.

Note: Some computers have a **Reset button** on the front of the system unit that can be used like Ctrl-Alt-Del to warm boot the computer when it is on. The Ctrl-Alt-Del method is available on all computers.

The DOS Prompt

After you have booted the computer, there are a variety of possibilities which you may see on the screen. For example, you might see a menu of choices which someone has set up for you. One of these choices might be DOS. If there is a menu from which you can choose DOS, do so now according to the menu instructions.

Or you might see at the bottom of the menu the DOS prompt, which may look like one of the following:

```
C>            C:\>      or        C:\DOS>
```

There may be no menu, but you will see one of the above prompts. Or you may see a message that says something like the following:

```
Current date is Fri 07-02-1994
Enter new date: (mm-dd-yy)
```

This is asking you to accept or change the date. You would then press [Enter]. The system will then display something like the following:

```
Current time is 8:06:59.01a
Enter new time:
```

This is asking you to accept or change the time. You would then press [Enter]. You may then see displayed one of the following:

```
C>              C:\>       or          C:\DOS>
```

The main idea is to get to what is called the DOS prompt, which may look like one of the drive C prompts above. It may be that you are working from a floppy diskette, and you would instead see:

```
A>                         or          A:\>
```

If your computer has a different display than those described above, ask for directions from your instructor on how to access the DOS prompt so that you can begin work!

DOS Commands

The instructions you give DOS are **commands** that the software can interpret and carry out. There are two types of DOS commands called **internal** and **external** commands. The internal commands are instructions contained in one large command file named COMMAND.COM. These instructions are **loaded** or read into the computer's RAM when you boot, or power up the computer. The internal instructions or commands stay in the computer's memory and are available for use until you turn off the power to the computer. If you are using DOS files on a floppy disk, you can remove the DOS disk and still work with the internal commands.

External commands, on the other hand, are smaller DOS files stored in the DOS directory. These commands are loaded each time they are needed for a specific task.

Displaying or Changing the Date and Time

Both the DATE and TIME commands are internal commands. When the computer is booted and DOS is loaded, the screen displays the date from memory. If the current date does not display, you will probably see:

```
Current date is Tues 01-01-80
Enter new date (mm-dd-yy):
```

Each time you boot a computer that does not have an internal battery-powered clock, it displays an incorrect date, January 1, 1980. If the system has an internal clock, you may not need to reset the date and time.

Keying the correct date and time to set the system clock is a good practice, as DOS records the date and time when you create or revise your data files. If the correct information is recorded, it helps you determine when the files were created and which version is the most recent.

To enter a new date on the line that reads "Enter new date (mm-dd-yy)," key:

A number from 1 to 12 representing the month, followed by a hyphen (-), a slash (/), or a period (.).

A number from 1 to 31 representing the day of the month, (-), (/), or (.).

The two digits representing the year. Press [Enter].

For example, 9-17-94 represents September 17, 1994.

When you have correctly entered the date, the current time in the computer's memory is displayed on your screen. The time display will be similar to the following:

```
Current time is 0:02:54.97
Enter new time:
```

The time is shown in hours, minutes, seconds, and hundredths of a second. The time is given using a 24-hour clock, commonly used by the military. With this clock, 0 is midnight, 12 is noon, 18 is 6 p.m., and so on. In DOS version 4.0 and later, you can indicate a 12-hour clock by keying the letter a or p for a.m. or p.m. after the time.

To set the time, key the following:

A number from 0 to 23 for the hour, followed by a hyphen (-), a slash (/), or a period (.).

A number from 0 to 59 for the minutes. It is unnecessary to key the seconds and hundredths of a second. Use the a or p if you wish to use a 12-hour clock. Press [Enter].

If the date and time displayed are correct, or if you wish to bypass entering the correct date and time, just press [Enter] at the date and time prompts.

If you do not receive prompts requesting you to enter the date and time, you may want to initiate them to be sure your files are correctly date and time stamped.

Practice: Setting the Date and Time

Again, your DOS prompt may look like any of the following:

C>   C:\>   *or*   C:\DOS>

To set the date, key the following at the DOS prompt:

■ C:\>**DATE 9-17-94** (or any date you wish)   [Enter]

To set the time, key the following:

■ C:\>**TIME 8:00a** (or any time you wish)   [Enter]

To confirm the date and time, key the following:

■ C:\>**DATE**   [Enter]

The date you entered is displayed. Press [Enter] to accept the date and return to the DOS prompt.

■ C:\>**TIME**   [Enter]

The time you entered is displayed. Press [Enter] to accept the time and return to the DOS prompt.

■ Reset the date and time to the current date and time.

Error Messages

If you make a mistake while performing tasks on the system, an error message will be displayed on the screen. DOS uses helpful messages to inform you about errors. You will learn what they mean and will use them as instant clues to what has gone wrong.

One common type of message is a device error message, such as "Not ready error reading drive A." When a device error occurs and this message is displayed, the system requires you to select an option from a list similar to the following:

```
Not ready reading drive A
Abort, Retry, Ignore?        or    Fail
```

You must key the initial letter for your choice: A to abort, R to retry, I to ignore, or F to fail. Abort means to abandon or end the attempted command. If you no longer wish to use that command, key **A** for abort. Keying **R** for retry instructs the computer to try again to execute the command. Keying **I** for ignore tells the computer to ignore the error and, if possible, continue execution of the command. If you are using DOS version 3.3 or later, you will see the option **F** for Fail in some of these error messages. Fail is equivalent to Ignore.

The usual reason for the "Not ready" error message is that you have forgotten to shut the door on the drive, do not have the disk fully inserted into the disk drive, or do not have a disk in the drive. If this is the case, correct the situation and key **R** to retry the command.

Another common error message generated from DOS is "Bad command or file name." This message tells you that you have entered a command or file name that DOS cannot recognize or find. When you see this message, carefully check the keyed command and reenter the command correctly.

DOS's cryptic error messages can be very helpful clues in working with the operating system.

Changing the DOS Prompt with PG

The A> or C> at which you keyed the DATE and TIME commands is called the **DOS prompt**. This all-important signal can tell you several things. The letter tells you what disk drive is the **current** or **default** drive. The default drive is the drive DOS will use unless you give other instructions. A much more efficient prompt is a prompt that not only tells you the disk drive that is current but also tells you the current **subdirectory**. A subdirectory is a subdivision of the hard disk or floppy diskette; you will learn in a later chapter how to create and work with subdirectories.

The number of files a hard disk or floppy disk will store can be increased by creating subdirectories to hold file information. Subdirectories can also make your disk and file management more effective by listing files in categories you create. This is especially helpful on hard disks, which often contain thousands of files. For example, you could place all DOS files in one subdirectory. When you install MS/PC-DOS 4.0 or a later version, a special subdirectory is created on drive C for the DOS files. When your computer is ready for your input, you want the DOS prompt to show the current drive as drive C and also indicate the current subdirectory.

The following prompts are more informative prompts showing not only the current drive but also the current subdirectory.

```
    C:\>              or              C:\DOS>
```

The C represents the current drive; the \ represents the root or main directory. The word DOS following the backslash (\) in the second example is the name of the subdirectory in which the DOS files are stored.

To change the prompt from C> or A> to also include the current subdirectory, key:

■ **PROMPT PG**   [Enter]

   Your prompt should now look like this:

      C:\>   *or*   C:\DOS>

When you are instructed to key something at the DOS prompt, these are the prompts to which the instructions refer. The blinking line or **cursor** to the right of the prompt indicates the point where anything you key will be displayed. In DOS you will usually key commands here. The line is called a "command" line.

Practice: **Setting the Prompt**

Regardless of what your prompt is, key the following:

■ **PROMPT**   [Enter]

This should make your prompt look like C>.

Change the prompt to display the current directory by keying the following:

■ **PROMPT PG**   [Enter]

This should display your prompt as one of the following: C:\> or C:\DOS.

Nice work on Chapter 1! Test your knowledge now with the Self-Check Quiz and Assignment.

CHAPTER 1 SELF-CHECK QUIZ

True/False (Write T if the statement is true, F if the statement is false.)

_____ 1.   ROM (read only memory) is temporary memory that the user can change.

_____ 2.   A hard disk can store more information than a floppy disk, but floppy drives access data faster than hard drives.

_____ 3.   The computer's internal clock tracks the date and time.

_____ 4.   To warm boot the computer, turn it off and back on.

_____ 5.   To show the current directory in the DOS prompt, key PROMPT PG.

Multiple Choice (Circle the correct answer.)

6. The microprocessor is a component of

   a. the disk operating system.   c.   the system unit.
   b. the monitor.   d.   optional adapter cards.

7. To retain a permanent record of the computer's output, it can be saved in

   a. random access memory.   c.   read only memory.
   b. RAM disk files.   d.   floppy or hard disk files.

8. The Ctrl and Alt keys are important in operating the computer because

   a. they are used in combination with other keys to give them special functions.
   b. they are toggle keys that turn the numeric keypad on and off.
   c. they control scrolling of the display on the monitor screen.
   d. they are used to perform the same special functions with all software.

9. Which of the following is NOT a hazard to floppy diskettes?

   a. magnetism   c.   heat
   b. light   d.   dust

10. A device that is commonly used for input and output is the

   a. monitor.   c.   printer.
   b. disk drive.   d.   keyboard.

ASSIGNMENT

To practice using the commands in this chapter, complete the following steps.
Check off each step when you understand its operation, or mark the step with a
question mark if it is not clear. Write the commands or keystrokes in the
space provided.

1. Cold-boot the computer.

   _____

2. If necessary, change the prompt to reflect the current directory.

   _____

3. Reset the date to your next birthday.

   _____

4. Reset the date back to today's date.

   _____

5. Reset the time to one hour earlier.

   _____

6. Reset the time back to the current time.

   _____

7. Perform a warm boot.

   _____

8. Reset the date if it is not correct.

   _____

9. Reset the time if it is not correct.

   _____

10. If necessary, change the prompt to show the current directory.

   _____

CHAPTER **2**

BASIC DOS COMMANDS

OBJECTIVES

When you have completed the activities and assignment in this chapter, you will be able to:

1. Clear the screen.

2. Print the screen.

3. Display a directory of a disk in several formats.

4. List the conventions for naming files.

5. Work with wildcards.

6. Use the DOS command VER (Version).

7. Use the HELP command and switch.

THINGS TO REMEMBER WHEN USING THIS TEXTBOOK

There are several important considerations that are unique to DOS and important to remember while using this textbook.

1. When using a floppy diskette, never open the drive door when the light on the front of the disk drive is on, indicating that the drive is in use.

2. DOS commands or instructions and file names may be keyed in upper- or lowercase. As a general rule, DOS is not case-sensitive. We will point out the exceptions when they occur.

3. A DOS operation can be stopped by holding down the Ctrl key and tapping the C key or the Break key.

4. DOS treats letters and numbers differently: the lowercase letter "l" cannot be substituted for the number "1" key. The uppercase letter "O" cannot be substituted for the number "0."

5. You will see a bullet (■) preceding any required input. You must press the Enter key when you have finished keying a command to signal DOS to execute the command. In this textbook, [Enter] denotes pressing the key marked Enter. (Do not key the [ ] or the word Enter.) Where commands to be keyed are shown, the letters in boldface indicate what should be keyed. In the following example, you would key the letters DATE and then press the key marked "Enter."

■   **C>DATE**   [Enter]

DOS commands are shown in uppercase letters throughout this text. However, you can key them in upper- or lowercase.

6. If your prompt reads C> instead of C:\>, key:

C>PROMPT PG

If your prompt reads C:\>, and you would like it to read C>, key:

C:\>PROMPT

7. If your prompt reads C:\DOS> instead of C:\>, key the following:

C:\DOS>CD \

This command is one you will learn in Chapter 6. The CD means Change Directory; the backslash represents the root directory. Therefore, using this command, you are requesting to change directories to the root directory.

8. It is important to know how to correct errors or delete characters when keying DOS commands. There are several ways to correct errors:

   a. Use the Backspace key and backspace once for each character to be deleted.

   b. When you have keyed a command at the DOS prompt and wish to cancel the entire line, press the Esc and [Enter] keys and the DOS prompt will again be displayed.

Practice: **Canceling a Line**

Again, your DOS prompt may look like any of the following:

C>   C:\>   *or*   C:\DOS>

To cancel a line, key the following at the DOS prompt:

■ **C:\>DOS is easy to learn.**

To cancel this line, you could backspace each letter off the screen, but a faster way is to press the Esc key. Do that now. The line will then display as:

```
C:\>DOS is easy to learn.\
```

The line is still there and is followed by a backslash (\) symbol. The backslash symbol is a result of your having pressed Esc. Press [Enter] to display the DOS prompt.

DOS COMMANDS—INTERNAL vs EXTERNAL

As you read in Chapter 1, the commands in DOS are either internal or external. It is important to know the difference between internal and external commands and to remember which commands are in each group. The internal commands are instructions contained in one large command file named COMMAND.COM. These instructions are **loaded** or read into the computer's RAM when you boot, or power up the computer. The internal instructions or commands stay in the computer's memory and are available for use until you turn off the power supply to the computer. If you are using DOS files on a floppy disk, you can remove the DOS disk and still work with the internal commands. Therefore, once you have loaded DOS, you can use any of the internal commands, such as **DIR** (directory of disk), **VER** (version of DOS), and **VOL** (volume label or name of disk).

External commands are smaller DOS files stored in the DOS directory. These commands are loaded each time they are needed for a specific task.

Study the following list to learn which commands are internal and which are external:

Internal   **External**

CHDIR or CD   PROMPT   CHKDSK   HELP
CLS   REN or RENAME   COMP   LABEL
COPY   RMDIR or RD   DEFRAG *, **   MIRROR
DATE   TIME   DISKCOMP   PRINT
DEL   TYPE   DISKCOPY   SCANDISK *
DIR   VER   DOSKEY   SYS
ERASE   VOL   E ***   TREE
MKDIR or MD   EDIT   UNDELETE
MOVE *, **   EDLIN   UNFORMAT
PATH   FC   XCOPY
                                     FORMAT

Commands: * MS-DOS 6.0   ** MS-DOS 6.2   *** IBM PC-DOS 6.1

CLEARING THE SCREEN

You may wish to work with a blank screen from time to time. To do so, key
at the C:\> prompt:

   CLS

The screen will be cleared and only the DOS prompt will be displayed. You
can then key another command.

Practice: Clearing the Screen

Of course, you remember that you can change from C> to C:\>, for example,
by changing the prompt with the PROMPT PG command as you learned in
Chapter 1. Regardless of what your DOS prompt is, try this new command by
keying the following:

■   C:\>**CLS**   [Enter]

PRINTING USING PRINT SCREEN

It is important that you begin to print some of your work. There are several
ways to print using DOS. The first method you will use is to print the contents
of the screen display; this is like taking a picture of what is currently on the
screen. This operation and the resulting print is called a **print screen**, screen
print, or screen dump.

Before you begin to print, make certain there is a printer connected to your computer, that the printer is turned on, and that it is on-line. You may need to ask for help if this is your first experience with printing or if you are unsure about the printer setup.

When you are ready to print, locate the key marked Print Screen, PrtSc, or a similarly marked key. On many systems, to print the contents of the screen, you must hold down one of the Shift keys and tap the PrtSc key. On some of the newer systems you need only to press the PrtSc key. You will see the cursor move across and down the screen as its contents are being printed. If the cursor does not move, but remains at the top left corner of the screen, the information to be printed is not going to the printer, or the printer is unable to print the information. Hold down the Ctrl key and press the Break key, then look for the problem. Many laser printers will not screen-print a partial page, and you will have to research the printer documentation for the method to screen-print. Some computers and printers do not work well together to print the screen. Read the printer documentation to research alternate methods.

Practice: **Printing with PrtSc**

Experiment with PrtSc in the following exercise. First, clear the screen:

- **C:\>CLS**   [Enter]

Next, check the date and time:

- **C:\>DATE**   [Enter] [Enter]

- **C:\>TIME**   [Enter] [Enter]

Now print the screen by pressing the PrtSc key (or hold down the Shift key and press the PrtSc key) on your keyboard. Your printed copy should match your screen.

FILENAMES AND EXTENSIONS

Programs and data are stored as files on a disk. Each file has a unique **file name** so that the user *and* the system can identify and locate the file. Below are the rules and conventions for naming files.

Filenames and extensions are shown by DOS in uppercase letters. If you key them in lowercase, DOS will convert them to uppercase.

A few words should not be used as file names. These words include the DOS commands and the **device names** listed in the following section—**Program**

Extensions and Device Names. Unpredictable results might occur if you were to use a DOS command or device name as a file name.

1. The first part of the file name is called the **filename** (one word). The filename can be from one to eight characters long. It can include any letter, number, or special character except:

   Blank spaces
   The following invalid characters:
   . " / \ [ ] : | < > + = ; , * ?

   Some examples of valid filenames are:

Irvine	Mary	07_02_94
1	ABC	ABC_1234

2. The second part of the file name is called the **extension**. The extension is optional— file names are not required to include an extension. The filename and extension are separated by a period or "dot." The same characters and symbols can be used in the extension as in the filename; however, the extension is limited in length to three characters, numbers, or symbols. Extensions are often used to provide additional information about a file. For example, the extension TXT is conventionally used to tell you that the file is a text file. The examples of file names with extensions are:

IRVINE.CA	NOV-28.94
JANKE.LTR	1993-94.BFS

PROGRAM EXTENSIONS AND DEVICE NAMES

1. Some software programs automatically add their own default extensions. By convention, certain extensions have special meanings. They can help you recognize the source of files and tell you what the files might contain. Here are a few examples:

BAK	Backup file
BAS	Program written in the BASIC programming language
BAT	Batch file
BMP	Bit-mapped graphics file from Windows Paintbrush
C	Program written in the C programming language
COM	Executable program command file
CO_	Compressed DOS COM file
DBF	dBASE data file
DOC	Text data file created in Microsoft Word
EXE	Executable program file
INI	Initialization file storing information for setting up software

PCX	Graphic format for Paintbrush files
PM5	PageMaker version 5.0 file
SYS	System file or file that enables use of a device such as a mouse
TIF	Graphics file storing a scanned image
TXT	Data file containing text
WK1	Lotus 1-2-3 spreadsheet file
ZIP	Compressed file

2. Device names that should not be used as file names include:

AUX	A communications port
COM1	The first communications port (interchangeable with AUX, PRN)
COM2	The second communications port (also COM3, COM4, etc.)
CON	The console (keyboard and screen)
LPT1	A parallel (line) printer port (interchangeable with PRN)
LPT2	A second parallel printer port (interchangeable with PRN)
LPT3	A third parallel printer port (interchangeable with PRN)
NUL	A dummy (nonexistent) device
PRN	The on-line printer

THE DIRECTORY

One of the most frequently-used internal commands is the DIR (directory) command, which displays a list of files and subdirectories on a disk. The DIR command, used without any parameters, displays the following information:

• The name (Volume label) of the disk.

• The Serial Number of the disk.

• The name of the directory.

and five columns of information for each file as follows:

• filename

• file extension

• size of file in bytes

• date the file or subdirectory was created or last revised

• time the file or subdirectory was created or last revised

At the end of the directory listing, you will find information about the total number of bytes in the files listed and the amount of free unoccupied space on the disk.

Practice: Displaying the Directory

Let's try displaying a directory from the DOS prompt of drive C. If you wish the prompt to display the current directory, key the following as you learned in Chapter 1:

- **C>PROMPT PG**   [Enter]

Now display the directory with the following command:

- **C:\>DIR**   [Enter]

You should see a directory such as the partial one that follows. Depending on your DOS prompt, your directory contents may be significantly different.

```
Volume in drive C has no label
Volume Serial Number is 1B63-B812
Directory of C:\

COMMAND    COM     54,619   06-19-92   12:00p
CONFIG     SYS        437   06-19-92   12:00p
DASDDRVR   SYS      1,170   06-19-92   12:00p
NUMOFF     COM         11   06-19-92   12:00p
AUTOEXEC   BAT        111   06-19-92   12:00p
WINA20     386      9,349   06-19-92   12:00p
TEXT1      TXT      5,349   06-20-94   01:00p
CHAPTER1   TXT     12,894   07-23-94   11:00p
BOOK4      DOC      4,098   08-19-94   12:00p
BANKLOT    XLS     22,450   06-20-94   02:30p
BKBAL      WK1     33,712   09-21-94   02:03p
BKDEP      XLS     45,067   08-21-94   10:00p
TAX93      TXT      3,128   05-22-94   11:05p
TAXCAL     WK1     12,986   04-19-94   10:00a
TAXUSCO    TXT        500   01-07-94   07:00p
ANAH       TXT      1,763   10-23-94   02:10p
NORD       TXT        879   07-18-94   05:07p
SEAR       DIV         50   01-12-94   10:10a
KIMBERY    BAB      4,590   09-30-94   09:06p
NOVELL     TXT     98,745   04-19-94   06:30a
PM         EXL      2,417   08-09-94   12:09p
HOME       TXT     32,123   10-30-94   07:45p
MARIA      TTE      7,000   02-15-94   12:00p
SCREEN     WK1        920   06-19-92   02:25p
etc.
```

The file names will not be the same but the format will show the name and serial number of the disk, and each file with its filename and extension, size, and date and time of creation or last revision.

Switches Used with Directory Commands

You can modify many DOS commands by adding optional "switches" that signal DOS to perform the command in a specific way. A **switch** is a special parameter that follows the command and always begins with a slash (/). The DIR command has several switches. Two that are frequently used to modify its operation are /P and /W.

Using the Pause Directory Switch (/P) with DIR

If the directory has more than 23 files in it, the entire directory will not fit on the screen at one time. The /P switch can be added to the DIR command to tell DOS to display the directory in screen-length portions. The slash tells the system to modify the command; the P tells DOS to pause the directory display after each 23 lines. When you are ready to see more of the directory, you can press any key and the next 23 lines will be displayed. Therefore, the command to pause the DIR command is as follows:

> C:\>DIR/P

Practice: Using the Pause Switch (/P) with DIR

Key the following to display the current directory of drive C with the /P switch.

■ **C:\>DIR /P**   [Enter]

The display will pause after the first 23 lines. Depending on your DOS prompt, the directory contents may be significantly different.

```
Volume in drive C has no label
Volume Serial Number is 1B63-B812
Directory of C:\

COMMAND     COM         54,619      06-19-92    12:00p
CONFIG      SYS            437      06-19-92    12:00p
DASDDRVR    SYS          1,170      06-19-92    12:00p
NUMOFF      COM             11      06-19-92    12:00p
AUTOEXEC    BAT            111      06-19-92    12:00p
WINA20      386          9,349      06-19-92    12:00p
TEXT1       TXT          5,349      06-20-94    01:00p
```

```
CHAPTER1    TXT             12,894      07-23-94    11:00p
BOOK4       DOC              4,098      08-19-94    12:00p
BANKLOT     XLS             22,450      06-20-94    02:30p
BKBAL       WK1             33,712      09-21-94    02:03p
BKDEP       XLS             45,067      08-21-94    10:00p
TAX93       TXT              3,128      05-22-94    11:05p
TAXCAL      WK1             12,986      04-19-94    10:00a
TAXUSCO     TXT                500      01-07-94    07:00p
ANAH        TXT              1,763      10-23-94    02:10p
NORD        TXT                879      07-18-94    05:07p
SEAR        DIV                 50      01-12-94    10:10a
KIMBERY     BAB              4,590      09-30-94    09:06p
NOVELL      TXT             98,745      04-19-94    06:30a
PM          EXL              2,417      08-09-94    12:09p
HOME        TXT             32,123      10-30-94    07:45p
MARIA       TTE              7,000      02-15-94    12:00p
```

```
Press any key to continue . . .
```

To continue the display of information, follow the screen prompt instructing you to press any key.

Using the Wide Directory (/W) Switch with DIR

Notice that with the directory commands you have used so far, the directory listing has included five columns of information about each file: the name of the file, the file extension, the size of the file (in bytes), and the date and time the file was created or last revised. You won't always need all of this information about the contents of the disk. There are occasions when just the file names are enough information. There are also times when you will want to see on one screen the names of all files on the disk. A wide directory obtained with the /W switch will usually display this. Key:

C:\>DIR /W

The same 23 filenames shown above are displayed in columnar form:

```
Volume in drive C has no label
Volume Serial Number is 1B63-B812
Directory of C:\

COMMAND.COM    CONFIG.SYS     DASDDRVR.SYS   NUMOFF.COM     AUTOEXEC.BAT
WINA20.386     TEXT1.TXT      CHAPTER1.TXT   BOOK4.DOC      BANKLOT.XLS
BKBAL.WK1      BKDEP.XLS      TAX93.TXT      TAXCAL.WK1     TAXUSCO.TXT
ANAH.TXT       NORD.TXT       SEAR.DIV       KIMBERY.BAB    NOVELL.TXT
PM.EXL         HOME.TXT       MARIA.TTE      etc.
```

Does your screen display look like the above? The files will not be exactly those listed here, but the format should be the same.

Practice: Using the Wide Switch (/W) with DIR

Key the following:

- **C:\>DIR /W**   [Enter]

Obtaining Directory Listings for Selected Files

Occasionally you will want directory information about only one file. You can ask DOS for a directory of just one file by specifying the file name as a parameter after the command DIR. For example, if you wanted information about the file COMMAND.COM in the default directory, you would key:

C:\>DIR COMMAND.COM

Five columns of information including the filename, extension, date and time the file was created or last revised, and the size of the file is displayed.

```
Volume in drive C has no label
Volume Serial Number is 1B63-B812
Directory of C:\

  COMMAND        COM  54,619     06-19-92    12:00p
```


Practice: Obtaining Directory Listings for Selected Files

Display information about the following files by keying:

- **C:\>DIR AUTOEXEC.BAT**   [Enter]

and

- **C:\>DIR CONFIG.SYS**   [Enter]

Five columns of information about each of the files are displayed.

Changing the Directory Order

Additional directory switches were introduced with DOS 5.0 to sort the directory in various orders. These commands display the files as follows:

DIR /ON   Arranges alphabetically in ascending order by name (A–Z).

DIR /OE	Arranges alphabetically in ascending order by extension (A–Z).
DIR /OS	Arranges by size (smallest to largest).
DIR /OD	Arranges by date (earliest to latest).
DIR /OG	Arranges subdirectories before files.
DIR /B	Displays each filename and extension on a line by itself with no other information.

Most of these commands begin with **O** which represents the word **order**. Most of these new switches also may be combined with the /P and /W switches. The combination DIR /ON /P will display a directory sorted by name in screenfuls of 23 lines.

To reverse the order of the above commands, insert a minus sign (–) after the /O. For example:

DIR /O-N	Sorts the directory files in descending order by name beginning with the letter Z.

Practice: Sorting the Directory

Display the directory of drive C:

■ **C:\>DIR**   [Enter]

Now display the directory of drive C in alphabetic ascending order by filename as follows:

■   **C:\>DIR /ON**   [Enter]

Do you see a difference in the order of the directory listing? Now sort by date with most current date first:

■ **C:\>DIR /O-D**   [Enter]

In both cases you should see the files listed in the appropriate order.

WILDCARDS

A wildcard can be a substitute for a filename or an extension. Wildcards are one of the most useful tools in DOS. There are two wildcards: The wildcard that represents a single character is the question mark (?); the wildcard that represents a group of characters is the asterisk (*). An example of a way to use a ? as a wildcard to display the directory listing for COMMAND.COM is to key:

DIR ?OMMAND.COM

Here the ? represents the C in COMMAND. You could also substitute question marks for other letters in the filename or extension such as the following:

DIR ??MMAND.?OM

Notice that one question mark is substituted for each unknown character in the name. COMMAND.COM fits this description.

The asterisk, or "star" as it is more often called, represents a number of characters. Used in the filename, one asterisk stands for any characters in the filename that come after it. For example, to display a list of all files in the directory that have any filename starting with the letter C and with the extension COM, you would key the following at the DOS prompt:

DIR C*.COM

One asterisk used in the extension represents all characters that come after it. To see a list of all files that have filenames beginning with F and that have any extension, you would key:

DIR F*.*

To see a list of all files with any filename and with the extension COM, the command would be

DIR *.COM

To see a list of all files with any filename that begins with the letter C with any extension, the command would be

DIR C*.*

Practice: **Working with Wildcards**

Key the following commands using wildcards. Depending on your configuration, you may or may not have files for some of the following.

■ C:\>**DIR *.SYS**   [Enter]

- **C:\>DIR *.S??**   [Enter]

- **C:\>DIR COMM*.?OM**   [Enter]

- **C:\>DIR C*.C***   [Enter]

- **C:\>DIR *.COM**   [Enter]

Print the screen.

THE VERSION (VER) COMMAND

As you learned in Chapter 1, there have been several versions of DOS. As
new capabilities in computer hardware and application software have required
new commands and operations, new versions of DOS have been released. The
first version of DOS was numbered 1.0 as is the convention for numbering
software releases. Minor revisions to a version are numbered with a decimal
number (1.1, 1.2, 1.3, etc.). When a major revision is made, the first number is
changed. For DOS this occurred when version 2.0 was introduced to handle
the hard drive of the IBM XT computer. The designers of the operating
system have been careful to keep the commands and operations of the new
versions compatible with the earlier ones. Therefore, you can use the older
versions when necessary. Sometimes it is important to know which version of
DOS you are using. Some software application packages require more recent
versions of DOS than others or might require upgrading to run with the newer
versions of DOS.

Another important reason for knowing the version of DOS you are using is that
DOS will not allow you to mix COMMAND.COM and most external
commands of various versions of DOS. The internal command VER (version)
provides an easy way to quickly determine the version of DOS used to boot the
computer. By keying VER at the DOS prompt and pressing [Enter], you can
obtain a report on the version of DOS currently residing in memory. VER is
an internal command.

Practice: Using the VER Command

At any DOS prompt, key

- **VER**   [Enter]

DOS will display a report similar to the following:

```
MS-DOS Version 6.2 (or whatever version you are using),
or IBM Version 6.1
```

ASKING FOR HELP

One of the important features of the latest versions of DOS is the addition of the HELP external command. You can obtain information on the DOS commands you specify in two ways. One way is to key the command HELP followed by the command you would like explained. For example, if you would like help on the DATE command, key:

C:\>HELP DATE

You can display on-line HELP information by keying:

C:\>HELP

You also receive on-line information using the /? switch, by keying:

C:\>DATE /?

The screen display shows a brief description of the command, the command syntax, and other information pertinent to the command.

To display a list of all the commands listed under the Help function, key the word HELP without any parameter. The DOS commands are listed alphabetically.

Practice: The HELP Command

Request information regarding the DIR command with:

■ **C:\>HELP DIR**   [Enter]

or

■ **C:\>DIR /?**   [Enter]

Good work! Now practice your newly found HELP skills as needed for your work on the Self-Check Quiz and Assignment.

CHAPTER 2 SELF-CHECK QUIZ

True/False (Write T if the statement is true, F if the statement is false.)

_____ 1.   The wildcard that represents a single character is the question mark (?).

_____ 2.   To display the list of HELP topics, key HELP.

_____ 3.   To cancel a line, depress the Alt and Del keys.

_____ 4.   Internal DOS commands are contained in the COMMAND.COM file.

_____ 5.   To determine the version of DOS on the computer you are using, key the following: VERSION

Multiple Choice (Circle the correct answer.)

6. Which of the following switches is used with the DIR command to sort the directory alphabetically by filename?

    a. /ON   c. /OG
    b. /OS   d. /OA

7. Which one of the following is a valid file name?

    a. @WASH-DC.DOC   c. SMITH,R.LTR
    b. INVOICES.1993   d. CON

8. Which command would you key to list all files with filenames beginning with COM and with any extension?

    a. COM ?.*   c. DIR /COM.*
    b. DIR COM*.*   d. DIR COM?.???

9. Which switch would you use to display the directory 23 lines at a time?

    a. DIR /23   c. DIR /P
    b. DIR /W   d. DIR /?

10. To clear the screen, key which of the following?

    a. CLEAR   c. CLS
    b. CLR   d. CLRSC

ASSIGNMENT

To practice using DOS commands in this assignment, complete the following steps. Check off each step when you understand its operation or mark the step with a question mark if it is not clear. Write the commands or keystrokes in the space provided.

1. Warm-boot the computer.

   _____

2. Change the prompt to reflect the current directory.

   _____

3. Display a directory sorted by file size from smallest to largest. Print the screen. Print the screen again of a directory sorted by file size from largest to smallest.

   _____

4. Clear the screen.

   _____

5. Determine the version of DOS the computer is using.

   _____

6. Print, using PrtSc, a list of the files in the root directory of drive C that begin with a C and have any extension.

   _____

7. Print, using PrtSc, a list of the files in the root directory of drive C that have any filename but have an extension which begins with an E.

   _____

8. Request HELP for the PROMPT command using a switch. Print the screen.

   _____

9. Clear the screen and display a directory showing each filename and extension with no other information. Print the screen.

   _____

10. Clear the screen and display a wide directory. Print the screen.

   _____

CHAPTER 3

DISK AND FILE PREPARATION

OBJECTIVES

When you have completed the activities and assignment in this chapter, you will be able to:

1. Set a search path.

2. Abort DOS commands.

3. Format disks with the system and volume label.

4. Use the FORMAT and Unconditional FORMAT command.

5. Use the LABEL command to name or rename a disk.

6. Use the VOL command.

7. Change the default drive.

8. Specify disk drives in commands.

9. Use the DOSKEY command.

10. Create text files.

11. Display and print text files.

12. Use echo printing.

FLOPPY DISKETTES

Unlike the fixed hard disks that are sealed in a metal casing and never seen by the user, floppy diskettes are routinely handled. Forming good habits for handling and storing floppy diskettes can be one of the most important outcomes of your study of DOS.

Important features of floppy diskettes are shown in Fig. 3-1. Both 5 1/4- and 3 1/2-inch floppy diskettes can be write-protected. **Write-protected** means that the disk can only be read, not written to, and that the files on it cannot be changed or erased. On 5 1/4-inch floppy diskettes, the write-protect notch is a square notch cut in one side of the diskette. The notch can be covered with a small adhesive tab to make the disk "read only" and prevent erasing, formatting, or overwriting files on the disk.

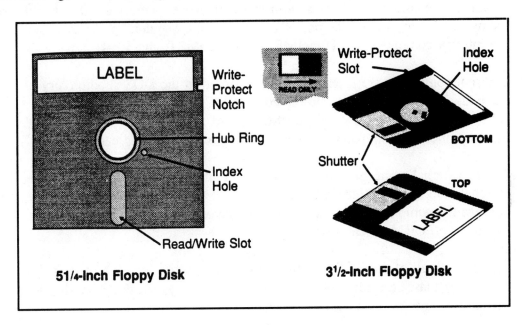

Figure 3-1. Features of floppy diskettes.

On the 3 1/2-inch diskette, the write-protect tab slides in a slot near one corner. To make this disk "read only" and prevent erasing, formatting, or overwriting files on the diskette, the sliding tab must be pushed toward the corner of the diskette so that the hole in the slot is open.

In many DOS operations accidental overwriting of files can easily occur. Because you seldom want to change application software program files, it is a good idea to always write-protect application software diskettes. Write-protecting your data diskettes helps safeguard your data but prevents you from adding to or updating the data. In this case, having a second copy as a backup may be a better security measure.

Both sizes of floppy diskettes have an indexing hole and a read/write slot in their protective sheath. The indexing hole is used by DOS to find locations on the diskette where files can be read and written. The read/write slot on both sides of the diskette jacket exposes the diskette surface for access by the drive read/write heads. On the 5 1/4-inch diskette, the Mylar surface is visible through these openings. On the 3 1/2-inch diskette, the read/write slot is protected by a metal shutter that slides to one side when the disk is inserted in the drive.

MORE ABOUT INTERNAL AND EXTERNAL DOS COMMANDS

As you know, the instructions you give DOS are **commands** that the software can interpret and carry out. You have learned that there are two types of DOS commands, **internal** and **external**. The internal commands are instructions contained in one large command file named COMMAND.COM. These instructions are **loaded**, or read into the computer's RAM, when you **boot** or power up the computer. They stay in the computer's memory and are available for use until you turn off the power supply to the computer. You have used the internal commands DATE, TIME, DIR, PROMPT, and VER.

External commands are smaller DOS files stored in the DOS subdirectory of drive C. They are not read into the computer's memory until you use the command. Unlike COMMAND.COM, most of these files do not stay in memory after the command is executed but must be reloaded each time.

To use external commands such as FORMAT, the DOS program file for the external command (in this case, FORMAT.COM) must be loaded each time you use the command. This is the file that gives the system the capability to execute the FORMAT command.

So it is with all of the DOS external commands. A file for each of these commands must be loaded into memory to give the system the capability to execute the specific external command.

SETTING THE SEARCH PATH TO THE DOS COMMAND FILES

Before DOS can load an external command file such as FORMAT.COM, the system must know where it is stored on the hard drive. If you want DOS to execute an external command, you must tell DOS the drive and directory where the DOS external command files are stored. Usually this directory is called DOS. If you are using PC/MS-DOS versions 4.0 or higher, the DOS external files were stored in a subdirectory called DOS on drive C during the installation process.

There are several ways to help DOS find the external command files. One way is to use the internal command PATH to tell DOS the drive or directory name where the files can be found. This is called "**setting the search path**." For example, if the files are on the hard disk in a directory named DOS, you can enter this command at any prompt to set the search path to the place where the files are stored:

    PATH C:\DOS

If the external command files are in a directory with a different name, you must use that name instead of "DOS." This PATH command will ensure that the system can find any DOS files in that directory and execute them from any DOS prompt.

The system stores the search path in memory until the computer is turned off or rebooted. You need to enter the PATH command only once during a computing session, unless you cold-boot or warm-boot the computer. After a warm or cold boot, you must reset the path by entering the PATH command line again.

Practice: Setting a Search Path

At the DOS prompt, key the appropriate PATH command to tell DOS where to look for external command files, such as FORMAT.COM. Again, your DOS prompt may look like any of the following:

C>   C:\>   *or*   C:\DOS>

If the DOS files are on the hard disk in a subdirectory, key

■ **C:\>PATH C:\DOS**   [Enter]

If the external DOS command files are stored in a directory with another name, substitute the drive and directory names for C:\DOS in the line shown above. Nothing apparent happens when you enter the PATH command, but DOS stores the entry in memory.

To check the current search path, key the following:

■ **C:\>PATH**   [Enter]

DOS displays the search path stored in memory.

```
C:\>PATH=C:\DOS
```

ABORTING DOS COMMANDS

If you discover that you are executing a command that you really don't want to complete, you can abort a command by holding down the Ctrl (Control) key and tapping the letter C. Using this key combination that stops any ongoing operation is sometimes referred to as "Pressing the Panic Button." You can also hold down the Ctrl key and tap the Break key. This tells DOS to abort the command process. However, if the process has already begun, any data on the disk may no longer be readable.

Practice: Aborting DOS Commands

For this exercise, you will key the DIR command and then decide to abort it as follows:

■   **C:\>DIR**   [Enter]

Quickly, press Ctrl-C or Ctrl-Break to stop the execution of the command. You may need to try this several times before you move quickly enough to be successful.

PREPARING DISKS FOR USE

Preparation of a floppy diskette and a hard disk is considerably different. To prepare a floppy diskette for use, simply format it. A hard disk often requires low-level formatting, partitioning, and formatting. The preparation of a hard disk is beyond the scope of this textbook. Prior to using a disk, there are several procedures which should be followed for maximum productivity.

Formatting a Disk

To make a disk ready for use on a DOS machine, the disk surface must be set up in a format that DOS recognizes for storing data. This setup process is called "formatting." Formatting is accomplished with the FORMAT command, an external DOS command. To use the FORMAT command, you must have the file FORMAT.COM in the DOS directory on the hard disk. Formatting does the following:

- Sets up a structure for the directory of the hard or floppy disk.

- Checks for defects in the disk.

- Makes previously recorded data or programs on the disk being formatted inaccessible.

- Prepares the disk so that the system can work with it by reading from and writing to its tracks and sectors with the disk drive read/write heads.

Data is stored on floppy and hard disks in the format shown in Fig. 3-2. On both types of disks, the tracks for recording data are arranged in concentric circles. The tracks are divided into sectors. A sector is a wedge-shaped section of the disk that is the basic unit of storage on a disk. When a disk is formatted, DOS maps the disk so that the operating system can find specific sectors and tracks. Each sector commonly stores 512 bytes. A 5 1/4-inch

Tracks   Sectors

360K double-density diskette is formatted with nine sectors numbered 0 through 8 and 40 tracks numbered 0 through 39 on each side of the disk. A 5 1/4-inch 1.2MB high-density disk has 80 tracks with 15 sectors per track on each side. A 3 1/2-inch 1.44MB high-density disk has 80 tracks with 18 sectors per track on each side. A 3 1/2-inch 2.88MB disk has 80 tracks with 36 sectors per track. DOS allocates space to files in groups of one to four (usually two) sectors called allocation units or clusters.

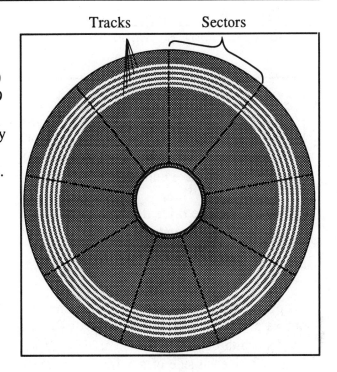

Figure 3-2. Information is stored on disks in sectors and tracks.

You can use switches to modify the FORMAT command, just as you used switches to modify the DIR command. You will use several switches available for the FORMAT command in the formatting activities later in this chapter.

The command syntax for formatting a disk from the DOS prompt is:

    C:\>FORMAT A: (or other drive letter)

Practice: Formatting a Disk

Be sure the path is set to the DOS subdirectory on drive C, and write the following on an adhesive label to affix to a diskette:

(Your name)
(Your class)

■ **C:\>FORMAT A:**   [Enter]

This command tells DOS to format a disk in drive A. DOS will prompt you to insert a new disk. Insert the labeled blank diskette (or one with data of no value) in drive A. First the system will find the file FORMAT.COM on the hard disk in the DOS subdirectory. Next, DOS will load FORMAT.COM into memory. When the command is loaded, DOS will prompt you as follows:

```
Insert new diskette for drive A:
and press ENTER when ready . . .
```

> **WARNING:** USE THE FORMAT COMMAND WITH CAUTION.
> NEVER FORMAT A DISK THAT CONTAINS DATA YOU WANT
> TO KEEP. Even though DOS has an UNFORMAT command, you
> don't want to take unnecessary risks!
>
> Always use the drive designator (A: or B:) as a parameter after the
> FORMAT command.

The operating system will begin formatting the disk and will keep you updated about its progress. During formatting, two write heads (0 and 1) prepare tracks (cylinders) 0 through 39 on each side of a 5 1/4-inch 360K diskette or tracks 0 through 79 on each side of a 5 1/4-inch 1.2MB diskette or a 3 1/2-inch 720K, 1.44MB, or 2.88MB diskette. The number of the active head and the cylinder being formatted are displayed by many versions of DOS. Other versions display the percentage of the disk that has been formatted.

When the formatting process is complete, DOS will report:

```
Format complete.
```

You will be prompted to enter a "volume label" or disk name as follows:

```
Volume label (11 characters, ENTER for none)?
```

Key the name you want the disk to have, or press [Enter] to leave the disk with no label. For now, press [Enter]. (If you are using an earlier version of DOS and you want to name the disk, read the section "Formatting with the System" that follows.) With any version, DOS will report the total disk space, the amount of unusable space, if any, and the amount of space available. For a 5 1/4-inch 360K disk, the following information will be displayed:

```
362496 bytes total disk space
362496 bytes available on disk
```

If there are any "bad" or unusable areas on the disk, DOS will report the number of bytes in any bad sectors and will prevent their being used. The size and number of **allocation units** is also displayed.

There will be a screen prompt asking if you wish to format another disk. Your options are to key Y to format another diskette or N to end the process. Key N for No.

Formatting with Two Floppy Drives

Some computer systems have two floppy diskette drives. In this case you may wish to format a disk in either of these two drives. You would key the command as shown:

    C:\> or C:\DOS>FORMAT A:
             or
    C:\> or C:\DOS>FORMAT B:

The first command tells DOS to format a diskette in drive A. The second command tells DOS to format a diskette in drive B. Because of the PATH command, the system finds the file FORMAT.COM in the DOS subdirectory and loads it into memory. DOS will prompt you as follows:

```
Insert a new diskette for drive A:    (or drive B:)
and press ENTER when ready . . .
```

When the formatting process is complete, DOS will report:

```
Format complete.
```

You will be prompted to enter a "volume label" or disk name as follows:

```
Volume label (11 characters, ENTER for none)?
```

Key the name you want the disk to have, or press [Enter] to leave the disk with no label. (If you are using an earlier version of DOS and you want to name the disk, read the section "Formatting with the System" that follows.) With any version, DOS will report the total disk space, the amount of unusable space, if any, and the amount of space available. For a 5 1/4-inch 360K disk, information similar to the following will be displayed:

```
362496 bytes total disk space
362496 bytes available on disk
```

There will be a screen prompt asking if you wish to format another disk. Your options are to key Y to format another diskette or N to end the process.

Formatting with the System

There are times when it is helpful to have on your data disk the three DOS system files that make it possible to boot the computer. If properly prepared with these files, a data disk can be inserted into drive A and used to start the computer. Such a disk is sometimes called a **self-booting** disk or a system disk, because it can be used in drive A instead of DOS files on a hard disk to boot the computer.

The three required system files are IBMBIO.COM and IBMDOS.COM in IBM PC-DOS, or their equivalent files in MS-DOS: IO.SYS and MSDOS.SYS, and COMMAND.COM. The first two are called **hidden files** because they do not appear in a directory listing. Nonetheless, they are present on the DOS disk or any self-booting disk. The third file COMMAND.COM appears in the directory listing. This file contains the internal commands that are loaded into memory when the computer boots and which stay there until the power is turned off.

The three system files can be added to a data disk when it is formatted. This is accomplished by modifying the FORMAT command with the system switch /S. To request DOS to format a data disk and install the system files on it from the hard disk, you would key the following at the DOS prompt:

   C:\> or C:\DOS>FORMAT A: /S

Note: If you are using a version earlier than 4.0, you can also add the /V switch to tell DOS you want to label the disk:

   C:\>FORMAT A: /S/V

Key the name you want the disk to have when prompted by the screen display.

Formatting with Different Floppy Disk Drive Configurations

In the years since DOS was introduced, many features and options have been added to DOS personal computers so that there is no longer a "standard" PC. Floppy disk drives are an example of this diversity. There are four configurations in common use: 360K and 1.2MB 5 1/4-inch drives, and 720K and 1.44MB 3 1/2-inch drives. Your computer may have drives in one or more of these configurations. If you work with more than one computer, you might be using different floppy drive configurations on each machine. Knowing how to format and manage disks in several configurations can be essential to DOS users particularly if you wish to work with the same disk in multiple computers.

The 1.2 and 1.44MB diskettes are called "high-density" or "high-capacity" disks. They can be used only in high-density drives: the 1.2MB drives introduced with the AT machines and the 1.44MB drives introduced with the PS/2 machines. The 5 1/4-inch 1.2MB diskettes and the 3 1/2-inch 1.44MB diskettes are certified for high-density storage and are usually labeled as "HD" disks. You may also be able to recognize the 5 1/4-inch HD disk by its lack of a hub ring and the 3 1/2-inch HD disk by the square hole cut in the corner opposite the write-protection opening.

Low-density disks can be formatted and used in low- or high-density drives. However, high-density disks cannot be formatted for high density and used in low-density drives. If a diskette is already formatted, a high-density drive detects whether the disk is a high- or low-density disk and reads and writes data in the disk's format. By default, a drive attempts to format a disk in the drive's native format—if you wish to format a low-density disk in a high-density drive, you must add switches to the FORMAT command to specify this. The two most common modifications to the command are:

To format a 5 1/4-inch 360K disk in a 1.2MB drive:

C:\>FORMAT A: /4
          or
C:\>FORMAT A: /F:360   (DOS 4.0 and later)

To format a 3 1/2-inch 720K disk in a 1.44MB drive:

C:\>FORMAT A: /N:9 /T:80
          or
C:\>FORMAT A: /F:720   (DOS 4.0 and later)

The /4 switch tells DOS to format a 5 1/4-inch disk as a low-density 360K disk. Many 1.2MB drives will not format a disk labeled high density with this switch. As a general rule, it is more reliable to format a 360K (low density) 5 1/4-inch disk in a low-density drive. In fact, the DOS manual warns that a disk formatted with the /4 switch or /F:360 (DOS 4.0 and later) may not be written to or read reliably in a low-density drive. Before storing data on a disk formatted in this way, make sure the low-density drive can write data to the disk and read data from it. Whenever possible, format and use 5 1/4-inch disks in the type of drive for which they were designed.

The /N:9 switch tells DOS to format a 3 1/2-inch disk as a low-density disk with 9 sectors per track; the /T:80 switch specifies 80 tracks. You can use the same switches in DOS 4.0 and later, or you can use the /F:720 switch to specify the size in kilobytes. Disks formatted in this way in a high-density drive are very reliable when used in a high- or low-density drive.

FLOPPY DISK CAPACITIES				
Size of Disk	Disk Capacity	Density	No. of Sectors	No. of Tracks
5 1/4-inch Disks				
	360KB	Double Density	9	40
	1.2MB	High Density	15	80
3 1/2-inch Disks				
	720KB	Double Density	18	80
	1.44MB	High Density	18	80
	2.88MB	High Density	36	80

Practice: Formatting a Disk with the System

Before formatting a floppy disk, check to see the size of the drive you have and make sure the diskette is compatible. Set the search path to the DOS files and then format with the following command:

This time, format the diskette with the system as follows:

■ **C:\>FORMAT A: /S**   [Enter]

Name the diskette CLASS when asked for a volume label.

Unconditional Format

By default, the DOS 5.0 and later versions of the FORMAT command perform a "safe" format, that is, one that can be unformatted. The directory and FAT **(file allocation table)** information of the existing format is stored as UNFORMAT information, and for the new format, a new directory and FAT are created to replace the old information. (The file allocation table is a special file created when the disk is formatted.) DOS uses the FAT to record the numbers of the clusters or allocation units where each file is located. When DOS erases a file, it changes the first character of the file name in the directory so that the file can no longer be accessed and revises the FAT to show that the allocation units are available for other files. The data in the allocation unit(s) where the file is stored is not erased, however.

You will see how this is used to good advantage when you learn to undelete a file or unformat a disk in a later section. In a safe format, the remainder of the data on the disk is not changed, but the files are no longer accessible without the directory or FAT. If other files have not been written to the disk after a safe format, the DOS command UNFORMAT (covered in a later section) can be used to restore the original directory and FAT and make the files accessible again.

However, for security purposes if you want to completely erase a disk so that the files cannot be restored, you can format the disk "unconditionally" by using the switch /U, as in FORMAT A: /U. In this case, all data is physically erased from the disk and the disk cannot be unformatted. The command, FORMAT /U, cannot be used on a hard drive.

Labeling a Disk

An adhesive disk label can be peeled off accidentally, so DOS permits you to record a disk name or label electronically in a hidden file on the disk itself. At one time, disks were referred to as "volumes," so the electronically recorded disk name is called the **volume label**. The volume label you give the disk can be used to quickly identify its contents.

How can you give a disk an electronic label? The volume label can be recorded during the format process. The FORMAT command switch for giving a disk a volume label is /V. Therefore, the command to format and name a disk is FORMAT A: /V. DOS versions 4.0 and later automatically ask for a volume label even when the switch is not used.

In version 3.0, the external command LABEL was introduced. With it, you can add or change a disk label whenever you want. This is useful when the contents of a disk have changed or when you did not elect to give a disk a name when you formatted it.

Practice: Labeling a Diskette

Insert the diskette you formatted and labeled CLASS in drive A. Key the following at the DOS prompt (remember that LABEL is an external command, and you must have access to the command file):

■   **C:\>LABEL A:**   [Enter]

When prompted for a volume label, name the disk PRACTICE. You can also label the diskette by using the command:

■ **C:\>LABEL A: PRACTICE**   [Enter]

Repeat the LABEL command once more and change the name of the disk back to CLASS.

THE VOLUME (VOL) COMMAND

Have you wondered how you might later check the volume label of a disk? One way to do this is to display the directory; here you will see the name of the disk as well as the names of the files on it. Another way is to use the **VOL** (VOLUME) command. The command displays the name of the disk when used as follows:

    C:\>VOL   or   C:\>VOL A:

Practice: Using the VOL Command

Check the volume label of the disk you just formatted with the following:

■ **C:\>VOL A:**   [Enter]

DOS will report the volume label as CLASS.

SPECIFYING DISK DRIVES IN COMMANDS

To instruct DOS to carry out an action, key a DOS command at the DOS prompt. As an example, use the command DIR. The DIR command instructs DOS to display a directory listing of the information stored on the disk in the drive shown in the prompt. DOS will display the directory for the disk in the default drive unless you specify otherwise. To show how this would work, key the command DIR at the prompt on your screen:

    C:\>DIR   or   A:\>DIR

If you key DIR at the C:\> prompt, you know that the information displayed is the directory listing for the disk in drive C. If you key DIR at the A:\> prompt, the information displayed is for the disk in drive A. So, whenever you key a DOS command, the system assumes you are referring to the drive named in the DOS prompt or the default drive, *unless you specify otherwise* in the command line.

You can designate or specify a different drive by adding the **drive designator** after the command. The drive designator is the drive name followed by a colon (A: or C:). The drive designator is a **parameter**, additional information keyed after the command to specify exactly what you want DOS to do.

Whenever you want DOS to operate on a disk in a drive that is not shown in the prompt, you can instruct the system to do this by including a parameter, the drive designator, after the command. If you have a floppy diskette, you may wish to take time now to check the DIR in both the disk drives of your computer.

Practice: Specifying Disk Drives in Commands

Try the following to display the contents of drive C with either of the following commands:

■ C:\>**DIR**   [Enter]   A:\>**DIR C:**   [Enter]

Now try either of the following commands to display the contents of the disk in drive A.

■ C:\>**DIR A:**   [Enter]   A:\>**DIR**   [Enter]

CHANGING DEFAULT DRIVES

It is important to be able to navigate among disk drives to execute commands. For example, you may be at the A prompt and wish to go to the C prompt, or conversely, be at the C prompt and wish to go to the A prompt. If you are at the A prompt and wish to go to the C prompt, key the drive designator C:

A:\>C:

You will see the C prompt display as:

C:\>

If you have a formatted diskette in drive A, you can access the drive by keying the following:

A:

Practice: **Changing Drive Prompts**

With the formatted diskette, CLASS, in drive A, let's change the drive prompt as follows:

■   C:\>A: [Enter]

You should see the A prompt display such as:

A>   *or*   A:\>

Now change back to drive C with:

■   A:\>C: [Enter]

USING DOSKEY

DOSKEY is a memory-resident program that records the DOS commands you have keyed in a **command history** buffer. From the buffer, you can recall, revise, and reissue commands. With DOSKEY you can access a long series of earlier commands.

Keys for Use with DOSKEY	
Up and Down Arrows	Recall commands
Escape	Clears command line
Page Up	Recalls first command in memory
Page Down	Recalls last command in memory
F6	Perform DOS editing key functions as do Ins, Del, and Backspace
F7	Displays a numbered list of commands in memory
Alt-F7	Clears the command history
F8	Searches command history for most recent command starting with character(s) you press next
F9	Selects command by number entered next

Practice: Using DOSKEY

Set a path to the DOS files and install DOSKEY in memory by keying the following at the DOS prompt:

- **C:\>DOSKEY**   [Enter]

DOS should display the message: `DOSKEY installed.`

Key the following:

- **C:\>CLS**   [Enter]

- **C:\>VER**   [Enter]

- **C:\>DIR/W**   [Enter]

Press the **up arrow key**; do you see DIR/W? Press **F7**. You should see the following numbered list of commands:

```
1.   CLS
2.   VER
3.   DIR/W
```

Key **F9** and **1** and press [Enter] to recall line 1, the CLS command. Press Enter to repeat the command.

DOSKEY uses the DOS editing keys which you will learn in a later chapter **and** other cursor control and function keys. See the following list.

You may wish to clear any former command history. To do so, key:

- **Alt-F7** to clear any former command history.

Use **Ctrl + T** (displays the symbol ¶) to string multiple commands on a line as in DIR A: ¶ DIR C:.

String multiple commands using DOSKEY with the following:

- **C:\>VER ¶ VOL A:**   [Enter]

WORKING WITH TEXT FILES

A text file is a file that, as the name implies, stores a document or other text—perhaps a short message, letter, or memo. An easy way to create text files for all of these purposes is to use the DOS internal command COPY with

CON, which is short for console. CON is the device name given to the keyboard and display screen. The command syntax is:

COPY CON [filename.ext]

This instructs the system to copy input from the keyboard (CON) and store the input in the file you named in the command line. After you key the command line and press [Enter], DOS will begin storing in memory the text you key. You can key lines of text, pressing [Enter] at the end of each line. Word wrap is not available in this command.

If you make a keying error and have not pressed [Enter] on that line, you can backspace until you have deleted the error and rekey that portion of the line. If, however, you have already ended a line by pressing [Enter], you won't be able to correct the error at this time but must edit the file with an editing program, such as EDLIN, EDIT (version 5.0 or later), E, or a word processor. Later chapters in this book will explain how to use EDLIN or EDIT, but for now, just ignore your typos.

When you have finished keying the text, hold down the Ctrl key and press the letter Z (Ctrl-Z) or the F6 function key to signal the system that you want to end the file. When you press [Enter], DOS will copy the text stored in memory to a disk file and give it the name you specified in the COPY CON command line.

Reminder: When you do not specify a disk drive, your command will apply to the drive shown in the prompt.

As you will see in this and later chapters, you can utilize a text file in a variety of ways. You can view it on the screen, print it, revise it, combine it with other files, and make duplicate copies of it.

Practice: Creating Text Files

Insert the CLASS diskette in drive A and create a text file. Key the following command at the A prompt:

■ **A:\>COPY CON DOC1.TXT**   [Enter]

After you key the COPY CON DOC1.TXT command line and press [Enter], the cursor returns to the left margin and is ready to receive your input. Key

the text shown in bold type that follows. Substitute your name and current
date. To create a blank line, simply press [Enter].

If you make a error while keying the document and have not pressed [Enter] at
the end of the line, backspace until you have deleted the error and rekey that
portion of the line. If, however, you have already ended a line by pressing
[Enter], you won't be able to correct the error. If you want to start over, use
Ctrl-C keys to cancel the COPY CON command and return to the DOS
prompt. Then rekey the command and the file from the beginning. Later you
will learn how to edit text files such as this:

   A:\>COPY CON DOC1.TXT
- **(your name)**   [Enter]
- **(the current date)**   [Enter]
                                     [Enter]
- **This is my first text file.**   [Enter]
- **It will be stored on my disk**   [Enter]
- **in drive A.**   [Enter]
                                     [Enter]

To end and store your file, hold down the Ctrl key and then press the letter Z
key (Ctrl-Z) and press [Enter].   Or you can press the F6 function key and
[Enter] to accomplish the same purpose. Either way, these lines will display:

- **^Z**   [Enter]
   1 file(s) copied

(When you press Ctrl-Z or F6 and [Enter] to end the file, watch for the drive A
light to flash signaling that the file is being written to disk.) You should be
back at the DOS prompt. Now look at the directory of the disk on which you
stored the DOC1.TXT file.

- **A:\>DIR**   [Enter]

You will see the name of your disk and a list of the files on the disk. In this
list you should see the new DOC1.TXT file. Notice that in the directory list of
files, the filename and extension are in separate columns with spaces between
the filename and extension. However, when you key the filename and
extension in a DOS command line, you must separate them only with a period
(called a "dot" in computer lingo), as in the following:

   DIR COMMAND.COM   *or*   DIR DOC1.TXT

Now try creating a text file and storing it on a disk that is *NOT* in the default
drive. Change to drive C and use the COPY CON technique to create a file
called DOC2.TXT.

- **C:\>COPY CON A:DOC2.TXT**   [Enter]
- **This is my second text file.**   [Enter]
- **I keyed A: in front of the**   [Enter]
- **file name so the file will be**   [Enter]
- **stored on my disk in drive A.**   [Enter]
- **(your name)**   [Enter]
                                                    [Enter]
- **[F6]** *or* **[Ctrl-Z]**   [Enter]

Use the DIR command to see if DOC2.TXT is on the disk in drive A. To tell DOS to look at the disk in drive A, you must key the drive designator A: as well as the file name DOC2.TXT. This combination of the drive designator and the file name is called a **filespec**. There are no spaces in a filespec.

- **C:\>DIR A:DOC2.TXT**   [Enter]

DOS will display the directory information for DOC2.TXT.

Displaying the Contents of Text Files with the TYPE Command

You have seen DOC1.TXT and DOC2.TXT listed in the directory of the disk in drive A, but to see if the system actually recorded the contents of what you keyed, you can use the DOS internal command TYPE. DOS provides this easy way to display the contents of files, both on the screen and printed on paper. To display the contents of the file DOC2.TXT on the screen, key the command as follows:

    A:\>TYPE DOC2.TXT *or* C:\>TYPE A:DOC2.TXT

Remember, if the file is not in the default drive shown by the prompt, you must include the drive designator as part of the filespec.

It is also possible to display DOS command files, such as FORMAT.COM, with the TYPE command, but these program files are written in machine language and stored in code that cannot be read by the layperson.

Practice: Displaying Text Files

Display the contents of DOC1.TXT with the following:

- **A:\>TYPE DOC1.TXT**   [Enter]
  or
- **C:\>TYPE A:DOC1.TXT**   [Enter]

PRINTING FILES

It is important to be able to record on paper what is on the screen or stored on disk. There are several ways to print files.

Print Screen

The first method you learned was to print the contents of the screen; this is like taking a picture of what is currently on the screen.

Echo Print

Echo printing is a method of continuous printing that "echoes" everything that appears on the screen. This works best with a dot matrix printer. While output to the printer is on, anything that you key or that DOS displays on the screen also goes to the printer and is reproduced as hard copy. To turn on the echo-print option, press the Ctrl key and the PrtSc or the P key (Ctrl-PrtSc or Ctrl-P).

These key combinations act as toggle switches. When you press the keys once, the echo or continuous print function is turned on; press the keys again, and the function is toggled off. If you turn off the printer, you turn off the echo-print function.

Not all printers are capable of echo printing. In some networked systems where many computers share a printer, echo printing cannot be used. If your system, for whatever reason, does not have the capability for echo printing, read this section but do not enter the commands.

Using the TYPE Command to Print

Previously you displayed the contents of a file using the DOS internal command TYPE. You can also use that command to print the file. First, you would be sure that a printer is connected to your computer, is turned on, and is on-line. Next, key the following command to print the file DOC2.TXT:

    A:\>TYPE DOC2.TXT > PRN
    or
    C:\>TYPE A:DOC2.TXT > PRN

In this command line, the greater-than sign (>) redirects the output of the TYPE command from the screen, where it would normally go, to the printer. PRN is the system's device name for the printer, like CON is the device name for the console. So here you are telling the system to TYPE or display the file DOC2.TXT on the printer, rather than on the screen.

Using the COPY Command to Print

You can also use the COPY command to display and print the file. To print the file using the COPY command, key the following:

    A:\>COPY DOC2.TXT PRN

This instructs the system to copy the file DOC2.TXT from the drive A disk to the printer. The message "1 file(s) copied" appears on the screen but not on the printed copy.

Practice: Printing Text Files

Try the various ways of printing you have learned so far with the following:

1. Clear the screen and key the command to display the directory of the disk in drive A. Print the screen.

- **C:\>DIR A:**   [Enter]

    Press the Shift and PrtSc keys or just PrtSc depending on your system.

2. Using the TYPE command, print the DOC1.TXT file as follows:

- **C:\>TYPE A:DOC1.TXT > PRN**   [Enter]

3. Using the COPY command, print the DOC1.TXT file as follows:

- **C:\>COPY A:DOC1.TXT PRN**   [Enter]

4. To echo print, while you are holding down the Ctrl key, tap the PrtSc or key the letter P. (With some systems, only one of these key combinations will work.) Nothing will happen until you key the next letter. The next letter you key will print. To print the directory, key

- **C:\>DIR**

To turn off the echo-print function, key the Ctrl + PrtSc or Ctrl + P key combinations again.

Great work on Chapter 3! Test your knowledge by answering the Self-Check Quiz and working through the Assignment.

CHAPTER 3 SELF-CHECK QUIZ

True/False (Write T if the statement is true, F if the statement is false.)

_____ 1.   The search path provides access to the internal DOS commands.

_____ 2.   To rename a disk without reformatting it, use the LABEL command.

_____ 3.   By default the FORMAT command performs an unconditional format.

_____ 4.   TYPE, PATH, and VOL are internal commands.

_____ 5.   DOSKEY will store a history of the commands used during the current computer session.

Multiple Choice (Circle the correct answer.)

6. The TYPE command can be used to:

    a. key text files.
    b. display any file on the screen.
    c. display only text files on the screen.
    d. determine what type of drive you are using.

7. If drive A is the default drive, what command would you use to create a file named MYDOC in drive B?

    a. B:COPY CON MYDOC   c. TYPE B:MYD
    b. COPY CON B:MYDOC   d. COPY B:MYDOC CON

8. Which of the following do you use to indicate the end of a text file?

    a. Ctrl-Z   c. Ctrl-T
    b. Ctrl-E   d. Ctrl-C

9. Which two commands will print a copy of the file DOC4.TXT?

    a. TYPE DOC4.TXT PRN   c. COPY DOC4.TXT PRN
    b. TYPE DOC4.TXT > PRN   d. COPY DOC4.TXT > PRN

10. Which command would you use to create a self-booting disk in drive A?

    a. FORMAT \S A: c. FORMAT A: /S
    b. COPY /S A: d. FORMAT A: SYS

ASSIGNMENT

To practice using the commands in this assignment, complete the following steps. Check off each step when you understand its operation or mark the step with a question mark if it is not clear. Write the commands or keystrokes in the space provided.

1. Change the prompt to show the current directory and set the search path to the DOS files.

    _____

2. Activate the DOSKEY command, or if it is already activated, clear the command history.

    _____

3. Format a second floppy diskette with the system; name it TEST.

    _____

4. Clear the screen. Display a directory of the disk in drive A. Print the screen.

    _____

5. Rename the diskette to LAB FILES. Display the volume label of the disk. Print the screen.

    _____

6. Create a text file named A-DOC.TXT on the LAB FILES diskette. Compose your own wording, but include your name and date in the file. Print the file using the COPY [filename.ext] PRN technique.

    _____

7. Display the contents of A-DOC.TXT using the TYPE command. Print the screen.

    _____

8. Display a directory of the LAB FILES data disk. Then check to see what version of DOS you are using. Print the screen.

    _____

9. Using the DOSKEY command, display a list of the commands used during this assignment. Print the screen.

10. Complete the following chart on printing techniques:

COMPARISON OF PRINTING METHODS		
METHOD	ADVANTAGES	DISADVANTAGES
Print Screen		
Echo Print		
Copy File to Printer (Using COPY Command)		
Redirect File to Printer (Using TYPE Command)		

CHAPTER 4

FILE-HANDLING COMMANDS

OBJECTIVES

When you have completed the activities and assignment in this chapter, you will be able to:

1. Make copies of files on the same disk.

2. Copy files onto a different disk.

3. Use wildcards with the COPY command.

4. Combine files with the COPY command.

5. Compare files with the COMP or FC command.

6. Rename files with the REN command.

7. Move files with the MOVE command.

8. Use the DOS Editing keys.

STRUCTURE FOR FILE-HANDLING COMMANDS

The file-handling commands described in this chapter (COPY, FC, COMP, RENAME, and MOVE) all use the same structure or syntax in the command line. For all of them, the command is followed by the **source** filespec and then the **destination** or target filespec. You can mentally translate the command line as including:

COMMAND   *SOURCE*   *DESTINATION*

COPY   (from)   FILE1.DOC   (to)   FILE2.DOC

The words "from" and "to" are represented by spaces separating the command and its two parameters, source and destination. With few exceptions, both the source and destination must be specified in the command line.

COPY FILE1 FILE2   COMP FILE1 FILE2   RENAME FILE1 FILE2

COPYING FILES

The COPY command is one of the most useful internal commands of DOS. You have already used a form of COPY to create and print text files; COPY will also duplicate files, make copies of files on other disks, and combine files. Duplicate files are useful when you want to back up or create variations of the same document. You can make several copies and modify each one with a word processor or with the DOS editors, EDLIN, EDIT, and E. For example, you could use this technique to create notes to clients or personalized thank-you messages. You will work with EDLIN in Chapter 8 and EDIT in Chapter 9. The text editor, E, is not covered in the text.

Or you might want to make a copy of a file you have created to give to someone else. You will often use COPY to make backup files for protection in case a floppy disk is lost or damaged. You can use COPY to move files from one disk to another or from one directory of a disk to another directory. And, you can use COPY to combine files into a new file and to add or append information to an existing file.

There are three options for using COPY to copy files:

- You can make a copy with the same name.
- You can make a copy with a different name.
- You can combine files into one file.

Here are some important file naming conventions you must remember when you use any of these options:

- Each file in a directory listing must have a unique name. If you are copying a file into the same directory of a floppy or hard disk, you must give the copy a different name from the name of the file being copied. Changing at least one character in the filename or extension will satisfy this requirement.

- If you are copying a file onto another floppy disk, you can use the same name or a different name. Copies of a file with the same name can reside on different disks, as they will appear in different directory listings.

> **Note:** One important caution about this command is that if there are
> any files on the target disk with names identical to names on the
> source disk, the files on the target disk will be overwritten.
> However, DOS 6.2 has added a prompt that advises that a file of the
> same name exists and gives you the opportunity to overwrite or not.

- More than one file with the same name can be stored on a disk if the files
  are in different directory listings. You will learn about creating and
  working with subdirectories in Chapters 6 and 7.

Copying Files to the Same Disk

When copying a file onto the same disk, you need to ensure that there is room
for the copy, that the file to be copied is on the source disk, that you give a
unique name for the copy, and that no file with the new name already exists on
the disk. Except for MS-DOS v6.2, files with the same name will be
overwritten without warning. Display the directory to be sure the file is listed
and that there is no file with the new name you plan to give to the copy. Since
the copy will be listed in the same directory as the source file, you must give
the copy a *new and unique name*. A name is different if you change one
character in the file name or the extension. In this case, you will change the
entire extension to change the file name, DOC1.TXT to DOC1.DOC with the
following:

    COPY DOC1.TXT DOC1.DOC

Remember that COPY is an internal command; therefore, you do not have to
access the DOS external command files.

Practice: Copying a File to the Same Disk

For this practice, insert the CLASS diskette, copy the file, and give the new
file a different extension, NEW:

- **A:\>COPY A:DOC1.TXT A:DOC1.NEW**   [Enter]
                    or
- **A:\>COPY DOC1.TXT DOC1.NEW**   [Enter]

You have asked the system to copy the existing (source) file DOC1.TXT *from*
the disk in drive A *to* the same disk and to give the destination file a different
name, DOC1.NEW.

Note that if your disk is in the default drive A and you want DOS to find the source file there and place the copy on the same disk, the drive designators (A:) before the file names are not necessary. With either entry above, the system will respond with the message

```
1 file(s) copied.
```

If, instead, you see the error message "Bad command or file name" or "File not found," carefully examine the command line you keyed. Did you spell the filename exactly as it is spelled in your directory? Did you key a period (not a comma) between the filename and the extension? If you used the drive designator, did you key a colon (not a semicolon) after the letter A? Did you space the command and filenames exactly as shown above, with spaces only after COPY and the first file name? DOS *insists* that command lines such as this be keyed perfectly! If you find an error, key the line again.

Clear the screen and use the TYPE command to verify that DOC1.NEW is indeed an exact copy of DOC1.TXT.

■   **A:\>TYPE DOC1.TXT**   [Enter]

■   **A:\>TYPE DOC1.NEW**   [Enter]

Do the two files look the same? Later in this chapter you will learn how DOS can verify that two files are identical.

Copying Files onto Another Disk

There are many times when you will want to copy a file onto a different diskette. Follow the instructions that fit your system's configuration of one or two floppy drives.

One Floppy Drive System

If your system has only one floppy drive, DOS will use that drive as both drive A and drive B. For example, if you would like to copy the file TEXT1.DOC to TEXT1.DOC on another diskette from the same floppy drive, you would key the following:

A:\>COPY A:TEXT1.DOC B:

Here you have asked the system to copy the source file, TEXT1.DOC, from the disk in drive A. The destination for the copy is the disk in drive B. Because you did not specify a new file name after the B:, the system knows you want the new file to have the same file name as the source. In this example, you must include the destination drive designator B:, but since the source file is in the default drive, keying A: before the source file name is optional.

The system will load the contents of the source file TEXT1.DOC into RAM and then will instruct you to exchange the floppy disks so that it can write the copy onto the destination disk. The system will prompt you with the following message:

```
Insert diskette for drive B: and press any key when
ready.
```

Remove the source diskette and insert a different disk (the destination or target disk) into drive A. After you press a key, DOS will write the file from memory onto the disk and report:

```
1 file(s) copied
Insert diskette for drive A: and press any key when
ready.
```

Do as prompted and insert the source diskette and press any key.

Practice: Copying a File Using a One Floppy Drive System

Let's practice! Insert the CLASS diskette and key the following at the A:\> prompt. Follow the prompts to insert the LAB FILES diskette as the target diskette.

- **A:\>COPY A:DOC1.TXT B:**   [Enter]
                    or
- **A:\>COPY DOC1.TXT B:**   [Enter]

Display the directory of both the CLASS and LAB FILES diskettes to see that DOC1.TXT is listed.

Two Floppy Drive System

Copying files is faster and easier if you have two floppy drives. It is *not* essential that these two drives be the same size to be able to copy files from one to the other. Insert the CLASS diskette into drive A. The destination drive will be drive B. To copy the file COMPUTER.FIL, you would key the following:

```
A:\>COPY A:COMPUTER.FIL B:
```

Here you have asked the system to copy the source file COMPUTER.FIL from the disk in drive A, to the destination disk in drive B. Because you did not specify a new file name after the drive B the system knows you want the new file to have the same file name as the source. In this example, you must include the destination drive designator B:, but if the source file is in the default drive, the A: before the source file name is optional. DOS will load the contents of COMPUTER.FIL into RAM and then write the file onto the drive B disk and report:

```
1 file(s) copied
```

Practice: Copying a File Using a Two Floppy Drive System

Try this operation after inserting the CLASS disk in drive A and the LAB FILES disk in drive B:

- **C:\>COPY A:DOC2.TXT B:**   [Enter]
                or
- **A:\>COPY DOC2.TXT B:**   [Enter]

Display the directory of the disk in drive B to see if DOC2.TXT is listed:

- **A:\>DIR B:**   [Enter]

Copying Files to the Hard Drive

The same principles apply when copying files to the hard drive. To copy the file, COMPUTER.CGM from drive A to the hard drive, key the following:

```
COPY A:COMPUTER.CGM C:
```

Here you have asked the system to copy the source file COMPUTER.CGM from the disk in drive A. The destination for the copy is drive C. Because you did not specify a new file name after the C:, the system knows you want the new file to have the same file name as the source. In this example, if you do not include the destination drive designator C:, the file will be copied to the default drive resulting in the error message, "A file cannot be copied onto itself.".

DOS will load the contents of COMPUTER.CGM into RAM and then write the file onto drive C. Then DOS will report:

```
1 file(s) copied
```

Practice: Copying a File to the Hard Drive

Be sure that the source disk, CLASS, is in drive A and the destination is drive
C. Key the following:

■ **C:\\>COPY A:DOC2.TXT C:**   [Enter]
          or
■ **A:\\>COPY DOC2.TXT C:**   [Enter]

Display the directory of drive C to see if DOC2.TXT is listed.

■ **A:\\>DIR C:**   [Enter]

Copying and Giving the Destination File a Different Name

You can also choose to give the destination file (the copy) a *different name*.
For example, you might wish to copy OLDNAME.TXT and give the file a new
name, NEWNAME.TXT, with the following:

    COPY A:OLDNAME.TXT C:NEWNAME.TXT

Here you told the system to copy the OLDNAME.TXT file from the disk in
drive A, to place the copy on drive C, and to give the duplicate file a different
name, NEWNAME.TXT.

Practice: Copying and Giving the Destination File a Different Name

Try this new concept by keying the following command:

■ **C:\\>COPY A:DOC2.TXT C:NEWNAME.DOC**   [Enter]
                or
■ **A:\\>COPY DOC2.TXT C:NEWNAME.DOC**   [Enter]

Another variation is to copy a file from another drive to the default drive.
From the A prompt, copy NEWNAME.DOC from drive C (source) to the disk
in drive A (destination) with this instruction:

■ **C:\\>COPY NEWNAME.DOC A:**   [Enter]
          or
■ **A:\\>COPY C:NEWNAME.DOC**   [Enter]

Both of the preceding command lines tell the system to make a copy of the file
NEWNAME.DOC in drive C, to place the copy in the default drive A, and to
give the copy the same name.

Copying Files Using Wildcards

A useful technique for copying files is that of using wildcards when specifying files for copying. Used with the COPY command, the wildcards ? and * function in the same way as when used to specify the file names with the DIR command as explained in Chapter 2.

Remember, the wildcard ? stands for a single character in a filename or extension; the wildcard * stands for all characters to the right of the * in the filename or extension.

By using wildcards, you can make copies of a series of files that have similar names by entering only one command. Understanding how wildcards are used can save time in copying files and will also help you make decisions about naming files to facilitate the use of wildcards. For example, if you have files for Mr. Johnson and have begun all his file names with J such as J-TXT1.DOC, J-TXT2.DOC, and so on, you would copy all the files with the following commands:

    COPY A:J-TXT?.DOC B: *or*   COPY A:J*.DOC B:

These would select all the files beginning with J-TXT or J and ending with the extension DOC regardless of the letters following J-TXT or J.

To copy all of the files with the DOC extension, from drive A to drive B, key the following:

    COPY A:*.DOC B:

Practice: Copying with Wildcards

To begin this activity, display the directory of your CLASS disk to see if you have files named DOC1.TXT and DOC2.TXT files. Use the following commands to copy both files:

■ **A:\>COPY DOC1.TXT A-DOC.TXT**   [Enter]

■ **A:\>COPY DOC2.TXT B-DOC.TXT**   [Enter]

Check your directory to see that you have the following files. (You may have more, but be sure you have these listed.)

```
DOC1.TXT              B-DOC.TXT
DOC2.TXT              NEWNAME.DOC
A-DOC.TXT             DOC1.NEW
```

Now you will see how wildcards can be used in making copies of files. First experiment with the ?, which stands for a single character in a file name. You can use it to make copies of the files A-DOC.TXT and B-DOC.TXT. You will name the new copies A-DOC.NEW and B-DOC.NEW. The ? will stand for the A and B at the beginning of each file name. Key the following command line:

■ **A:\>COPY ?-DOC.TXT ?-DOC.NEW**   [Enter]

You have told DOS to copy all the files that have any first letter followed by DOC as a filename and the extension TXT. DOS is to give the files the same filename but change the extension to NEW. A list of the files is displayed as they are copied:

```
A-DOC.TXT
B-DOC.TXT

2 file(s) copied
```

Note that you could not use the * wildcard in place of the ? in this command because the * would substitute for all characters to its right in the filename. This would have been the same as entering the command

A:\>COPY *.TXT *.NEW

and would have copied every file with the extension TXT.

Next, copy all the files that begin with DOC and have TXT as the extension. In addition to copying them, change their extension to NEW.

At the A:\> prompt, key:

■ **A:\>COPY A:DOC*.TXT A:DOC*.NEW**   [Enter]
                    or
■ **A:\>COPY DOC*.TXT DOC*.NEW**   [Enter]

The system will identify all the files on the disk that begin with DOC and have the extension TXT, make copies of them on the disk, and give the copies the same filename but a different extension, NEW. A list of the files is displayed as they are copied. Display the directory to see the file copies listed.

Try another example. Copy all the files that have the extension NEW onto the same disk, give them the same filename, but give them your initials as the extension. Mary Todd Lincoln would use this command:

COPY *.NEW *.MTL

Practice using your own initials with

■ **A:\>COPY *.NEW *.[your initials]**   [Enter]

Display a directory of the disk to see a listing of your files.

Combining Files into a New File

Another application of the COPY command is to **combine** the contents of two or more small files into one larger file. For example, if you had several text files that contained memos written during the week, you might want to archive them as a group into a single file. Wildcards can be used in this process.

Given two files, NEWNAME.DOC and OLDNAME.DOC, you would combine the files by keying the command below. Key a plus (+) between the file names, and leave a space between these file names (the source files) and the name of the new, combined file (the destination file):

    COPY NEWNAME.DOC + OLDNAME.DOC TOGETHER.DOC

The system will respond with the following message:

    NEWNAME.DOC
    OLDNAME.DOC

     1 file(s) copied

The two files listed were combined into one file; therefore, the system reports that one file was copied.

Use the TYPE command to display TOGETHER.DOC. You will see that both files have been combined into a single file.

Practice: **Combining Files into a New File**

Insert the CLASS diskette in drive A. Use the TYPE command to see what the two files, DOC1.TXT and DOC2.TXT, contain. Then combine DOC1.TXT and DOC2.TXT and put the results in DOC3.TXT.

■ **A:\>TYPE DOC1.TXT**   [Enter]

■ **A:\>TYPE DOC2.TXT**   [Enter]

■ **A:\>COPY DOC1.TXT + DOC2.TXT DOC3.TXT**   [Enter]

The system will respond with the following message:

```
DOC1.TXT
DOC2.TXT

1 file(s) copied
```

Use the TYPE command to display DOC3.TXT. You will see that both files have been combined into a single file.

C:\>TYPE A:DOC3.TXT   [Enter]

Now use the copy command to combine DOC3.TXT and A-DOC.TXT and put the results in DOC4.TXT:

■   **A:\>COPY DOC3.TXT + A-DOC.TXT DOC4.TXT**   [Enter]

Use the TYPE command to display DOC4.TXT. Does it contain the contents of both DOC3.TXT and A-DOC.TXT?

Using Wildcards When Combining Files

To combine groups of files, you can also use wildcards in the command. You would key this command line to combine all files with the DOC extension:

A:\>COPY *.DOC LINKED.DOC

As DOS combines all the source DOC files into the destination file, LINKED.DOC, the system displays the list of files being merged. Use the DIR command to verify that LINKED.DOC is listed. This process does not change or remove the original files; you will see all of the DOC files also.

Use the TYPE command to be sure that LINKED.DOC is a combination of all the files with the DOC extension.

Practice: Combining Files with Wildcards

Try combining files with wildcards by using the following command with the CLASS diskette in drive A:

■   **A:\>COPY *.TXT COMBINE.DOC**   [Enter]

Use the DIR and TYPE commands to check to see that all files exist and contain what they should.

Appending Files

You can also combine files adding information to an existing file. This is called **appending**. For example, you could append or add a file containing a list of references to a résumé file. In this case, the *first* file listed in the command line is the file to which the contents of the other file(s) should be added.

To see how this works, use the TYPE command to view the contents of NEWDOC.TXT and then OLDDOC.TXT. After you see what each file contains, add the file OLDDOC.TXT to NEWDOC.TXT by keying the following command:

COPY NEWDOC.TXT + OLDDOC.TXT

DOS will add or append the *second* file listed to the first file. After this operation, the file OLDDOC.TXT will be unchanged, but its contents will have been added to the end of NEWDOC.TXT.

Note: The sequence of files is very important when combining files into an existing file. The contents of the second file is added to that of the first.

Practice: Combining Files without Creating a New File

Now, with the CLASS diskette in drive A, add A-DOC.TXT to DOC3.TXT as follows:

- **A:\>COPY DOC3.TXT + A-DOC.TXT**   [Enter]

Use the TYPE command to confirm that DOC3.TXT does now indeed contain both files. Note that if one of the files had been on another disk, you could have combined them simply by adding the drive designator in front of the file name. The contents of the appended file will be placed in the file in the location shown in the prompt.

If you want the file to be placed on the disk in another drive, add the drive designator at the end of the command line. For example, if you would like the above example to be placed in a disk on drive B, key the following:

- **A:\>COPY DOC3.TXT + A-DOC.TXT B:**   [Enter]

If you have a one-floppy diskette system, you will need to exchange the diskettes. Use the DIRectory command to see that the new file is on the disk in drive B.

You can use this append technique to print two or more files as if they were one file. Display DOC1.TXT and DOC2.TXT again with the TYPE command. Then make sure your printer is on-line and enter:

- **A:\>COPY DOC1.TXT + DOC2.TXT PRN**   [Enter]

Both files will be printed as one file. Neither file will be changed, as the output went to the printer (PRN) and was appended in the printed copy only.

DOS places an invisible marker at the end of a combined or appended file. If you combine this file again with a command that uses wildcards, the marker is not always removed. If this happens, there will be an erroneous end-of-file marker in the middle of the combined file! DOS stops any operation on a file when it encounters an end-of-file marker. Because portions of such a file would be ignored, using wildcards to combine *previously combined files* is not a reliable method. *Always* check the file contents when you use this technique.

COMPARING FILES

There will be occasions when you will want to compare one file to another. If there are differences in the two files, the COMP command will tell you.

COMP is not available in MS-DOS prior to version 3.3. Use the command FC instead of COMP. In IBM PC-DOS, only COMP is available prior to version 5.0, which has both commands. In IBM PC-DOS, version 6.1, both FC and COMP can be used. In the case of IBM PC-DOS, version 6.1, when you use FC the contents of each file are actually shown for your review. The external commands COMP and FC compare two files, byte for byte.

If a difference is found, you will be told where the difference occurs and the contents of the bytes that differ. By default, COMP compares files until it finds ten mismatches, then it concludes that further comparison is useless and reports:

```
10 mismatches - ending compare
```

By default, COMP and FC will not compare two files of different sizes. If you attempt to compare files of different sizes, the system may beep and will display a message like:

```
Files are different sizes.
```

A comparison is made until the end-of-file (EOF) marker Ctrl-Z is found. If there is no mark, the system reports this. Sometimes discrepancies in compared files occur after the unmarked "end" of the file; therefore, COMP reports when there is no end-of-file marker.

Since COMP and FC are external commands, you must set a search path for DOS to find the external command files. *If you are using DOS files on the hard drive*, enter the following PATH command:

    A:\>PATH C:\DOS

If the DOS files are in another directory on the hard disk, substitute its name in the command line.

Compare OLDDOC.TXT with NEWDOC.TXT with the appropriate command depending on your version of DOS:

    COMP OLDDOC.TXT NEWDOC.TXT
            or
    FC OLDDOC.TXT NEWDOC.TXT

Practice: Comparing Files

Display a directory of your CLASS diskette and copy the largest file you have listed. This will probably be the file called COMBINE.DOC. Name the copy COMBINE2.DOC. To compare the two files, key the appropriate command for your version of DOS:

■ **A:\>COMP A:COMBINE.DOC A:COMBINE2.DOC**   [Enter]
            or
■ **A:\>FC A:COMBINE.DOC A:COMBINE2.DOC**   [Enter]

The system compares the files. Did it report that an EOF (end of file) mark was not found? Did the files compare OK? Key N and press [Enter] at the prompt Compare more files (Y/N)?

Using COMP with Wildcards

Versions of FC prior to DOS 5.0 will not compare files selected with wildcards. If you are using MS-DOS 4.0 or earlier, read this activity for possible use in the future.

Groups of files selected with wildcards can be compared by using the COMP or FC commands with the various versions of MS/PC-DOS.

Practice: **Comparing Files with Wildcards**

You previously copied all files with the extension NEW and gave the copies your initials as the extension. If you were Mary Todd Lincoln, you would have used the command:

COPY *.NEW *.MTL

Now, with the CLASS diskette in drive A, compare the original files and the copies. Simply substitute COMP for COPY in the command line. (Use your own initials.)

■   **A:\>COMP *.NEW *.[your initials]**   [Enter]

Key N and press [Enter] to the prompt Compare more files (Y/N)?

RENAMING FILES WITH RENAME

In addition to renaming files when they are copied, DOS will rename an existing file without duplicating it if you use the internal command RENAME or REN. The command RENAME does exactly what it says: It changes the file name in the directory listing; it does not make a copy of the file with a new name or change the contents of the file in any way.

Since RENAME is one of the internal commands loaded into memory with COMMAND.COM, it is always available. You do not need access to the DOS external command files on a disk to use this command.

To rename a file, you can use RENAME or the shortened version, REN. Here is a typical rename command:

REN WHYDOS.NOW STUDYDOS.DOC

The original name of the file is given first, followed by a space and the new name. When you have renamed a file, the original name of the file no longer appears in the directory and can be used for another file. After the preceding command is entered, the name WHYDOS.NOW will no longer appear in the directory.

Apart from changing your mind about what a file should be called, you will find this command useful when you want to reserve and reuse a file name for a special purpose. For example, you might use COPY CON to write a daily list of things to do and name the file TO-DO. On rare occasions you may not complete all the tasks listed and need to save the list to refer to later. You could rename the file TO-DO.OLD and continue to use the name TO-DO for your current list.

Practice: Renaming Files

To rename the file called DOC1.TXT to FILE1.TXT on the CLASS diskette, key the following at the DOS prompt:

- **C:\>RENAME A:DOC1.TXT FILE1.TXT**   [Enter]
    or
- **C:\>REN A:DOC1.TXT FILE1.TXT**   [Enter]

Note that the command can be shortened to REN or spelled out. Also note that you did *not* use a disk drive designator with the new file name. DOS will not allow such a disk drive designator with a new file. This is logical because the system is only changing the name of the file in the directory of the disk. REN does not rename a file and move it to a different disk (that would be copying the file).

When you press [Enter], the drive light comes on briefly. DOS is changing the directory. Then DOS displays the DOS prompt on the screen. To verify the absence of DOC1.TXT and the existence of FILE1.TXT, try to display the DOC1.TXT file using the TYPE command:

- **C:\>TYPE A:DOC1.TXT**   [Enter]

DOS informs you that the file was not found. You can also display a directory of the disk in drive A to see that FILE1.TXT is there and that DOC1.TXT is not. Then display the contents of FILE1.TXT using the TYPE command. Do you recognize the contents of the old DOC1.TXT file?

Change the name back to DOC1.TXT by keying

- **C:\>REN A:FILE1.TXT DOC1.TXT**   [Enter]

To rename a file on a disk that is not in the default drive, specify the drive designator before the original file name. If necessary, change to drive C and key the following command line to rename a file in drive A:

- **C:\>REN A:B-DOC.TXT RECORD.ABC**   [Enter]

Examine the directory of the CLASS diskette in drive A to verify that the name change for the file was made.

Using Wildcards to Rename Groups of Files

Using wildcards, * and ?, it is possible to rename a group of files with one command entry. Check the directory of the disk in drive A for files with an extension TXT.

C:\>DIR A:*.TXT

The following command will give all files with the extension TXT the extension ABC:

C:\>REN A:*.TXT *.ABC

***Practice:* Renaming Files with Wildcards**

To practice renaming all files with the extension TXT on the CLASS diskette, key:

- **C:\>REN A:*.TXT *.XYZ**   [Enter]
          or
- **A:\>REN *.TXT *.XYZ**   [Enter]

In response to this command, the system gives all files with the extension TXT the new extension XYZ. The filenames are not changed.

To verify the change, key:

- **C:\>DIR *.TXT**   [Enter]

The system reports that no files are found. Now request a directory listing files with the XYZ extension. The system displays a list of the files that formerly had the TXT extension and that now have the XYZ extension.

DOS MOVE COMMAND

Introduced with DOS 6.0 is the capability to move a file from one location to another and delete the file from its original place. This command is similar to the COPY command in syntax. With the COPY command, a duplicate file is made; with the MOVE command, the file location is changed. The MOVE command will move files only to existing drives and directories. If you move a file and neglect to give a destination, the system will prompt with the following:

```
Required parameter missing
```

To move the file COMPUTER.TXT from drive A to drive C, you would key the following command:

MOVE C:COMPUTER.TXT A:

The screen displays the new location of the file with this message:

```
a:\computer.txt => c:\computer.txt [OK]
```

Note: This command requires special attention to the files in the target subdirectory. If there is a file with the same name as the file you are moving, the file in the target subdirectory will be overwritten without any warning message. However, MS-DOS 6.2 has added a protective warning which asks for confirmation before overwriting the file.

Practice: Moving Files

To move a file, DOC3.XYZ, from the CLASS diskette in drive A to drive C, key the following command:

- **C:\>MOVE A:DOC3.XYZ C:**   [Enter]

The screen displays the new location of the file with this message:

```
a:\doc3.xyz => c:\doc3.xyz [OK]
```

Practice your newly-found skills by moving the file DOC3.XYZ back from the hard disk to the floppy disk in drive A. Also, move the files DOC2.TXT and NEWNAME.DOC copied to drive C earlier back to the CLASS diskette.

DOS EDITING KEYS

Have you found that when you key a command and DOS reports "Bad command or file name," it is tedious to rekey the whole command to correct one small mistake? The DOS editing keys can be used to make corrections in the most recent command line after you have entered the command. You can also use them to repeat commands.

When you key a command and press [Enter], the system retains the line you just keyed in an **input buffer**, a special segment of memory. The line in the buffer can be used as a **template** or pattern for a new line. You can copy the template line and edit it with the DOS editing keys. You can also repeat the line with the editing keys.

The DOS editing keys are the function keys F1, F2, F3, F4, F5, F6, and the Del, Esc, Ins, Backspace, and right and left arrow keys. They operate as follows on the last command line entered and stored in the input buffer.

F1	Copies one character from the last command or template line and displays the character on the screen.
F2	Copies and displays the command line up to the character keyed after pressing F2.
F3	Copies and displays the entire previous command line or the remainder of the line.
F4	Skips over (deletes) characters in the line to the character keyed after pressing F4.
F5	Copies the current command line to the template, but does not carry out the command.
F6	Places a Ctrl+Z (^Z) in the current command line.
Del	Removes one character from the command line template. The display does not change.
Esc	Cancels the line displayed; the template remains unchanged.
Ins	Inserts characters in the template and the display at the cursor. Press any editing key to stop inserting.
Backspace	Erases the last character from the display, but not from the template.
Right Arrow	Same as F1.
Left Arrow	Same as Backspace.

Practice: Using the DOS Editing Keys

Try using some of these timesaving keys. Key the following:

■ **DIR /W**   [Enter]

Suppose you had meant to use the Pause switch instead of the wide switch. It's easy to correct as follows:

Press the **F3** key to recall this most recent command.

Do you see the DIR /W command you keyed earlier? Backspace to erase the "W" and key "P." Of course, you would need to press [Enter] to execute the command.

A way to use the Ins key is to insert A: between the "R" and "/W" as follows:

Press the **F1** key three times to display the DIR portion of the previous command. Next, press the **Ins** key to tell DOS to allow you to insert characters without erasing any of the previous command.

Press the **[spacebar]** once, then key **A:**

Finally, press the **F3** key to display the remainder of the previous command. The command line should be: DIR A:/P. Of course, you need to press [Enter] to execute the command.

Another way you might have corrected this would have been to use the F1 key. Try the same scenario in reverse.

Press the **F1** key.

Do you see the "D" on the command line? This is the "D" in the DIR A: /P you corrected in the last activity.

Press **F1** enough times to display through DIR A:/. Then key the "W" which you would like to change back to. Of course, you would have to press [Enter] in order to execute the command.

Now try the F2 and Del keys using editing techniques as follows:

Press the **F2** key and then **A** to display the characters up to, but not including, the **A**. Next, press the **Del** key three times to delete from the buffer the A:. Finally, press **F3** and [Enter].

These are good examples of the use of the DOS editing keys. You will work with more examples later.

Very nice work! Test your knowledge with the Self-Check Quiz and Assignment.

CHAPTER 4 SELF-CHECK QUIZ

True/False (Write T if the statement is true, F if the statement is false.)

_____ 1. When you rename a file with REN, the original file name is still in the directory.

_____ 2. When copying files with wildcards, the more common wildcard is the asterisk or "star."

_____ 3. It is possible to copy files by using wildcards in the command parameters.

_____ 4. Files can have the same name if copied to a different disk.

_____ 5. The command COMP compares two files byte by byte. After the first mismatch, the system will halt the COMP program.

Multiple Choice (Circle the correct answer.)

6. Which one of the following function keys copies up to the character keyed?

    a. F1   c. F4
    b. F2   d. F3

7. To combine the contents of FILE1.TXT with FILE2.TXT into a new file named FILE3.TXT, which command would you key?

    a. COPY FILE1.TXT FILE2.TXT + FILE3.TXT
    b. COPY FILE1 + FILE2.TXT FILE3.TXT
    c. COPY FILE2.TXT + FILE1.TXT=FILE3.TXT
    d. COPY FILE1.TXT + FILE2.TXT

8. To append the contents of FILE2.DOC to FILE1.TXT, which command would you key?

    a. COPY FILE1.TXT FILE2.DOC
    b. COPY FILE1.TXT + FILE2.DOC FILE3.DOC
    c. COPY FILE1.TXT + FILE2.DOC
    d. COPY FILE2.DOC + FILE1.TXT FILE3.DOC

9. To compare the file FILE1.TXT to FILE2.TXT, which command would you key?

   a. COMP FILE1.TXT FILE2.TXT
   b. COMP FILE1.TXT + FILE2.TXT
   c. COPY FILE2 COMP FILE1.TXT
   d. COMP FILE*.*

10. Which of the following is true about the DOS 6.2 MOVE command?

   a. The file will not overwrite an existing file of the same name in the destination directory without a warning.
   b. The file will remain in both locations.
   c. The file destination must not be a different disk drive.
   d. If you try to move a file and neglect to name the target location, the system will prompt with "Required parameter missing."

ASSIGNMENT

To practice using the commands in this chapter, complete the following steps. Check off each step when you understand its operation, or mark the step with a question mark if it is not clear. Write the commands or keystrokes in the space provided.

1. Print a directory of your CLASS diskette.

   _____

2. Create a text file describing the advantages of DOS. Name the file TEXT1.TXT.

   _____

3. Copy the TEXT1.TXT file to TEXT2.TXT on the same disk.

   _____

4. Compare TEXT1.TXT and TEXT2.TXT.

   _____

5. Copy all the files with names that begin with TEXT and that have a TXT extension and give them an ABC extension.

   _____

6. Copy all the files that begin with TEXT and that have an ABC extension and give them the same filename but an XYZ extension. Print a directory of the files.

   _____

7. Compare all the files with an ABC extension with those having an XYZ extension.

   _____

8. Rename the file TEXT1.XYZ to a file with an extension of your initials. Print a directory of the disk.

   _____

9. Move the file TEXT1.[your initials] to drive C. Print the screen or a directory of the CLASS disk.

   _____

10. Move the file TEXT1.[your initials] back to the CLASS disk in drive A. Print the screen or a directory of the disk.

CHAPTER 5

MANAGING FILES AND DISKS

OBJECTIVES

When you have completed the activities and assignment in this chapter, you will be able to:

1. Erase files with the DEL and ERASE commands.

2. Undelete files.

3. Unformat disks.

4. Use the DISKCOPY command to copy disks.

5. Use the COPY *.* and DISKCOPY commands at appropriate times.

6. Use the DISKCOMP command to compare disks.

7. Use the CHKDSK command to check disks.

8. Use the SCANDISK command to repair disk problems.

9. Use the DEFRAG command.

DELETING FILES

You have learned how to create, copy, rename, and move text files; now you will learn how to delete or erase them. The commands ERASE and DEL can be used to erase any file (text or program) that is not protected with read-only status or that is not hidden.

ERASE and DEL are internal DOS commands. You do not need access to the DOS external command files to use them. Simply enter the command followed by the name of the file you want to remove. ERASE and DEL work identically for erasing files.

Practice: Deleting Files

Use the DEL or ERASE command to delete DOC1.XYZ on your CLASS disk in drive A. At the DOS prompt, key

CAUTION: Use ERASE and DEL carefully. Even though DOS 5.0 and later versions contain UNDELETE capabilities, you do not want to take unnecessary risks!

- **DEL A:DOC1.XYZ**   [Enter]
  or
- **ERASE A:DOC1.XYZ**   [Enter]

Note that the drive designator is optional if the file is on the disk in the default drive. However, if there is ever a time when you want to be as specific as possible, it is when you are erasing files.

The drive light will come on briefly when you press [Enter]. DOS will display a new prompt on the screen.

Request a directory listing for the deleted file:

- **A:\>DIR A:DOC1.XYZ**   [Enter]

The display will show that the file is not found.

You can use wildcards with ERASE and DEL to delete or erase a group of files; however, you should make it a practice to always check wildcard entries by using them with the DIR command first. In this way, you can review the list of the files that will be erased when you enter the ERASE or DEL command line. First use:

- **A:\>DIR *.DOC**   [Enter]

When you have checked all the files on your disk with any filename and the extension DOC and have decided that you want to erase all the files shown in the directory listing, key:

- **A:\>DEL *.DOC**   [Enter]

You can use the UNDELETE command to retrieve these files, if necessary.

THE UNDELETE COMMAND

Prior to DOS 5.0, DOS could not reverse the changes made by DEL, ERASE, or FORMAT. Special utility programs could do this, but DOS did not have the capability. In version 5.0, the new command UNDELETE was introduced to restore deleted directory entries. In the later versions, some improvements were made on these capabilities.

As you read in an earlier chapter, on every disk there is a special file called the file allocation table (FAT) that was created when the disk was formatted. When DOS deletes a file, it does two things: (1) it changes the FAT to mark the disk space used by the file as available, and (2) it changes the first character of the filename in the FAT to σ (the Greek letter Sigma). Therefore, the FAT is revised to show that the allocation units are available for storage of other files, and the file can no longer be accessed using its former name. However, by replacing σ with a first letter for the filename, the file can be undeleted until any part of the disk space occupied by the file is overwritten.

Practice: Undeleting Files with DOS 5.0

Since UNDELETE is an external command, you will need to set the search path to the external DOS command files. To have access to these on the hard disk, key:

■ **A:\>PATH C:\DOS**   [Enter]

First undelete a file you deleted earlier, DOC1.XYZ, as follows:

■ **A:\>UNDELETE A:DOC1.XYZ**   [Enter]

DOS responds with messages similar to the following:

```
Directory:  A:\
FILE SPECIFICATIONS:  DOC1.XYZ
Deletion-tracking file not found.
MS-DOS directory contains   1 deleted files.
Of those,    1 files may be recovered.

Using the MS-DOS directory method.
 ?OC1.XYZ    16    7-03-94    12:50p  ...A  Undelete
(Y/N)  ?
```

At this point, key **Y** for yes to confirm that you want to undelete the file. DOS will then ask you to key the first character for DOC1.XYZ. Key the first character, **D**. When you do so and if you have not written any new files on the disk, DOS can restore the file.

To undelete all the files you have deleted, key

■ **A:\>UNDELETE /ALL**   [Enter]

DOS undeletes all files. However, the first character of the filenames which are undeleted has a # or a ? representing the first letter in the directory listing.

If you wish to supply the first character of each file as it is undeleted, key:

- **A:\>UNDELETE *.***   [Enter]

In this case, you have already undeleted all files. However, DOS will be able to undelete the files after you supply the first character of each filename.

USING MIRROR WITH DOS 5.0 TO UNDELETE FILES

The UNDELETE command is very useful. By using the DOS 5.0 external command MIRROR, you can set up a deletion-tracking file for the disk. Thereafter, when you delete a file, its name and related information are stored in the deletion-tracking file. UNDELETE, the command for restoring a deleted file, uses this information to restore deleted files.

When using UNDELETE, if you have installed the MIRROR.FIL on your disk drive, you will not be prompted to key the first character of the filename. If you have installed the MIRROR command before using the UNDELETE command, just follow the screen displays to successfully undelete the file.

Each disk must have its own deletion-tracking file. To tell DOS you want to track file deletions on your disks in drives A, B, and C, use the MIRROR command with the tracking switch /T and the drive name for each drive as in the following:

    MIRROR /TA /TB /TC

This command creates the file MIRROR.FIL and a small system file named MIRRORSAV.FIL in the root directory of the disks located in the drives you have named. MIRROR.FIL contains a copy of the disk's FAT and directory. When you delete files from the disk, another system file named PCTRACKR.DEL is created. Thereafter, when you delete files from the disk, DOS adds the file information to the PCTRACKR.DEL file. The PCTRACKR.DEL file keeps track of only a limited number of files. When the tracking file is full, the names of the files deleted first are removed to make room for new files. The size of the PCTRACKR.DEL file is relative to the size of the disk: 25 files for a 360K drive and up to 303 files for a drive with more than 32MB.

Practice: Using Mirror to Undelete Files (DOS 5.0)

If you are using PC-DOS 6.1 or MS-DOS 6.0/6.2, skip to the undelete section using those versions.

To use the MIRROR command to create MIRROR.FIL and to instruct DOS to perform deletion tracking on drives A, B, and C, key the following. (Note that there is no colon after the drive name.)

■ **C:\>MIRROR /TA /TB /TC**   [Enter]

MIRROR informs you that it is creating an image of the system area for drives A, B, and C and that it is installing the deletion-tracking software.

Display the directory and look for MIRROR.FIL. Do you find it in your default directory?

■ **C:\>DIR MIRROR.FIL**   [Enter]

Insert your CLASS disk in drive A and display the directory. Key the following command line to delete the files from the disk:

■ **C:\>DEL A:*.***   [Enter]

Did it take longer for the DOS prompt to reappear this time? DOS was creating PCTRACKR.DEL.

Now use the UNDELETE command to restore COMBINE.DOC.

■ **C:\>UNDELETE A:COMBINE.DOC**   [Enter]

DOS responds with a message similar to:

```
Directory:  A:\

File Specifications:  COMBINE.DOC

   Deletion-tracking file contains      1 deleted files
   Of those          1 files have all clusters
   available,
             0 files have some clusters available,
             0 files have no clusters available.

   MS-DOS directory contains      1 deleted files.
   Of those,   1 files may be recovered.

Using the deletion-tracking file.

   COMBINE.DOC  715 02-07-94  10.29p...A  Deleted:
```

```
   5-5-94 11:25a
All of the clusters for this file are available.
Undelete (Y/N)?
```

When you key **Y** for Yes to restore the file, DOS reports:

```
File successfully undeleted.
```

When UNDELETE can use the deletion-tracking file, there is no need to supply the first letter of the file name. Just key **Y** for each file.

Use the UNDELETE switch **/LIST** to display the files available for deletion.

- **C:\>UNDELETE A: /LIST**   [Enter]

Now retrieve all of the files on your CLASS diskette. Can you remember how?

- **C:\>UNDELETE A:*.***   [Enter]

To retrieve all the files without confirmation of each file, key:

- **C:\>UNDELETE A:/ALL**   [Enter]

Run a directory to assure yourself that the files on your diskette have been completely restored.   Use the TYPE command to confirm that their contents are unchanged.

UNDELETE USING MS DOS 6.0/6.2

DOS 6.0 and 6.2 provide three levels of protection for retrieving files previously deleted. The most efficient level is called Sentry; the second level is deletion tracking like that available in DOS 5.0; and the third level is DOS protection, which is also offered in DOS 5.0.

Since Sentry is the highest level of protection, that is the technique we will use. The Sentry level, introduced in MS-DOS 6.0, creates a special directory where all deleted files are placed. This directory is a hidden directory and is created as soon as any files are deleted from the drive. The deleted files are available until they are replaced by newer deleted files, or because the time frame for saving the files has expired. These are options contained in a file named UNDELETE.INI that can be changed if the defaults do not suit your needs.

To provide the Sentry protection to the disk in drive A, key

    C:\>UNDELETE /SA

Note that this command also protects drive C. You may include protection for other drives on the same command line. For example, to load the Sentry protection for both drive A and drive C at the same time, key:

    C:\>UNDELETE /SA /SC

To view the status of the protection of the drives, key:

    C:\>UNDELETE /STATUS

The status of Sentry displays. To see the number of files available for UNDELETE, key:

    C:\>UNDELETE /LIST

Practice: Undeleting Files Using MS-DOS 6.0/6.2

Display a directory of the DOS subdirectory on drive C to see the UNDELETE.INI file.

-   C:\DOS>**DIR UNDELETE.INI**   [Enter]

Unless you have installed UNDELETE or deleted a file using the UNDELETE /SA /SB /SC command, you should not find the file.

Next install the first level of protection, Sentry, for drives A, B, and C by keying:

-   C:\>**UNDELETE /SA /SB /SC**   [Enter]

The UNDELETE.INI file has been created and should now be listed in the directory. To check, key:

-   C:\DOS>**DIR UNDELETE.INI**   [Enter]

Insert your CLASS disk in drive A and key the following line to delete the DOC1.NEW file from the disk:

-   C:\>**DEL A:DOC1.NEW**   [Enter]

To see if the file has been deleted, check the directory of drive A.

■   **C:\>DIR A:DOC1.NEW**   [Enter]

You should receive a message stating that the file is not found.

To retrieve the file DOC1.NEW, key

■   **C:\>UNDELETE A:DOC1.NEW**   [Enter]

Again, if you wish to check the directory for the file, key:

■   **C:\>DIR A:DOC1.NEW**   [Enter]

This time the file should be listed.

View the status of the protection of each drive by keying:

■   **C:\>UNDELETE /STATUS**   [Enter]

To delete all files from the CLASS disk in drive A, key the following:

■   **C:\>DEL A:*.***   [Enter]

To see the number of files that are available now to be undeleted, key:

■   **C:\>UNDELETE A:/LIST**   [Enter]

To finish this practice session, undelete all the files and run a directory of the disk in drive A. Use the following commands:

■   **C:\>UNDELETE A:*.***   [Enter]

■   **C:\>DIR A:**   [Enter]

UNDELETE USING IBM PC-DOS 6.1

IBM PC-DOS 6.1 provides three levels of protection for retrieving deleted files. However, the Sentry level, which creates a special directory where all deleted files are placed, is the one we will use as the preferred level. When deleted, the files are available until they are replaced by newer deleted files.

To provide the Sentry protection to the disk in drive A, key

   C:\>UNDELETE A: /S

Note that this command can also be used to protect drive C as follows:

    C:\>UNDELETE C: /S

To view the status of the protection of the drives, key:

To see the name, date, time, size, and the condition of the file for UNDELETE, key:

    C:\>UNDELETE /LIST

Practice: Undeleting Files Using IBM PC-DOS 6.1

Insert your CLASS disk in drive A and install the Sentry level of protection for drive A by keying:

- **C:\>UNDELETE A: /S**   [Enter]

Key the following command to delete the DOC1.NEW file from the disk:

- **C:\>DEL A:DOC1.NEW**   [Enter]

To see if the file has been deleted, check the directory of drive A.

- **C:\>DIR A:DOC1.NEW**   [Enter]

You should receive a message stating that the file is not found.

To retrieve the file DOC1.NEW, key

- **C:\>UNDELETE A:DOC1.NEW**   [Enter]

You will need to provide the first character of the filename, and the file will be undeleted. Again, if you wish to check the directory for the file, key:

- **C:\>DIR A:DOC1.NEW**   [Enter]

This time the file should be listed.

To delete all files from the CLASS disk in drive A, key the following:

- **C:\>DEL A:*.***   [Enter]

To see the number of files that are available now to be undeleted, key:

- **C:\>UNDELETE /LIST**   [Enter]

To finish this practice session, undelete all the files and run a directory of the disk in drive A. Use the following commands:

■   C:\>UNDELETE A:*.*   [Enter]

■   C:\>DIR A: [Enter]

UNFORMATTING DISKETTES

If you reformat a disk accidentally and are using DOS 5.0 or later, you may be able to use the UNFORMAT command to restore the disk.

By default, the DOS 5.0 and later FORMAT command performs a "safe" format. As explained in Chapter 3, if you haven't written files to a disk since accidentally formatting it, then you will likely be able to unformat the disk. The command to unformat a disk in drive A is:

UNFORMAT A:

Practice: Unformatting a Disk

Let's restore a disk. First, format the CLASS disk, which you should have in the A drive. Key:

■   FORMAT A: [Enter]

Label the disk again with the name, CLASS.

Display a directory to assure yourself that no files are listed and that the disk has, indeed, been formatted. Then use the UNFORMAT command as follows:

■   UNFORMAT A: [Enter]

After asking for the disk to be inserted, DOS will deliver warning messages about the disk's being restored. The MIRROR image is located and the date and time it was last used is noted. You are then asked to confirm that you wish the disk to be updated and the unformat process begins.

When the unformat process is complete, display a directory to see that all files have been recovered and that the disk is just as it was before you formatted it.

COPYING DISKS

Often you will need to copy disks. They may be copied sector by sector using the DISKCOPY command, or they may be copied file by file using the COPY command.

THE DISKCOPY COMMAND

As you use the COPY command to duplicate files, you use the command DISKCOPY to duplicate floppy diskettes so that if the original disk is lost or damaged, you can use the copy in its place. Another application is to make several copies of a disk containing data or program files you have created and want to distribute to others. DISKCOPY will copy the contents of floppy diskettes onto diskettes *of the same size and capacity*. You cannot use DISKCOPY to copy a 360K floppy onto a 1.2MB floppy or to copy a 3 1/2-inch floppy onto a 5 1/4-inch floppy or a hard disk. If you specify an incompatible disk with the DISKCOPY command, DOS will display an error message.

The system refers to the disk from which you are copying as the **source**, master, or original. The disk that will hold the copy may be called the **target**, backup, or destination disk. Make sure that the source and target disks are distinctly labeled. Write-protect the source disk. Then, if the source is accidentally used for the target, DOS will alert you that the wrong disk is inserted because it cannot write to the disk.

CAUTION: DISKCOPY formats (erases) as it copies files onto a disk. Use this command only when you do not want to save any existing files on the target disk that will hold the disk copy.

Do not use Ctrl-C or Ctrl-Break to interrupt the DISKCOPY process when the target drive light is on.

DISKCOPY is one of the few DOS commands other than FORMAT that have formatting capabilities. When you attempt to make a disk copy on an unformatted disk, the system detects this and DISKCOPY formats the target disk during the copy operation. As a result, disk copying takes longer with unformatted disks. DOS will display a message similar to "Formatting while copying."

When formatting a disk with the FORMAT command, the system tells you if there are any defective areas (bad sectors) on the disk and locks out the bad sectors so that they will not be used. When a disk is formatted during the DISKCOPY process, if there are bad sectors the copy may or may not be usable, depending on what data were affected. For this reason, it is a good practice to format disks with the FORMAT command before using them for backup copies and to use only disks with no bad sectors when you make copies with DISKCOPY.

The syntax for copying diskettes is as follows:

    C:\>DISKCOPY A: A: *or*   C:\>DISKCOPY A: B:

Use the first command if you are copying with only one drive; use the second command for copying diskettes from drive A drive to drive B.

Because most computers today have different size and/or capacity disk drives, and the DISKCOPY command requires disk drives of the same size and/or capacity, you will most likely copy diskettes using one floppy drive. This is, however, untrue with MS-DOS 6.2. With this new version and the appropriate switch, you can work with the hard drive as interim storage using the DISKCOPY command.

Practice: Copying a Disk Using DISKCOPY

Using One Floppy Drive with DOS Files in Drive C

Because DISKCOPY is an external command, you must have a search path set to the drive or directory where your DOS files are located. Check this with the PATH command below, and reenter the search path if it is not set correctly.

■ **C:\>PATH**   [Enter]

If you do not have a PATH, enter:

■ **C:\>PATH C:\DOS**   [Enter]

Now make a copy of the CLASS disk. It will be the *source* disk. You will need to use a compatible disk with no useful files on it (LAB FILES) for the *target* disk. Place the *source* disk in drive A and key the following:

■ **C:\>DISKCOPY A: A:**   [Enter]

After DOS has read the DISKCOPY.COM file into memory from the DOS directory of the hard disk in drive C, the system will prompt:

```
Insert SOURCE diskette in drive A:
Press any key to continue . . .
```

The source disk (CLASS) is in drive A. Strike any key. The in-use light on the front of the disk drive will come on as the system reads the contents of the source diskette into the computer's random access memory. DOS will display a message such as:

```
Copying 80 tracks
9 sectors per track, 2 side(s)
```

When the disk contents have been read into memory, the system will prompt:

```
Insert TARGET diskette in drive A:
Press any key to continue . . .
```

Remove the source disk and insert the target disk (LAB FILES). Press any key to begin the writing process. Again, the in-use light on the disk drive will come on. If the target disk has not been formatted, DOS will inform you that it is being formatted during the copy process. After the information has been written from memory, DOS will prompt you for the next step.

Note: If the source diskette has more information that the computer's memory can hold at one time, the system will instruct you to exchange the source and target diskettes more than once to copy the entire disk.

When copying is complete, DOS will ask:

```
Copy another diskette  (Y/N)?
```

If you wish to copy the same disk or another disk, key **Y** for yes; if not, key **N** for no.

Using Two Compatible Floppy Drives with DOS Files in Drive C

With the CLASS disk in drive A, key at the prompt:

■ **C:\>DISKCOPY A: B:**   [Enter]

After DOS loads the DISKCOPY command file into memory from the DOS files on drive C, the system prompts:

```
Insert SOURCE diskette in drive A:
Insert TARGET diskette in drive B:
Press any key to continue . . .
```

The source disk (CLASS) is in drive A. Place the compatible target disk (LAB FILES) in drive B. Remember that the information on the disk in drive B will be erased. When you are ready, press any key.

The in-use light on drive A comes on as the system reads the contents of the source diskette into the computer's memory. The drive B light comes on as the system writes the contents of memory onto the target diskette.

While the disk is being copied, you will see a message similar to:

```
Copying 80 tracks
9 sectors per track, 2 side(s)
Formatting while copying     (unless the disk was previously
formatted)
```

When the copy is complete, you will see a message similar to:

```
Copy another diskette    (Y/N)?
```

If you wish to copy the same disk or another disk, key **Y** for yes; if not, key **N** for no.

> **Note:** Backup copies made with DISKCOPY provide reliable protection against loss *providing* you store the originals and backups in separate locations. If both copies are subject to the same calamity, having a duplicate will be of no help. Plan your disk storage with this in mind.

COMPARING DISKS USING THE DISKCOMP COMMAND

The DISKCOMP command enables you to compare entire disks, as well as to determine if a disk was correctly copied. Use this command when you want to be sure that two disks match exactly—track by track and sector by sector. Because DISKCOMP compares two disks exactly, it is not possible to compare

a floppy disk to a hard disk or to compare floppy disks of different capacities
or sizes.

DISKCOMP is useful if you need to make several copies of the same disk and
want to verify that they are exact duplicates. Use each copy as the source disk
for the next copy, then compare the last copy with the first disk copied. If
these two disks compare ok, all the copies must be identical.

DISKCOMP is an external command. You must have a search path set to the
drive or directory where your DOS files are located.

The syntax for comparing diskettes is as follows:

    C:\>DISKCOMP A: A: *or*   C:\>DISKCOMP A: B:

Use the first command if you are comparing using only one drive; use the
second command for comparing diskettes in drive A and drive B.

Practice: Comparing Disks

Using One Floppy Drive with DOS Files on Drive C

Check to see if the search path is set and, if not, set a path to the external
command files with a command such as PATH C:\DOS.   To begin the disk
comparison process, key:

■   C:\>**DISKCOMP A: A:**   [Enter]

After DISKCOMP.COM is loaded into memory, the system prompts you to
insert the first diskette and then to exchange it for the second diskette. Follow
the prompts to insert the source (CLASS) and target (LAB FILES) disks. If
the comparison is successful, the system will report:

```
Compare ok
Compare another diskette (Y/N)?
```

If you do not have another disk to compare, key **N**.

Depending on the amount of memory available in the computer, you may need
to insert the diskettes more than once. DOS will prompt you.

If the disks do not compare, the screen display will report the locations where
errors are found in a message similar to the following:

```
Compare error(s) on side 0, track 1
```

Press Ctrl-C or Ctrl-Break to interrupt the compare process. You will need to use DISKCOPY again to obtain an exact copy. Then use DISKCOMP to compare again.

CAUTION: Do not use Ctrl-C or Ctrl-Break to interrupt the disk comparing process when the target drive light is on.

Using Two Floppy Drives with DOS Files on Drive C

Key at the A:\> or C:\> prompt:

- **A:\>DISKCOMP A: B:**   [Enter]
  or
- **C:\>DISKCOMP A: B:**   [Enter]

After DOS loads the DISKCOMP command into memory, the system prompts you to insert the first diskette and the second diskette. Follow the prompts, using the CLASS disk in drive A and the LAB FILES disk, the copy you just made of the CLASS disk, in drive B. Wait until the system reports the following:

```
Compare ok
Compare another diskette  (Y/N)?
```

If you do not have another disk to compare, key **N**.

DISKCOPY also copies the volume name of the source diskette to the target diskette. It is necessary to change the name of the target diskette to LAB FILES using the LABEL command as follows:

- **LABEL B: LAB FILES**   [Enter]

COPY *.* COMPARED TO DISKCOPY

Because you may want to copy from one disk to another without erasing the contents of the target disk, it is important to know an alternative to the DISKCOPY method. One is COPY *.* or COPY "Star-dot-star," as this command is usually stated. This process is also called making a **file-by-file** copy of a disk. If you were to key the following command, you would copy

all the files from the source disk in drive A to drive C without erasing the
existing files on drive C, the target disk.

    A:\>COPY *.* C:

One important caution about this command is that if there are any files on
drive C with names identical to files on the source disk in drive A, the files on
drive C will be overwritten. However, DOS 6.2 has added a prompt that
advises of a file of the same name and gives you the opportunity to overwrite
or not.

Another consideration for using COPY *.* is that there must be enough space
remaining on drive C to hold all the files on the drive A disk.

With DISKCOPY, the source and target disks must be identical in size and
capacity. With COPY *.*, the source and target disks can be different sizes
and capacities. For example, COPY *.* can be used to copy from a 5 1/4-inch
360K floppy diskette to a 3 1/2-inch 144MB floppy diskette.

Another circumstance where COPY *.* may be preferable to DISKCOPY is
when you are making backup copies of data files. As data files are created,
erased, revised, and added to a disk, the system may write portions of the same
file in widely scattered locations on the disk. DOS must keep track of these
locations and find the file segments each time you work with the file. Working
with **fragmented files,** or "non-contiguous" files, slows down the system. One
way to correct this condition is to back up the files onto a blank, formatted
disk with COPY *.*. When you use the COPY command to back up files onto
a fresh diskette, the system can copy the fragments of each file into a
contiguous, unfragmented file. On the other hand, DISKCOPY makes an *exact*
copy of the source disk and will reproduce any fragmentation.

Certain files cannot be copied with the COPY command. For example, hidden
files, such as the hidden system files (IBMBIO.COM and IBMDOS.COM or
MSDOS.SYS and IO.SYS) and the files MIRRORSAV.FIL and
PCTRACKR.DEL cannot be duplicated with COPY. Software manufacturers
may include hidden files on their disks. In cases like this, DISKCOPY must
be used to obtain a complete backup or working copy.

Practice: Using COPY *.* to Copy Disks

Use the CLASS diskette as the source and the LAB FILES diskette as the
target with the following command:

■ **A:\>COPY A:*.* B:**   [Enter]

Remember that DOS will use the A drive as both A and B if you have only one drive. However, you will have to exchange diskettes for each file. If you have two floppy disk drives even if they are different size and/or capacity, files can be copied between them. Each file will be listed as it is copied. If you would like to be sure that the files have copied correctly, use the COMP *.* command to compare files.

CHECKING A DISK WITH CHKDSK

To receive a status report on the amount of space left on your disk and in your computer's memory, use the CHKDSK command. This versatile command reports the total disk space; the amount of space used for hidden files, directories, and user files; the space occupied by defective sectors on the disk, if any; and the space available for use. CHKDSK also reports how much internal memory is available in the computer and how much memory is not in use.

CHKDSK has two switches that add to its usefulness. The /F switch tells the system to fix any errors found in the checking process. The /V switch causes all files and their paths on the disk to be listed, including hidden files.

You can also use CHKDSK to check for fragmented, or non-contiguous, files on a data disk. Earlier we described how portions of data files can become scattered over the disk as the files are revised and enlarged. The system must collect the fragments of these files from the disk and reassemble them in memory when you use the files. This increases the file access time and slows system performance. As you will see in the next activity, you can determine how many files are fragmented by using the CHKDSK command and correct this condition by copying the files to a newly formatted disk.

Practice: Checking the Diskette

CHKDSK is an external command; be sure your search path is set correctly. To check the disk in drive A, key

■   **C:\>CHKDSK A:**   [Enter]

Your screen will display information similar to the following:

```
Volume CLASS created (date and time)
Volume Serial Number is (number)

362494 bytes total disk space
71680 in 2 hidden files
54272 bytes in (26) user files
236544 bytes available on disk
```

```
1024 bytes in each allocation unit
354 total allocation units on disk
231 available allocation units on disk

655360 bytes total memory
586848 bytes free
```

If you are using DOS 6.2, you will also see the following:

```
Instead of using CHKDSK, try using SCANDISK. SCANDISK
can reliably detect and fix a much wider range of disk
problems.  For more information, type HELP SCANDISK
from the command prompt.
```

The first lines identify the disk being checked. The serial number line appears in version 4.0 and later.

The next block of lines refers to the disk space. The number of bytes of total disk space indicates whether the disk is a single-sided (183,296 bytes), double-sided (362,494 bytes), or high-capacity 5 1/4-inch (1,213,952 bytes) or a 3 1/2-inch double-sided (730,112) or high capacity (1,457,664 bytes) floppy disk.

The next block of lines in the example is reported only by DOS 4.0 and later versions. It tells how many allocation units are available on the disk and how large they are. An allocation unit is the smallest amount of space a single file can occupy. Files will use space in multiples of this size.

The last block of lines in the example refers to the computer's RAM. The amount of total memory and the amount of memory not in use are shown.

Now use the /V switch with the CHKDSK command to check for a listing of all files including the hidden files. Use the Pause key to pause the display.

■   **A:\>CHKDSK /V**   [Enter]

Does this command display the three hidden files on the disk? Look for the two system files IBMBIO.COM and IBMDOS.COM or their MS-DOS equivalents, MSDOS.SYS and IO.SYS in the list.

The /F switch is used with CHKDSK to find and fix "lost" file sectors on the disk. It is more likely to be helpful if you are checking a hard disk, which may contain thousands of files and may have errors in the file location information that can be corrected with this switch. If lost sectors are reported by CHKDSK, use the /F switch to combine the sectors into a file. Try the following:

■   **C:\>CHKDSK /F A:**   [Enter]

If there are lost sectors, you should answer yes to combine them into a file.

To check for any fragmented, or non-contiguous, files on the disk in drive A, key:

■   **C:\>CHKDSK A:*.***   [Enter]

You will see a listing of the fragmented files containing non-contiguous blocks. If there are some, the system will display a report like this:

```
A:\><Filename>
Contains 2 non-contiguous blocks.
```

You can also use CHKDSK to check individual files or groups of files for fragmentation by keying the file name after the CHKDSK command at the DOS prompt.

■   **C:\>CHKDSK A:DOC1.NEW**   [Enter]
      or
■   **C:\>CHKDSK A:*.DOC**   [Enter]

to check for a group of files with the extension DOC.

If a data disk contains a large number of fragmented files with non-contiguous blocks, it is good practice to copy its contents onto an empty, formatted disk with COPY *.*. Remember, if you want the disk copy to be self-booting, format it with the /S switch to copy the hidden system files to the disk. COPY *.* will not copy hidden files.

SCANDISK (DOS 6.2)

SCANDISK is a disk analysis and repair utility that was introduced with MS-DOS 6.2. It checks for errors on the disk and provides an opportunity to correct problems that it finds.

SCANDISK will test the file structure on the drive. If there are lost clusters or sectors, SCANDISK will put them into files with a CHK extension similar to CHKDSK/F. You then can check the file using the TYPE command to see if the file is an important one. If it is not, you can delete the file.

The syntax for SCANDISK is:

C:\>SCANDISK

Practice: SCANDISK Using MS-DOS 6.2

If you have DOS 6.2 and would like to check and fix the current drive, key the following:

■ C:\>SCANDISK   [Enter]

THE DEFRAG COMMAND IN PC-DOS 6.1 and MS-DOS 6.2

You will be surprised how quickly you fill your disk with tens, if not hundreds, of files. As these files are written to your disk over time, you will have files that are fragmented. Fragmented files are broken into sections that are stored in different locations on the disk. Fragmentation doesn't affect the data, but it can slow your system down noticeably. If you have checked your disk and know that you have fragmented files, you can use the PC-DOS 6.1 and MS-DOS 6.2 command, DEFRAG.

The syntax is DEFRAG A:

Practice: Defragmenting a Disk

It is important to be sure you are at the DOS prompt and not in any programs, including Windows or the Shell, a graphic representation of DOS. Key the following:

■ C:\>DEFRAG A: [Enter]

When you issue the DEFRAG command, the system displays a screen showing all the drive options. Select the drive that holds the disk you want to defrag and press [Enter]. After the drive selection, the system tells you whether or not the disk needs to be optimized. If it has no fragmentation, the system tells you that defragmentation is not necessary. If there is fragmentation, the system will mark a recommended optimization method. You will have the option to use the Optimize or Configure setting. The system will show its preference. While the files are being defragmented, you can see the progress on the display screen.

Nice work on Chapter 5! Test your knowledge and skills with the Self-Check Quiz and Assignment.

CHAPTER 5 SELF-CHECK QUIZ

True/False (Write T if the statement is true, F if the statement is false.)

_____ 1. The PC-DOS 6.1 and MS-DOS 6.2 DEFRAG command will make non-contiguous files contiguous.

_____ 2. To see how much space is still available on your disk use the CHKDSK command.

_____ 3. DEL and ERASE both erase files and can be used with wildcards.

_____ 4. The COMP command compares two disks.

_____ 5. It was possible to use the UNDELETE command prior to DOS version 5.0.

Multiple Choice (Circle the correct answer.)

6. Which of the following is an advantage of using COPY *.* instead of DISKCOPY?

   a. Files can be copied without erasing the target disk.
   b. All files, including hidden files, can be copied with COPY.
   c. The target disk does not need to be formatted.
   d. All existing files on the target disk are erased.

7. Which two of the following can be true concerning the DISKCOPY command?

   a. Disks of different sizes can be copied using the DISKCOPY command.
   b. DISKCOPY formats as it copies.
   c. DISKCOPY will not copy the label of a disk as it copies the files.
   d. DISKCOPY does not erase the target disk.

8. Which command would you use to back up all files on the disk in drive A and to add the backup files to a new disk in drive B?

   a. COPY A: A: c.   COPY A:*.* B:
   b. DISKCOPY A:*.* B: d.   DISKCOPY A: A:

9. Which command will erase only the files with the extension MOS?

   a. ERASE *.MOS   c.   DELETE *.MOS
   b. DEL *.M?   d.   DEL *.*

10. SCANDISK, like DEFRAG, looks similar to a(n) _____ on the
     screen.

      a.   directory   c.   subdirectory
      b.   utility   d.   attribute

ASSIGNMENT

To practice using the commands in this chapter, complete the following steps. Check off each step when you understand its operation, or mark the step with a question mark if it is not clear. Write the commands or keystrokes in the space provided.

1. Copy all files with the XYZ extension from your CLASS diskette to a new diskette named LAB FILES. Print a directory of the LAB FILES diskette. Format the LAB FILES diskette. Print a directory of the LAB FILES diskette.

    _____

2. Unformat the LAB FILES diskette. Print a directory of the LAB FILES diskette.

    _____

3. Set up Sentry or deletion tracking protection (depending on your version of DOS) for the LAB FILES diskette. Delete all the files with the XYZ extension. Print the directory of the LAB FILES diskette.

    _____

4. Undelete the files with the XYZ extension. Print the directory of the LAB FILES diskette.

    _____

5. Diskcopy the CLASS diskette onto the LAB FILES diskette. Print a wide directory of both diskettes.

    _____

6. Compare the CLASS diskette with the LAB FILES diskette. Print a wide directory of both diskettes.

    _____

7. Check the CLASS diskette for fragmentation using the CHKDSK command.

    _____

8. Use the DEL command to erase all files from the CLASS diskette in one operation. Print a directory of the diskette.

    _____

9. Use the COPY command that will copy all the files from the LAB FILES diskette to the CLASS diskette using wildcards.

    _____

10.   If you have PC-DOS 6.1 or MS-DOS 6.2, check the CLASS diskette to
       look for fragmentation using the DEFRAG command. Print a copy of the
       results.

CHAPTER 6

CREATING AND USING SUBDIRECTORIES

OBJECTIVES

When you have completed the activities and assignment in this chapter, you will be able to:

1. Describe the purpose of subdirectories.

2. Create subdirectories.

3. Specify paths to directories.

4. Change the current directory and display its path and name.

5. Create and store files in directories.

6. Print subdirectory listings.

7. Locate a file in any directory of a disk.

INTRODUCTION TO SUBDIRECTORIES

When a floppy or hard disk is formatted, a file directory structure is established that allows for the description of each file on the disk. The description includes the file name, size, and time and date of creation or last revision, as well as information about the file's location on the disk and other attributes. The directory created during formatting is called the main or **root directory**. The size of the root directory file is fixed. The root directory can hold a limited number of file entries because of its fixed size: 64 entries on a single-sided 180KB diskette, 112 on a 360KB or 720KB double-sided diskette, 224 on a 1.2MB or 1.44MB high-density disk, and 512 or more on a hard disk. For this reason, you can have bytes free on a disk but cannot add files to the disk because adding a file would exceed the maximum number allowed in the root directory.

You can increase the number of files a floppy diskette or hard disk will store by creating **subdirectories** to hold file information. Subdirectories can also make your disk and file management more effective, by listing files in categories you create. This is especially helpful on hard disk systems, which often contain thousands of files. Since subdirectories can be used to organize the files into different groups, you may want to use subdirectories to segregate different application software files and data files. For example, you could place all DOS files in one subdirectory, as was done in the installation of DOS 5.0 and 6.x versions. You might create a subdirectory for word processing program files and one for database program files. In addition, you might want to create directories by subject area for your data files. For instance, documents created for different projects or classes could be separated into different subdirectories for easy access.

A main or root directory exists on every floppy and hard disk. Subdirectories and then subdirectories of each subdirectory can be added to the directory structure. This file structure is often called a **tree-structured file system,** since the structure resembles an upside-down tree, with the main or root directory branching to several levels of subdirectories as shown in Figure 6-1. A more appropriate analogy might be a family tree. You can also think of subdirectories as filing cabinet drawers each containing the files you place there.

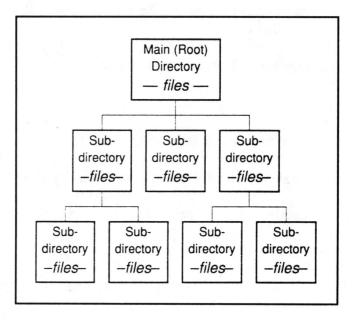

Figure 6-1. A tree-structured file system branches from the root directory.

Of course, it is important that you set up a directory structure and name your directories in a logical way in order to work with them easily. Keep the branching as simple as possible so that you won't have to search through a complex tree structure to access the files you need.

Subdirectory names follow the same naming conventions as the names of other files—a maximum of eight characters with no spaces. Although you can add an extension to a subdirectory name, this is seldom done. Instead, it is a good practice to keep subdirectory names as short as possible. As you will see, short directory names can save many keystrokes.

When you use DIR to display a directory listing of a subdirectory, you will see the same information about the files in that subdirectory as you see displayed for the files in the root directory, and in the same format: the filename and extension, size, and date and time of creation or last revision. A subdirectory is actually a file, like the root directory, that contains information for each file listed in the subdirectory. However, the files storing subdirectory information are not limited in size like the file storing the root directory information. Therefore, there is no limit to the number of entries that can be placed in a subdirectory. In actual practice, you may want to limit the number to what the command DIR /W will display on a single screen.

You cannot use the command COPY or DEL to create or remove a subdirectory. In this chapter and the next, you will learn DOS commands for creating and removing subdirectories.

To access files in subdirectories, you will sometimes need to change the default directory from the root to one of the subdirectories. You can think of this as "moving around" in the tree structure.

CREATING A SUBDIRECTORY STRUCTURE

A common reason for setting up subdirectories on a hard disk or floppy diskettes is to segregate software or data files. For example, you may set up one subdirectory for word processing, one for spreadsheets, and one for desktop publishing.

The syntax for creating these subdirectories is MD (directory name). To create a subdirectory named WP, key the following from the DOS prompt:

    A:\>MD WP

Practice: Setting Up a Subdirectory Structure

Even though you will do this exercise on a floppy diskette, the principles apply identically to a hard disk. To prepare for creating a tree-structured diskette, reformat the LAB FILES diskette with the system. Name it TREE DISK.

Create three subdirectories in which you could install software. One directory is for word processing software; name this directory WPRO. The second directory is for spreadsheet software used for accounting work; name this directory ACCT. The third directory is for desktop publishing software; name this directory DTP. Thus your tree structure will have three subdirectories named WPRO, ACCT, and DTP. These directories will all be subdirectories of the root directory. For now, the data files or documents relating to each application can be stored in the application's directory. The tree can be visualized as shown in Figure 6-2.

To create the three
directories shown in
Figure 6-2, key:

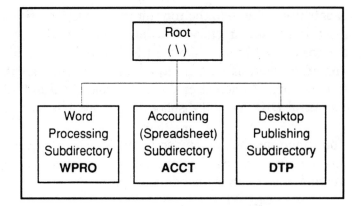

- **A:\\>MD WPRO**
  [Enter]

- **A:\\>MD ACCT**
  [Enter]

- **A:\\>MD DTP**
  [Enter]

Figure 6-2. The structure for TREE DISK.

To see the directories you
created on the disk in drive A, key

- **A:\\>DIR**   [Enter]

The system displays:

```
Volume in drive A is TREE DISK
Volume Serial Number is _____
Directory of A:\

COMMAND     COM  52589  06-29-93      12:00p
WPRO        <DIR>        09-17-94      10:15a
ACCT        <DIR>        09-17-94      10:16a
DTP         <DIR>        09-17-94      10:17a
            4 file(s)   52589 bytes
                       727040 bytes free
```

Note that the directories are identified by <DIR> and that no size is shown for
them. The backslash in the line that says "Directory of A:\" refers to the root
directory of the disk. The line below the list of directories shows that there are
four files—DOS counts the directories as files.

If you make a mistake and want to remove a directory, key the command RD
(remove directory) and the directory name.

- **A:\\>RD <directory name>**   [Enter]

You will learn more about removing directories in the next chapter.

SPECIFYING THE PATH TO A DIRECTORY

Because WPRO is a directory, the contents can be displayed with the directory
command DIR, just as you display the contents of the root directory. However,

it is necessary to tell DOS the route to follow to find the WPRO directory; this route is referred to as the **pathname** or **path**. The pathname specifies the way to a directory, usually starting from the root directory. Notice in the command line in the next Practice section that a backslash (\) is used before the WPRO directory name. The backslash means that the path starts at the root directory, represented by the backslash. The command line instructs DOS to start at the root directory, to go from there to the WPRO directory, and to display a directory listing of the WPRO directory.

Practice: **Specifying Paths to Directories**

Key the following command line:

■ **A:\>DIR \WPRO**   [Enter]

The contents of the WPRO directory are displayed as:

```
Volume in drive A is TREE DISK
Volume Serial Number is ____
Directory of A:\WPRO

    .                   <DIR>  09-17-94        10:15a
    ..                  <DIR>  09-17-94        10:15a
            2 file(s)            0 bytes
                        727040 bytes free
```

It looks as though WPRO contains two directories named . (one dot) and .. (two dots). However, these are not true directories; they are **subdirectory markers** used to access directories. Remember that we said that directories are actually files containing information about files? The subdirectory marker file .. contains the name of the **parent** or next higher directory (in this case, the root directory). The marker file . contains the name of the **current** directory, in this case, WPRO. More about the markers later.

The display tells you that you are looking at the directory listing of A:\WPRO. The path is shown as going from the drive A root directory to WPRO.

The pathname will continue with another backslash if you add a file name. For example, if the directory WPRO contained a file named LETTER.JRB, the pathname with the drive and file name attached would be A:\WPRO\LETTER.JRB. Here the second backslash is a separator—it does not signify the root directory. Notice there are no spaces in this entry, which is called a **filespec**. This filespec includes the drive designator, pathname, and file name.

When the default directory is the root directory, it is *not* mandatory that you begin the path with the backslash (\). For example, if you are in the root directory and want to display a listing of the DTP directory, which is in the next level below the root, the backslash is not necessary. You can key

■ A:\>**DIR DTP**   [Enter]

You can also key

■ A:\>**DIR \DTP**   [Enter]

Try both of these options.

CHANGING THE CURRENT (DEFAULT) DIRECTORY

When you want to work with files in a directory other than the default shown by the prompt, it is often more efficient to change to that directory—that is, to make it the current or default directory. To do this, use the change directory command, CHDIR or CD. CD is shown in this textbook. It must be followed by the path to the directory you want to make current.

Practice: Changing the Current Directory

For example, if you want to change the current directory from the root directory to the subdirectory named WPRO, you can do so by keying

■ A:\>**CD \WPRO**   [Enter]

This is another example of a time when the backslash is optional. Since you are in the root directory, it is not mandatory.

After you enter the CD command to change to the WPRO directory, notice that the prompt has changed to show that the current directory is now WPRO.

   A:\WPRO>

Now key the directory command to display the directory and verify that you are in the WPRO directory.

■ A:\WPRO>**DIR**   [Enter]

You will see the following:

```
Volume in drive A is TREE DISK
Volume Serial Number is ___
Directory of A:\WPRO

    .              <DIR>  09-17-94        10:15a
    ..             <DIR>  09-17-94        10:15a
         2 file(s)        0 bytes
                   727040 bytes free
```

You have seen how the DOS prompt and top lines of the directory display tell you where you are in the tree structure. There is a third way to determine the name of the current directory: If you enter the change directory command CD with no parameters, rather than change the directory, the system will check the current directory and display its path and name.

To verify this, key the following check directory command at the DOS prompt:

- **A:\WPRO>CD**   [Enter]

The system should respond with:

```
A:\WPRO
```

To check the current directory on another drive, add the drive designator as a parameter to the CD command. Try

- **A:\WPRO>CD C:**   [Enter]

To review, the CD command can be used to *change* or *check* directories. If you use CD with a path or directory name as the parameter, the system will change to the directory specified. If you use CD without a parameter, the system will identify the current directory on the default drive by drive and pathname. If you use CD with a drive designator as the parameter, the system will identify the current directory on the drive specified.

When you are in a subdirectory and want to work with another subdirectory that is part of another "branch" of the tree, you must always specify the full path including the backslash. This tells DOS that the path begins at the root directory.

- **A:\WPRO>DIR \DTP**   [Enter]

Without the \ , DOS would assume that DTP was at the level below WPRO in the tree structure. Remember, the backslash is always needed unless you are in the root directory and/or want to specify a path to a directory that is listed in the current directory. In other words, if the directory you want to list is a child

of (one level below) the current directory shown by the prompt, you do not
need to use the backslash.

Since the backslash is used to signify the root directory, you can change back
to the root directory using the CD command and the backslash. Change to the
root directory with:

■   **A:\WPRO>CD **   [Enter]

The prompt will change to:

    A:\>

Now the prompt tells you that you are working in the root directory and that
commands you enter will apply to the root directory of the diskette in drive A.

Change to the ACCT subdirectory:

■   **A:\>CD ACCT**   [Enter]

The prompt will change to:

    A:\ACCT>

The entries in the ACCT directory are displayed when you key:

■   **A:\ACCT>DIR**   [Enter]

Practice: **Creating Files in the Directories**

Now you can work with files in some of the subdirectories. Change to the
WPRO directory. To create a file for this directory using the COPY CON
technique, key the following text while in the WPRO subdirectory:

■   **A:\WPRO>COPY CON SUB.TXT**   [Enter]
■   **I am creating a file for the WPRO subdirectory.**   [Enter]
■   **It is easy!**   [Enter]

Press the F6 key or Ctrl-Z and [Enter] to end the file and save it.

Since you instructed the system to create the file SUB.TXT and placed it in the
current directory, you should see the new file listed when you list the WPRO
directory. Try it.

■   **A:\WPRO>DIR**   [Enter]

The contents of the WPRO directory are displayed.

```
Volume in drive A is TREE DISK
Volume Serial Number is _____
Directory of A:\WPRO

   .              <DIR>  09-17-94      10:15a
   ..             <DIR>  09-17-94      10:15a
SUB      TXT         62  09-17-94      10:55a
         3 file(s)          62 bytes
                        724992 bytes free
```

Now, from the WPRO subdirectory, create a file for the root directory and place it there *without* changing to the root directory. Key the following:

- **A:\WPRO>COPY CON \REVIEW.TXT**   [Enter]
- **I am creating a file for the root directory.**   [Enter]
- **I keyed a backslash before its name so it**   [Enter]
- **will be stored there.**   [Enter]

Press the F6 key or Ctrl-Z and [Enter] to end the file and save it.

Notice that you instructed the system to put the file REVIEW.TXT in the root directory by placing the backslash before the file name.

Check to see that REVIEW.TXT is in the root directory by using the backslash as a parameter for the DIR command.

- **A:\WPRO>DIR **   [Enter]

The system lists the entries in the root directory, including the new file REVIEW.TXT. (Your listing may have additional entries.)

```
Volume in drive A is TREE DISK
Volume Serial Number is _____
Directory of A:\

COMMAND    COM    52589   06-29-93      12:00p
WPRO           <DIR>      09-17-94      10:15a
ACCT           <DIR>      09-17-94      10:20a
DTP            <DIR>      09-17-94      10:25a
REVIEW   TXT       112    09-17-94      11:00a
         5 file(s)     52701 bytes
                      723968 bytes free
```

The root directory of the disk in drive A contains at least three subdirectories and the file you just created. Note that you are still in the WPRO subdirectory.

Create another file for the WPRO directory. Key the following:

- **A:\WPRO>COPY CON ADD.TXT**   [Enter]
- **This file belongs in the WPRO directory.**   [Enter]
- **^Z**   [Enter]

Now display the directory listing of the current directory:

- **A:\WPRO>DIR**   [Enter]

Move to the root directory as follows:

- **A:\WPRO>CD **

You may want to see a list of only the subdirectories with no files included.
To display a directory listing of the subdirectories, key

- **A:\>DIR *.**   [Enter]

With this command you request a listing of files with no extension in their file
name. Since the directory names have no extension, they will be selected. If
the directory contained other files named without an extension, such as
TODOFORM, these would be included in the listing.

Create a file of your own called FILE1.ABC for the ACCT directory.   You
can do this from the WPRO directory. Change to the WPRO subdirectory and
key the following command:

- **A:\WPRO>COPY CON \ACCT\FILE1.ABC**   [Enter]

The pathname \ACCT tells DOS to place the new file in the ACCT directory
below the root directory. The second backslash is a separator between the
directory name and file name.

You can also change to the ACCT directory and create a file as follows:

- **A:\WPRO>CD \ACCT**   [Enter]

- **A:\ACCT>COPY CON FILE2.ABC**   [Enter]

Note that you do not have to specify the path for the file when you are in the
ACCT directory. Use this technique to create a short file and store it in the
ACCT directory. Display the ACCT directory listing to see that your two new
files are listed.

Next, create two files for the DTP directory called JOB1.DOC and JOB2.DOC
using the same techniques. First create JOB1.DOC for the DTP directory while

you are in the ACCT directory. Then change to the DTP directory and create
the file JOB2.DOC. List the directory of the DTP directory to see that your
two new files are there.

Practice: Copying Files from Floppy Diskettes to the Hard Disk

You may need to copy from one floppy diskette to another using the same
floppy drive. For example, you may have only one floppy drive. You could
use the following command to do this copying (remember, if you are using a
system with only one floppy, DOS will use that drive as both A and B).

- A:\>COPY *.* B: [Enter]

If you are working with a system with only one floppy drive, the command
will require that you swap the source disk and target disk for each file copied.
To avoid this tedious process, you can set up a directory on the hard disk and
copy the files from the source floppy to this directory with COPY *.*. Then,
after exchanging floppy disks, copy the files from the hard disk directory to the
target floppy disk. Finally, erase the files from the hard disk and remove the
directory.

To make a temporary directory on the hard disk named TEMP, key the
following at the C:\> prompt:

- C:\>MD TEMP   [Enter]

Insert the CLASS disk in drive A from which you would like all the files
copied. Copy all the files on the disk in drive A into the TEMP directory with
this command:

- C:\>COPY A:*.* TEMP   [Enter]

Next, insert the TREE DISK diskette in the A drive and use the following
command to copy the files to this floppy diskette:

- C:\>COPY TEMP*.* A: [Enter]

If you would like to be sure that the files have copied correctly, use the COMP
. command to compare files.

Erase the files in the TEMP directory and remove the directory with these
commands:

- C:\>DEL TEMP   [Enter]

- C:\>RD TEMP   [Enter]

PRINTING DIRECTORY LISTINGS

You can print directory listings by using the redirect process. The **right redirect**, the greater-than sign (>), redirects output from the default device to another device. The default device for the display of the directory is the screen. You can redirect the display from the screen to the printer by using the right redirect symbol between the command DIR and the device name PRN.

Practice: Printing Directory Listings

Make sure the printer is on-line. Change to the root directory and key these command lines:

■ **A:\>DIR > PRN**   [Enter]

■ **A:\>DIR WPRO > PRN**   [Enter]

■ **A:\>DIR ACCT > PRN**   [Enter]

■ **A:\>DIR DTP > PRN**   [Enter]

SEARCHING FOR FILES IN A TREE STRUCTURE

Now that you are working with subdirectories, you may find that it is sometimes difficult to locate files. For example, you might not remember in which directory you placed a file or be uncertain about the exact name of a file. DOS 5.0 introduces a new directory command that will help you locate files in these circumstances. The switch /S tells DOS to list the files in all subdirectories where the file is found.

Practice: Using /S to Search for Files in a Tree Structure

To find the file ADD.TXT, change to the root directory and key the following command line:

■ **A:\>DIR ADD.TXT /S**   [Enter]

DOS will begin looking in the root directory and search in all subdirectories for the file. If a copy is in more than one directory, all the locations of the file will be listed.

Suppose you remember creating a file named JOB1, but have forgotten what its extension is and where you placed it. You can search for it with a wildcard.

■ **A:\>DIR JOB1.* /S**   [Enter]

The /S switch can be used to display all the directories and files on your disk in one step.

- **A:\>DIR /S**   [Enter]

Also, you might try

- **A:\>DIR /B**   [Enter]

Notice that you have the directory listing with only a portion of the information, specifically the filename and extension.

You can redirect the directory list to the printer in the same way that you did previously:

- **A:\>DIR /S > PRN**   [Enter]

Nice work on your introduction to subdirectories! Test your knowledge of the chapter with the Self-Check Quiz and Assignment.

CHAPTER 6 SELF-CHECK QUIZ

True/False (Write T if the statement is true, F if the statement is false.)

_____1. Subdirectories have a fixed number of entries.

_____2. Use the DIR /S command to locate a file anywhere on drive C.

_____3. The root directory is created during the formatting process.

_____4. You must always include the backslash when you specify a path to a subdirectory.

_____5. The contents of a subdirectory can be printed using the right redirect (>) technique.

Multiple Choice (Circle the correct answer.)

6. Which represents the maximum number of files that can be placed on a 3 1/2-inch double density diskette?

   a. 512   c. 112
   b. 224   d. No limit

7. What command can you use to change from the TEXT directory to the root directory?

   a. A:\TEXT> CD ROOT   c. A:\TEXT> CD
   b. A:\TEXT> CD \   d. A:\TEXT> CH DIR

8. Which command would you enter to create the subdirectory named GRAPHS branching from the root directory?

   a. A:\>MD GRAPHS   c.   A:\TEXT>MKDIR GRAPHS
   b. A:\>MAKE GRAPHS   d.   A:\GRAPHS>MAKE GRAPHS

9. What are the naming conventions for subdirectories?

   a. The same naming conventions as for a file
   b. A maximum of eight letters including spaces
   c. There are no naming conventions for subdirectories
   d. A maximum of eight letters, no spaces allowed

10. What command would you enter to create a file named DOC7.TXT in the WPRO subdirectory from the root directory?

   a. A:\>COPY CON DOC7.TXT\WPRO
   b. A:\>COPY CON WPRO DOC7.TXT
   c. A:\>WPRO\COPY CON \DOC7.TXT
   d. A:\>COPY CON WPRO\DOC7.TXT

ASSIGNMENT

To practice using the commands in this chapter, complete the following steps. Check off each step when you understand its operation, or mark the step with a question mark if it is not clear. Write the commands or keystrokes in the space provided.

1. Change to the A drive and change the prompt to reflect the root directory.

   _____

2. Clear the screen. To store communication software and data, create a subdirectory named COMM below the root directory of the TREE DISK.

   _____

3. Change to the COMM subdirectory and create a text file named COMMDATA.TXT. Compose the wording of the text file and save it.

   _____

4. Print the root directory of the disk. Print the COMM directory listing.

   _____

5. Locate the file COMMDATA.TXT from the root directory using the directory search command. Print the screen.

   _____

6. Create a new subdirectory named TEMP on the root directory of drive C. Print a directory of the TEMP subdirectory.

   _____

7. Create a file named REPORTS.TXT in the COMM directory of drive A. Use your own wording to compose the file. Print the file.

   _____

8. Copy the file REPORTS.TXT to the TEMP subdirectory on drive C. Print the TEMP directory.

   _____

9. Move and overwrite the file, REPORTS.TXT, from the TEMP directory of drive C back to the COMM directory on the TREE DISK diskette in drive A. Print the directory of the TREE DISK listing the REPORTS.TXT file.

   _____

10. Remove the TEMP directory on drive C. Print the screen.

    _____

CHAPTER 7

WORKING WITH A TREE STRUCTURE

OBJECTIVES

When you have completed the activities and assignment in this chapter, you will be able to:

1. Copy files from one directory to another.

2. Make subdirectories within existing subdirectories.

3. Specify the path to a file.

4. Use subdirectory markers to change directories and to delete all files in a directory.

5. Remove a subdirectory with the remove directory (RMDIR or RD) command.

6. Display and print the directories on a disk with the TREE command.

7. Use the DOS 6.0 DELTREE command to delete a directory and all subordinate directories and files.

8. Use the DOS 6.0 MOVE command to rename a subdirectory.

9. Use the XCOPY command to copy files within a tree structure.

DIRECTORY AND FILE MANAGEMENT

Managing files on a hard disk often requires that you move from one directory to another and specify file locations within a multi-level tree structure. To expand your file management skills and practice using them in a more complex tree structure, you will learn to copy files from one directory to another. You will create a third level of directories and copy files into these directories.

Practice: Copying Files from One Directory to Another

A file can be copied from one directory to another. Use the COPY command with the necessary parts of the filespecs (drive, pathname, and file name) for the source and destination files.

First, insert the TREE DISK diskette and change to the WPRO directory with the following command:

■   **A:\>CD WPRO**   [Enter]

Display a directory of the root to see if REVIEW.TXT is there.

■   **A:\WPRO>DIR \REVIEW.TXT**   [Enter]

To copy REVIEW.TXT from the root directory to a file named LESSON.TXT in the WPRO directory, key:

■   **A:\WPRO>COPY \REVIEW.TXT LESSON.TXT**   [Enter]

The system responds with:

```
1 file(s) copied
```

You included the pathname (the backslash meaning the root directory), the source file name (REVIEW.TXT), and the new file name for the copy (LESSON.TXT); you did not include a pathname for LESSON.TXT because it is the same as the path shown in the prompt. You did not include the drive because you wanted the copy to be on the disk in the default drive shown in the prompt.

Now display the default directory WPRO. Does the list have three TXT files in it?

A:\WPRO>**DIR**   [Enter]

```
Volume in drive A is TREE DISK
Volume Serial Number is _____
Directory of A:\WPRO


 .                 <DIR>   09-17-94        10:15a
 ..                <DIR>   09-17-94        10:15a
SUB      TXT          63   09-17-94        10:55a
ADD      TXT          45   09-17-94        11:05a
LESSON   TXT         112   09-17-94        11:00a
            5 file(s)          220 bytes
                           713728 bytes free
```

The subdirectory markers also count as a file since they represent directory files.

You learned earlier that a file copied into the same directory must have a different name. This is another advantage of using subdirectories. Two (or more) files on the same *disk* can have the same name providing *each is stored in a different directory*. Since their filespecs are different, the system can tell them apart.

You can verify this by copying the file named LESSON.TXT from the WPRO directory into the ACCT directory, using the same file name. Be sure you are in the WPRO directory. Key the following:

■   **A:\WPRO>COPY LESSON.TXT \ACCT**   [Enter]

The file name is not repeated for the destination directory because you want the file in the ACCT directory to have the same name as the original file. You must, however, give the new file's complete pathname starting at the root directory, since the file is to be placed in a directory that is another branch of the tree structure.

Check to see that the file was copied. Display the directory of ACCT by keying at the DOS prompt:

■   **A:\WPRO>DIR \ACCT**   [Enter]

Now there are two files named LESSON.TXT on the same disk, but they are in different directories. The different pathnames give them different filespecs and make them as different to the system as if they had different file names.

ADDING SUBDIRECTORIES TO CREATE A THIRD LEVEL

Subdirectories can contain any type of file, including other subdirectories. Like putting dividers between dividers in a file drawer, this further structuring narrows the subject of a storage compartment and makes file and disk management easier.

A common practice is to store data files in directories a level below the application software directories. For example, you could divide the work you do with each software application by type or by project. You could add the subdirectories shown in capital letters in the following lists and then place data files pertaining to each type of work or project in those directories. Complete your tree structure by creating the third level of subdirectories as indicated:

Word Processing	Accounting	Desktop Publishing
WPRO	ACCT	DTP
REPORTS (reports)	CORP (corporate)	TEXT (text)
CORRES (letters)	PROJ1 (project 1)	ART (graphics)
MISC (miscellaneous)	PROJ2 (project 2)	PUBS (publications)

Practice: Creating Subdirectories on a Third Level

If necessary, insert the TREE DISK diskette. To create the third level of
subdirectories under WPRO, be sure you are in the WPRO subdirectory and
key these commands to create the three subdirectories:

- **A:\WPRO>MD REPORTS**   [Enter]

- **A:\WPRO>MD CORRES**   [Enter]

- **A:\WPRO>MD MISC**   [Enter]

Display the WPRO directory. You should see the three new directories just
made plus the files copied previously.

Change to the ACCT subdirectory and create the third level of subdirectories
(CORP, PROJ1, PROJ2). Then change to the DTP directory and create the
third level of subdirectories for DTP (TEXT, ART, PUBS). When you have
finished, compare your structure to that shown in Figure 7-1.

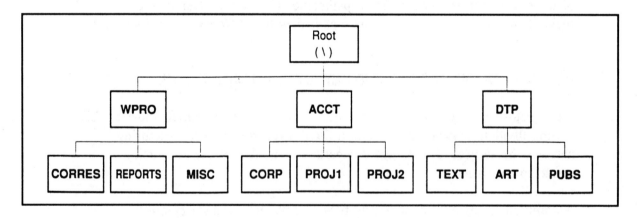

Figure 7-1. Three-level TREE DISK tree structure.

USING THE CD COMMAND WITH ANOTHER DRIVE

The change directory command (CD) has two parameters, drive and pathname
or path. Drive is the disk drive designator (A:). Path includes the names of

any directories through which DOS will be passing, ending with the directory you want to be current. If you omit the drive, the default drive is used. If you specify a drive, DOS looks for the path you specify on the disk in the drive you specify.

Practice: Using the CD Command

To verify that DOS will look for the path you specify on the disk in the drive you designate, change to drive C and key the following:

■ **C:\>CD A:\WPRO\REPORTS**   [Enter]

The system will look at the disk in drive A, since you specified that drive. DOS will begin looking there in the root directory (\) for a directory named WPRO. Next, DOS will look in the WPRO directory for a directory named REPORTS. DOS will change the current directory for drive A to the REPORTS directory. It is important to note that DOS will check the REPORTS subdirectory in the A drive, but that your prompt will still reflect the C drive.

Note that *there are no spaces* in the path. If you key a space following WPRO, as C:\>CD A:\WPRO \REPORTS, the system will change to the WPRO directory and will ignore the portion of the pathname keyed after the space.

If you omit the drive and pathname and just enter CD, DOS will display the current directory name. If you enter the drive and omit the path, DOS will report the current directory of the other drive. To see the current directory of drive A, key:

■ **C:\>CD A:**   [Enter]

DOS will report the status of the A drive; however, the prompt will still reflect the C drive. This trick can be a timesaver when you are copying files between tree-structured disks and want to know the current directories on both the source disk and the target disk.

USING SUBDIRECTORY MARKERS

Remember the markers . (one dot) and .. (two dots) listed in each subdirectory? The marker . represents a file containing the name of the current directory. The marker .. represents a file containing the name of the parent directory. You can use this marker with the CD command to move to that directory—that is, to move up one level in the tree structure. You can use the . marker to perform operations on the current directory, such as copying, displaying, or deleting its contents.

Practice: Using Subdirectory Markers

If necessary, change to drive A; then change to the REPORTS directory by keying

■   **A:\>CD WPRO\REPORTS**   [Enter]

To move from this directory up one level toward the root directory, key:

■   **A:\WPRO\REPORTS>CD ..**   [Enter]

  A:\WPRO>   (This will be the new prompt.)

As you can see, the current directory has changed to the parent directory WPRO, which is one level above REPORTS. By pressing F3, you can repeat the command CD .. to return to the root directory.

REMOVING A DIRECTORY

When you want to delete directories from your tree structure, you will use the remove directory (**RMDIR** or **RD**) command. Most users use RD because it requires fewer keystrokes. In this textbook RD is used as the command to remove subdirectories.

There are two requirements for removing a directory:

• A directory cannot be deleted if it lists any subdirectories or files other than the subdirectory marker files. This is to ensure that no files or directories are left without a directory structure.

• The current directory cannot be removed. You must change to another directory before issuing the remove directory command. DOS will not allow you to saw off the limb you are sitting on!

The remove directory command has two parameters: drive and pathname or path. These are used in the same way with RD as with the CD and MD commands.

If you want to remove a directory but need some of the files it contains, copy the files you need to another directory or disk, then erase all the files in the obsolete directory and remove the directory.

There are two ways to remove all files from a directory. One method is to use the DEL or ERASE command with the wildcards that select all files:

A:\>DEL WPRO\REPORTS*.*   *or*   A:\>DEL WPRO\REPORTS\ .
  or
A:\>WPRO\REPORTS>DEL *.*

Another method is to use the DEL or ERASE command with the directory name alone to remove all files in the specified subdirectory:

A:\WPRO>DEL REPORTS
  or
A:\WPRO\REPORTS>DEL .

The last example shows how you can use the one-dot directory marker (.). Remember that this marker is for a file that stores the name of the directory where the marker appears. DOS interprets the dot in the command DEL . as the current directory name, in this case, REPORTS.

ERASE can be used in place of DEL in the preceding examples. Either command tells DOS to erase the files in the specified directory.

Practice: Removing Directories

Change to the appropriate directory and use either the DEL or ERASE command to remove the files from the REPORTS directory. Both of the following commands will provide the same results: All files are deleted from the REPORTS directory.

- A:\WPRO\REPORTS>**DEL** *.*   *or*   A:\WPRO\REPORTS>**DEL** . [Enter]
    or
- A:\WPRO>**DEL REPORTS**   [Enter]

When the system asks if you are sure you want to erase the files, key **Y** for yes. This will not remove the directory; it simply erases the files within the directory. Display the REPORTS directory to confirm that it has no files.

When the REPORTS directory is empty, make sure that it is *not* the current directory; then delete the REPORTS directory by keying

- A:\WPRO>**RD REPORTS**   [Enter]
    or
- A:\>**RD WPRO\REPORTS**   [Enter]

Display the WPRO directory to ensure that REPORTS no longer exists. Remember: You use ERASE or DEL commands to remove files and the RD command to remove directories.

USING THE TREE COMMAND TO DISPLAY THE TREE STRUCTURE

When you create a tree structure with several levels, you may not remember exactly what subdirectories you created or exactly where they are. You might display the contents of each directory on the disk to find the files marked <DIR>, but there is a quicker way to display the complete structure. Use the TREE command to view a graphical representation of the contents of your disk.

Practice: Displaying the Tree Structure

Since TREE is an external command, you must be sure your search path is set to the DOS external command files. Check to be sure you are in the root directory and then key:

■ **A:\>TREE**   [Enter]

This instructs DOS to find the TREE command file, load the command into memory, and display a tree of the disk in drive A.

You can also request DOS to display the tree structure of a disk in another drive. To view the tree structure of the C drive, key:

■ **A:\>TREE C:**   [Enter]

Notice that there are no files included in the display. The TREE command has a switch that modifies the command to list all files in all directories for a complete listing of every file on the disk, except hidden files. To display the tree of the disk in drive A and include the files in the root directory and each subdirectory, key:

■ **A:\>TREE /F**   [Enter]

To display the tree and file listing for a different disk that is not in the default drive, key:

■ **A:\>TREE C:/F**   [Enter]

When you use the /F switch, the displayed tree includes the name of every file in every directory. This can be quite a long list if you have many small files or are displaying the tree of a hard disk. A printed copy of such a report can be helpful, especially if your filing system has several levels. You can use the right-redirect symbol (>) to send the output of the TREE command to the printer.

■ **A:\>TREE /F > PRN**   [Enter]

Still another option is to redirect the output of the TREE command to a file, to obtain a permanent record on disk. Try this:

- **A:\>TREE /F > TREEFILE**   **[Enter]**

Similar to the technique used to print the directory with the command DIR > PRN, you have redirected a tree listing to a file.

To send the file TREEFILE to the printer, key:

- **A:\>COPY TREEFILE PRN**   **[Enter]**

You could also use

- **A:\>TYPE TREEFILE > PRN**   **[Enter]**

DOS 6.0 DELTREE COMMAND

DOS 6.0 has a new command that eliminates the need to delete all files and subdirectories below a given subdirectory before removing a directory. With the command DELTREE it is possible to delete all levels of subdirectories below the directory including the files in one command. For example, if you want to delete all branches of the DTP directory, key:

   A:\>DELTREE DTP

Answer the screen prompt `Delete directory DTP and all its subdirectories? (Y/N)`. When you respond **Y** for yes, all files and subdirectories of the DTP directory will be removed.

It is also possible to remove only one subdirectory without first removing the files by keying the name of the subdirectory. To remove all files and the subdirectory CORP from the ACCT directory, key:

   A:\ACCT>DELTREE CORP

As you can see, this is a command to be used with extreme caution. You cannot use UNDELETE to restore the files deleted with DELTREE.

Practice: **Using the DELTREE Command**

Look at the directory structure of the TREE disk again with the following command:

- **A:\>TREE /F**   **[Enter]**

With the TREE DISK in drive A, remove a branch of the directory structure with the following command:

- **A:\>DELTREE DTP**   [Enter]

Respond to the screen prompt and all the subdirectories and files below DTP will be deleted.

Now erase one subdirectory and its files with the following command:

- **A:\>DELTREE A:\ACCT\CORP**   [Enter]
  or
- **A:\>CD ACCT**   [Enter]
- **A:\ACCT>DELTREE CORP**   [Enter]

Run a tree structure to ensure that the CORP subdirectory has been deleted.

Use the DELTREE command to delete the TEMP subdirectory from drive C.

RENAMING DIRECTORIES

In DOS 5.0 you were able to rename a subdirectory only by using the SHELL, a graphic interface to DOS, but in DOS 6.0 the MOVE command will rename a directory. It is not possible to rename the current directory just as it is not possible to remove the current directory. To rename the directory SMYTH to SMITH, key:

   A:\>MOVE SMYTH SMITH

The use of this command will rename the SMYTH directory to SMITH.

Practice: Using the RENAME Directory Command

Access the ACCT directory with the following:

- **A:\>CD \ACCT**   [Enter]

Rename the PROJ2 directory to TRANSPROJ with the following command:

- **A:\ACCT>MOVE PROJ2 TRANSPROJ**   [Enter]

USING THE XCOPY COMMAND

XCOPY is a very powerful command for copying files that was added to DOS version 3.2. XCOPY is more versatile than COPY, as it can copy files that exist in different directories and will create those directories while copying the files. XCOPY is an external command that has the same basic syntax as COPY:

XCOPY source file(s)   destination file(s)

The files to be copied are specified just as you would with the COPY command. You can use wildcards with XCOPY. A number of useful switches are available for controlling file transfer with XCOPY. Suppose that scattered throughout your hard disk directories were files with the extension LTR containing correspondence. You want to copy these files to a backup diskette in directories that correspond to the source directories. With the COPY command, you would have to create each directory on the target disk and then copy the source files from the source directory to the corresponding destination directory on the target disk, working with one directory at a time.

With XCOPY, you would simply enter the following command with the switch /S:

A:\>XCOPY C:*.LTR A: /S

This command line issues the following instructions to DOS:

- Search through the root directory and all subdirectories of the source disk in drive C for files with the LTR extension.

- Create the necessary subdirectories on the target disk in drive A.

- Copy the LTR files to the appropriate destination directories on the target disk.

XCOPY does not limit the copy process to one size or capacity disk. Therefore, you can XCOPY to and from hard disks and floppy diskettes of any size or capacity provided you do not exceed the capacity of the target disk.

XCOPY can be used with the following switches:

/A   Copies files that have the archive attribute on; does not reset the attribute to off.

/D   Copies only the files created on or after a date you specify.

/E   Duplicates subdirectories on the target disk that are on the source disk even if they are empty.

/M   Copies files that have the archive attribute on; resets the attribute to off.

/P   Prompts you before each file is copied for selective copying of files.

/S   Copies the current directory and its subdirectories.

/V   Verifies the correct copying of files.

/W   Waits for you to insert a source disk if you are copying to the same drive.

Another important advantage of XCOPY for systems with one floppy drive is that XCOPY reads as many files as possible into memory and then writes them to the target disk. Thus, XCOPY can be used to copy a group of files from one floppy disk to another on a one floppy drive system without swapping disks after each file, as you must do with the COPY command.

Note: One important caution about this command is that if there are any files on the target disk with names identical to the files on the source disk, the files on the target disk will be overwritten. However, DOS 6.2 has added a prompt that advises if a file of the same name exists and gives you the choice to overwrite it or not.

Practice: Using the XCOPY Command

Put the TREE DISK diskette in drive A and have a blank formatted diskette named FILES BACKUP disk handy to serve as the target diskette. Use XCOPY to make a backup of the TREE DISK diskette as follows:

■ A:\>XCOPY A:*.* B: /S /E   *or*   A:\>XCOPY A: B: /S /E   [Enter]

You have instructed DOS to copy files in the default (root) directory and all subdirectories of the drive A source disk to the target disk in drive B. In the process, XCOPY will create the subdirectories if they do not exist on the target disk. The /E switch tells DOS to create the directories even if the source disk directories are empty.

Read the screen messages and prompts. XCOPY will read a series of files into memory and then write them to disk. If you are using one floppy drive, watch for instructions to exchange disks. You may need to swap disks several times, but not nearly as often as you would with the COPY *.* command.

The result of this process will be a backup copy of your work disk with the same tree structure. Note that the source and target disks do *not* have to be the same size and capacity. If you want to verify the contents of the disks, insert the source disk in drive A, and key:

■   **A:\>TREE /F > PRN**   [Enter]

Now insert the target disk and key the same command. Compare the printouts.

Nice work with subdirectories! Test your knowledge with the Self-Check Quiz and Assignment.

CHAPTER 7 SELF-CHECK QUIZ

True/False (Write T if the statement is true, F if the statement is false.)

_____ 1. To redirect the screen display of the TREE command to the printer, use the right redirect (>).

_____ 2. The root directory, subdirectories, and their files make up the tree structure.

_____ 3. The complete tree structure, including file names, can be displayed but cannot be printed.

_____ 4. The same file can exist in two subdirectories but must have different names.

_____ 5. You cannot delete a subdirectory unless named files are still in it.

Multiple Choice (Circle the correct answer.)

6. Which *two* of the following commands are valid commands for copying ADD.TXT to the root directory of drive A?

    a. A:\>COPY ACCT\CORP\ADD.TXT
    b. A:\>COPY CORP\ADD.TXT
    c. A:\ACCT\CORP>COPY ADD.TXT \ ..
    d. A:\ACCT>COPY CORP\ADD.TXT \

7. Which *two* of the following are valid commands for moving up one level in the tree structure?

    a. A:\WPRO\TEXT> CD..
    b. A:\WPRO\TEXT>CD \
    c. A:\WPRO\TEXT>CD \WPRO
    d. A:\WPRO\TEXT>MD \

8. Which command would you use to rename the subdirectory WPRO to WP?

    a. REN WPRO WP
    b. COPY WPRO WP
    c. MOVE WPRO WP
    d. RD WPRO WP

9. Which of the following is true of the DELTREE command?

   a. DELTREE is available only in DOS 5.0 and later.
   b. All files must be removed from the subdirectories before the DELTREE command can be used.
   c. The DELTREE command will not delete files.
   d. The DELTREE command will delete the directory and all levels of the directory below it, including all files, in one command.

10. Which command would you use to copy all files on the disk in drive A, including all its subdirectories to the disk in drive B?

    a. XCOPY A:\ A /S   c. XCOPY A:*.* B:/S
    b. XCOPY A:S B: d. XCOPY A:\ A:/D/D

ASSIGNMENT

To practice using the commands in this chapter, complete the following steps.
Check off each step when you understand its operation, or mark the step with a
question mark if it is not clear. Write the commands or keystrokes in the
space provided.

1. Clear the screen. Using the TREE DISK, make the root directory of drive
   A the current directory. Use the redirect function to print the directory
   listing for the root directory.

   _____

2. Without changing the directory, use the redirect function to print a directory
   listing of the COMM directory on the disk.

   _____

3. Copy REVIEW.TXT from the root directory to the COMM directory. Copy
   SUB.TXT from the WPRO directory to the COMM and the ACCT
   directories. Do you see any different messages displayed when copying
   this file to the two different subdirectories?

   _____

4. Using the redirect function, print the disk's tree structure with files.

   _____

5. Remove the WPRO directory and print a copy of the tree structure with
   files.

   _____

6. Using XCOPY, back up the TREE DISK diskette onto the FILES BACKUP
   diskette.

   _____

7. Use the MOVE command to rename the ACCT subdirectory to
   NEWACCT. Print a copy of the tree with files.

   _____

8. Create a subdirectory of the NEWACCT directory. Name the directory
   STOCK. Compose a short file for the STOCK subdirectory called JAN.94.
   Use your own wording.

   _____

9. Print a tree showing all directories and files.

   _____

10.   Remove the NEWACCT subdirectory using the DELTREE command.

CHAPTER 8

An Introduction to EDLIN, the DOS Line Editor

OBJECTIVES

When you have completed the activities and assignment in this chapter, you will be able to:

1. Describe uses for EDLIN.

2. Create and edit text files in EDLIN.

3. Use EDLIN commands to list a text file.

4. Use EDLIN commands to append, insert, and delete lines.

5. Use the DOS editing keys for editing in EDLIN.

6. End editing and save the file or quit without saving.

DOS EDITING TECHNIQUES

MS-DOS has two **text editors** to help you create and revise files. One program, EDLIN, is available in all versions of MS-DOS and PC-DOS. The other text editor, EDIT, is available in MS-DOS Versions 5.0 and later and PC-DOS 5.0.

In **EDLIN**, files are created and edited line by line by keying EDLIN commands, specifying lines of text by line number, and keying or modifying individual lines of text. **EDIT**, described in Chapter 9, gives you more flexibility in working with blocks of text, has drop-down menus, and can be used with a mouse.

IBM PC-DOS 6.1 introduces another **text editor** named **E** which is similar to the EDIT program in MS-DOS. If you would like to use the E program, research your PC-DOS documentation for further information.

By using any of the DOS text editors, you produce files that are stored in ASCII format. As you read in Chapter 1, ASCII is a standardized code used for translating text characters into numbers that all computers can process. ASCII files can be used by almost every computer and software program that processes text.

In previous chapters, you learned to create short text files using the COPY CON method which also produces ASCII text. A disadvantage of this method is that there is no way to correct or edit a line after you have ended the line by pressing [Enter]. In EDIT, EDLIN, and E, you can edit any ASCII text file, including those created with COPY CON or with other text editing software.

This chapter introduces you to some features of EDLIN; others will not be covered. Check your documentation if you want additional information. Chapter 9 will help you get started with EDIT. If you complete both this chapter and Chapter 9, you will be able to use both.

USES FOR EDLIN

EDLIN is useful for writing or correcting short lists, messages, and other text files without loading a word processing software package. Using EDLIN is usually preferable to using the COPY CON technique for creating text files longer than a few lines because of the editing capabilities of EDLIN. You can use EDLIN to revise files such as batch files created with COPY CON.

While EDLIN is not a substitute for a word processing software package, you will find it useful when you want to create or revise a short text file without loading a word processor. And, because it is one of the DOS command files, it will always be available when you are using a DOS machine. The EDLIN command file is small compared to the combined size of the command files for that are required for using EDIT. This might be a significant advantage if you need to have a text editor available on a floppy disk.

CREATING A TEXT FILE WITH EDLIN

To access EDLIN, you would key the following:

    C:\>EDLIN <filename>

If the file is new, you will be given the message that you are creating a new file. At that point, you will use EDLIN's initial letter commands.

EDLIN uses initial letter commands. They are easy to remember because they all stand for the action they cause, as in D to delete. In this introduction, you'll learn the most commonly used commands: I (insert), L (list), D (delete), C (copy), M (move), P (page), E (end edit and save), and Q (quit without saving). The DOS editing keys are also useful in editing with EDLIN.

You key text one line at a time and press [Enter] to end each line. While a line can be up to 253 characters in length, you will want to limit line length to a screen width. Form the habit of pressing [Enter] before the text reaches the right edge of the screen and the line wraps to the next line. Revisions are made to one line at a time. Lines can be copied, deleted, or moved singly and in blocks of adjacent lines.

Practice: Creating a Text File with EDLIN

Begin by keying a new text file using EDLIN. EDLIN is an external command and therefore must be accessed in the hard disk directory where DOS files are stored. If necessary, set a search path to the DOS files.

- **C:\>PATH C:\DOS**   [Enter]

Place your TREE DISK diskette in drive A. If necessary, change the prompt to display the current drive and directory.

- **C:\>PROMPT PG**   [Enter]

To practice using your tree-structured filing system, change to the COMM directory and store the text files you will be creating there.

To load EDLIN and begin a new file, key the command EDLIN, a space, and the file name.

- **A:\COMM> EDLIN TEXTMSG.DOC**   [Enter]

The system finds the EDLIN command file in the DOS directory in your search path and loads EDLIN into memory. EDLIN responds with the message New file because there is no existing file named TEXTMSG.DOC. The "New file" message is often helpful because it tells you there is no file by that name.

New file
*

Notice the asterisk below the "New file" message. The * is the EDLIN prompt. Just as DOS uses a prompt to show you where you can key DOS commands, EDLIN has its own command prompt, the asterisk.

The EDLIN screen is divided into two areas (Figure 8-1). At the far left is the command area. When the asterisk prompt and blinking cursor are in this area, you can enter EDLIN commands. Actual text editing takes place in the center and far right of the screen, where text is displayed. When the blinking cursor is in this area, you can revise or add lines.

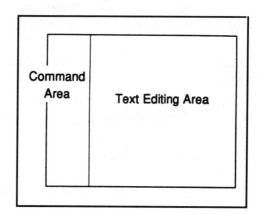

To start keying text, it is necessary to be in the insert mode. To get into the insert mode, key the insert command initial letter **I** (or **i**) at the * prompt and press [Enter].

Figure 8-1. The two areas of the EDLIN screen.

    New file
■   ***I**   [Enter]

Now the line number 1: followed by an asterisk appears in the text editing area. You are ready to key lines of text. Each time you finish a line, press [Enter] and the next numbered line will appear for keying additional text. Backspace to erase errors that you catch before you press [Enter]. Each line is placed in memory when you press [Enter]. The completed lines of text in memory will comprise your TEXTMSG.DOC file.

Key the lines shown in bold type, ignoring any errors you discover after you have pressed [Enter]. You will learn to correct them soon.

■   1:***Today is Monday, the day after Sunday.**   [Enter]
■   2:***Today is Monday, the first day of the week.**   [Enter]
    3:*

The text lines are automatically numbered by EDLIN. Later you will see that when you use EDLIN's delete or insert functions, the lines have been automatically renumbered. The line numbers that appear on the EDLIN screen are not saved with the file and will not appear when it is printed or displayed on the screen. The numbers are displayed only in EDLIN.

Notice that each new line number is followed by an asterisk signifying that this is the line of the file with which you are currently working. In the text editing area, the last asterisk always indicates which line is the **current line** of entry or the last line entered. The current line (3:) is the line EDLIN will work on next, unless you give other instructions.

Continue to key the lines shown. Do *not* press [Enter] at the end of line 4.

- 3:**Today is Tuesday, the second day of the week.**   [Enter]
- 4:**Today is Wednesday, the fourth day of this month.**

At the end of line 4, backspace to "the" and rewrite the sentence as follows:

- 4:*Today is Wednesday, the **third day of the week.**   [Enter]

Then continue:

- 5:**Today is Thursday, the fourth day of the week.**   [Enter]
- 6:**Today is Friday, TGIF.**   [Enter]
     7:*

You are now finished keying text and are ready to exit the insert mode because you have no more new lines to key. You must exit the insert mode on a new line so that you retain all keyed lines. Be sure the cursor is at the *beginning* of line 7. Then hold down the Ctrl key, tap the letter Z (Ctrl-Z), and press [Enter].

- 7:**^Z**   [Enter]

You can press the F6 function key and [Enter] instead of Ctrl-Z and [Enter] to exit the insert mode. F6 also places ^Z on the line. This code is the DOS end-of-file mark. If you use Ctrl-Z or F6 anywhere except at the beginning of a line, you will still be in the insert mode after you press [Enter]. The characters ^Z will appear on the line where you pressed [Enter], and the cursor will move to the next line. If you save a file with ^Z in it and then reload the file into EDLIN, only the portion of the file before the end-of-file mark will be loaded. The exception to this is in DOS 5.0 and 6.1, where you can use the switch /B when you load the file to instruct EDLIN to ignore end-of-file marks.

Other options for exiting from insert mode are to press Ctrl-C or Ctrl-Break. Be sure the cursor is on a blank line—using these options will cancel the current line, the line the cursor is on, erasing it from the file buffer.

When you exit the insert text mode, EDLIN returns to the command mode with an asterisk prompt in the command area. Now list the lines of text you keyed. At the * prompt, key the **list** command initial letter **L** (or **l**) and press [Enter].

■ ***L**   [Enter]

EDLIN lists the file. The six lines of text are displayed. EDLIN then returns to the command mode with a * prompt at the left of the screen.

Did you notice that in the list there is no asterisk marking a current line? This is because line 7, the last line you worked on, is still the current line. Since you canceled this line with Ctrl-Z, EDLIN does not display it.

EDLIN can list 23 lines (one screenful) at a time. What if your file were longer or if you wanted to list only a part of it? To list from line 5 to the end of the file, key:

■ ***5L**   [Enter]

If the file were longer, the command above would list through line 27.

You can also list from a starting point through a specific line. For example, if you want to list lines 2 through 5, key at the * prompt in the command area: the beginning line number, a comma, the ending line number, and the letter L.

■ ***2,5L**   [Enter]

Now end editing and save the completed file. At the command * prompt, key the end edit command initial letter **E** (or **e**) to end editing and exit. When you press [Enter], the file is saved and you are returned to the DOS prompt.

■ ***E**   [Enter]

If, for some reason, you decide *not* to save text you have written or edited in EDLIN, you can exit from the EDLIN program without saving the file by keying the quit command, initial letter **Q** (or **q**). Do this only when you do not want to save the text you have entered or edited.

■ ***Q**   [Enter]

When you use Q, you are required to confirm that you want to "Abort edit (Y/N)?" Key **Y** to return to DOS or **N** to continue working on the file.

Use the TYPE command to display the TEXTMSG.DOC file. Notice that the line numbers do not appear.

EDITING A TEXT FILE WITH EDLIN

Now edit the file you saved. First you must reload the file into memory. When you load an existing file, EDLIN displays the message, "End of input file." Be sure to key the correct file name or EDLIN will tell you that you are creating a new file. If you try to retrieve an existing file for editing and receive a "New file" message, you will know the system was not able to find your file. Recheck the file name, pathname, and drive designator; then check to see if you have the correct disk in the drive.

Practice: Editing a Text File with EDLIN

In order to edit the file you created, recall the document to the display screen by keying EDLIN followed by the name of the file you want to edit.

- A:\COMM>**EDLIN TEXTMSG.DOC**   [Enter]

The screen displays "End of input file." This tells you that such a file exists and that the entire file is loaded into memory. You have seen how EDLIN informs you if the file is a new file or if it already exists by displaying either "New file" or "End of input file." COPY CON does not give you this information. With COPY CON, you could accidentally overwrite a file by giving a new file the same name as an existing file.

DOS 5.0 and 6.1 users can display an EDLIN help screen by keying a **?** at the EDLIN prompt. The displayed information is valid for all versions of EDLIN:

```
*?
Edit line               line#
Append                  [#lines]A
Copy                    [startline],[endline],toline[,times]C
Delete                  [startline][,endline]D
End (Save file)         E
Insert                  [line]I
List                    [startline][,endline],L
Move                    [startline],[endline],tolineM
Page                    [startline][,endline]P
Quit (throw away changes)        Q
Replace                 [startline][,endline][?]R[oldtext]
                        [Ctrl+Znewtext]
Search                  [startline][,endline][?]Stext
Transfer                [toline]T[drive:][path]Filename
Write                   [#lines]W
```

Study the EDLIN help screen displayed above to review the commands you have used so far. (Remember, parameters shown in brackets are optional.) Then key the list command (L or l) to list the file and display the numbered lines you will be editing.

■ *L   [Enter]

To change to a specific line, first make it the current line by keying its line number at the * prompt in the command area. To change to line 1, key:

■ *1   [Enter]

When you select a line for editing, two versions of the line are displayed. EDLIN lists the line as it currently exists and, under that line, displays a blank line where you can key the line as you want it to appear.

```
    1:*Today is Monday, the day after Sunday.
    1:*
```

At the blinking cursor on the bottom line, key the bold type below:

```
    1:*Today is Monday, the day after Sunday.
```
■ **1 : *Today is Monday, the day following Sunday.**   [Enter]

Now list the file to see that line 1 reflects your change.

Inserting Lines

Insert a blank line before line 1. To do this, key at the * prompt in the command area the line number 1 followed by the letter i (for insert).

■ **1i**   [Enter]

At the 1:* in the text area, enter the following text:

■ **1:*Days of the week move by very quickly.**   [Enter]

Exit the insert mode by pressing Ctrl-Z and [Enter] at the beginning of line 2. List your file to see that the new line 1 is inserted and the remaining lines are renumbered.

To insert a blank line just above line 2 of your text, at the command prompt key the line number 2 followed by the letter i (for insert).

■ *2i   [Enter]

At the 2:* in the text area, press the [Enter] key.

■ 2:*   [Enter]

Press Ctrl-Z and [Enter] at the beginning of line 3 to return to the * prompt in
the command area. When you list the file, there is a new blank line 2 between
lines 1 and 3, and the remainder of the lines are renumbered.

Appending Lines

When you want to append (add) lines to the end of a file, at the command
prompt key the pound sign (#) and i (for insert).

■ *#i   [Enter]

This takes you to the next blank line at the end of the file. Key the following
in the text area:

■   9:*Saturday--the weekend is here!   [Enter]
■ 10:*Sunday--are you ready for Monday?   [Enter]

Press Ctrl-Z and [Enter] at the beginning of line 11 to return to the command
area.

Remember: You can also use Ctrl-C or Ctrl-Break to exit from the
Insert mode. Whenever you press Ctrl-C while on a line, you cancel
any changes made to that line. If you press Ctrl-C on line 10, for
example, you would cancel the entry you just made on that line. For
this reason, you should go to a blank line to exit the Insert mode with
Ctrl-C as you must with Ctrl-Z.

Deleting Lines

Before deleting lines, always list them to make certain you are entering the
correct line numbers. To delete a line, at the * command prompt key the line
number followed by the delete command initial letter **D** (or **d**).

To delete line 4, key the following at the * prompt:

■ ***4D**   [Enter]

To see the revised file with the line deleted, list the file. The former line 4 has been deleted and the remaining lines have been automatically renumbered. Line 4 is marked with the * indicating that it is the current line.

It is a good practice to always list a file after you have deleted lines and before you go on to the next step. In this way, you can be certain that you are using the correct line numbers when you issue the next command.

To delete several adjacent lines, key this sequence: the number of the first line to be deleted, a comma, the number of the last line to be deleted, and the command initial D or d. Press [Enter] to carry out the command.

Delete lines 1 and 2 with this command:

■ ***1,2D**   [Enter]

List the file. The first two lines have disappeared and the remaining lines are renumbered.

Now exit the file and save it with the end edit command (E or e). Display a listing of the COMM directory to see the file listed. Notice that EDLIN also saved the earlier version of the file as TEXTMSG.BAK. Each time you edit a file with EDLIN, the earlier version is saved as a backup and is renamed with a BAK extension.

Copy the TEXTMSG.DOC file to the printer so that you can see the results of all your hard work!

Practice: Creating and Revising Text

1. Create this file named TEXTLTR.DOC in the COMM directory. Key:

   ■ **A:\COMM>EDLIN TEXTLTR.DOC**   [Enter]

   You will see:

   *
   New file

   Key **I** for Insert. Continue with the document as follows:

- 1:*(Your Name)   [Enter]
- 2:*(Your Address)   [Enter]
- 3:*(Your City, State, and ZIP)   [Enter]
- 4:*   [Enter]
- 5:*   [Enter]
- 6:*Trabuco Valley College   [Enter]
- 7:*1311 Alicia Allyson Avenue   [Enter]
- 8:*Orland Park, IL 60462   [Enter]
- 9:*   [Enter]
- 10:*   [Enter]
- 11:*Dear Friends: [Enter]
- 12:*   [Enter]
- 13:*I would like to attend your college this   [Enter]
- 14:*fall. My brother attends now and he is very   [Enter]
- 15:*pleased with the classes, particularly those   [Enter]
- 16:*in the computer department.   [Enter]
- 17:*   [Enter]
- 18:*Please send me the schedule of classes for   [Enter]
- 19:*the coming fall semester.   [Enter]
- 20:*Thank you,   [Enter]
- 21:*   [Enter]
- 22:*(your name)   [Enter]

2. Save and print the file.

   a. End editing and save the file.

   b. Copy TEXTLTR.DOC to the printer.

   c. Redirect a listing of the COMM directory to the printer.

3. Edit TEXTLTR.DOC as follows. Remember to list the file after each change.

   a. Delete one blank line after the college address.

   b. Add one blank line before the complimentary close, "Thank you,"

   c. Exit the edit mode and save the file.

   d. Make a copy of the file for use in the next activity. Name the copy TEXTLTR1.DOC.

4. Compose three of your own revisions to TEXTLTR1.DOC:

a. Append a line at the end of the letter giving your title as "Student."

b. Delete a line.

c. Insert several lines of text in the body of the letter. Press [Enter] to end each line before it wraps.

d. Save and print the revised file. Mark the revisions.

5. Compose a short text file named MYFILE using EDLIN. Remember to end each line before it wraps. Print the file.

6. Revise the file you created in step 5 and print it. Mark the revisions. Redirect a listing of the COMM directory to the printer.

EDLIN COMMAND SUMMARY CHART		
EDLIN Command	Examples	Action
I or **i** (insert)	2i	Inserts a line at line 2, renumbers lines below
#	#i	Appends a line at end of file
L or **l** (list)	1L 2,8L	Lists file beginning at line 1 Lists lines 2 through 8
D or **d** (delete)	5d 4,7d	Deletes line 5, renumbers lines below Deletes lines 4 through 7, renumbers lines below
E or **e** (end edit)	e	Exits from EDLIN and saves file
Q (quit)	q	Quits (aborts) edit, does not save file

Revising Files with a BAK Extension

As you learned, EDLIN stores a backup file when you revise an existing file. For example, when you recalled TEXTMSG.DOC, revised it, and stored the revised version by keying the end edit command (E or e) and pressing [Enter], the original version was not replaced, but was left unchanged on the disk. When you saved the new version, the original version's file name extension was changed to BAK (for backup). The new version was stored as revised, but with the original's filename and extension, TEXTMSG.DOC.

There is one important thing to remember about the backup file. EDLIN will not access any file with a BAK extension. If you wish to edit the backup file, *you must rename the file*. For example, to revise TEXTLTR.BAK, you could rename it TEXTLTR.OLD. The exception to this is PC-DOS version 3.3, which will load BAK files into EDLIN.

THE DOS EDITING KEYS FOR EDITING IN EDLIN

The DOS editing keys work exactly the same way for editing in EDLIN as they do for editing DOS commands. As you have seen, the EDLIN commands operate on *complete lines* within a file or document. The function keys and other editing keys are used to edit *within a line*.

There is a special section in the computer's memory called an input buffer. The last line you enter from the keyboard is retained in this buffer when you press [Enter]. When you are working in EDLIN, the current line is stored in the buffer. EDLIN identifies the current line for you by displaying an asterisk (*) after its line number. Because the current line is in the input buffer, you can use it as a template or pattern for editing.

Use the DOS editing keys to repeat or modify lines in EDLIN just as you use them to repeat or modify DOS command lines. At the EDLIN command prompt, key the number of the line you wish to revise and press [Enter]. EDLIN will display the requested line as a template line with a blank line below it. The DOS editing keys operate on the template line in the following ways:

F1 The F1 key copies one character at a time from the template line in the buffer and displays it on the screen. For example, to copy the first part of the line, press **F1** until you reach the point of change.

F2 The F2 key copies the line up to the character you specify. For example, in the line "The quick brown fox jumps over the lazy dog," to change the word fox to cat, press **F2** and the letter "**f**" in the word "fox." This will copy "The quick brown ." Key "**cat**"; then press **F3** to complete the line.

F3 The F3 key copies the entire current line or the rest of the line from the buffer to the display screen. For example, to add something to an existing line, press **F3** to copy the entire line. Then simply key what you want to add to the line. Or, if you have made a revision in the beginning of a line and want to use the rest of the line unchanged, press **F3** to quickly copy the remainder of the line.

F4 The F4 key deletes letters up to the character you specify after pressing **F4**. In the line "The quick brown fox jumps over the lazy dog," if you press **F4** and the letter "**b**," the characters up to b in "brown" will be erased from the buffer. When you press **F3**, the line will begin "brown fox jumped . . ."

Right and Left Arrow Keys The right and left arrow keys can also be used. The right arrow key acts like the F1 key, copying one character at a time from the buffer onto the display screen. The left arrow key acts like the Backspace key, erasing one character at a time and moving to the left. The character erased remains in the buffer, however.

Delete A pointer accesses the same place on the template line in the input buffer as the cursor's position in the current line on the screen. Each time you press the Del key, one character showing on the display screen is deleted from the buffer. No change appears on the screen until you press **F1** or **F3** to display the next character(s) in the line. The deleted characters do not appear.

Insert When you press the Ins key, the next character(s) you key will be placed on the screen and in the buffer at the cursor location, and all following characters in the line will move to the right. The insert mode is turned off by pressing any function key, any other DOS editing key, or [Enter].

Practice: Using the DOS Editing Keys to Edit a File

Retrieve the file TEXTLTR.DOC. It should be stored in the COMM subdirectory. This time, rather than changing to that directory, use the file's pathname to tell the system where the file is:

■   **C:\>EDLIN A:\COMM\TEXTLTR.DOC**   [Enter]

If all goes well, you will see this message:

```
End of input file
*
```

If not, check to see if you keyed the path name and file name correctly. If your entry is correct, next check the COMM directory to make sure the TEXTLTR.DOC file is there.

List the file by keying **L** at the EDLIN prompt. Then with EDLIN commands and the DOS editing keys, make the changes described in the following steps.

Use **F2** and **2** to change the ZIP in the inside address for the college to 60464. To do this, first make line 8 the current line by keying **8** and pressing [Enter] at the * command prompt. EDLIN displays line 8 with a blank line below it.

```
8: Orland Park, IL 60462
8:*
```

Press **F2** and **2** to copy line 8 up to line 2. Then key **4** to change the ZIP to 60464. Press [Enter] to return to the command prompt.

Now make line 10 the current line by keying **10** at the * prompt and pressing [Enter]. When line 10 displays, press **F1** five times to copy "Dear" and the space. Key a new salutation, "**Ladies and Gentlemen:**" and press [Enter].

Make line 12 the current line. Press **F1** twice to copy the "I" and the space; then change the rest of the first line of the letter to:

- **I hope to enroll in and attend your college**   [Enter]

Make line 12 the current line by pressing [Enter] again. Press **Ins** and key the word "this" and a space at the beginning of the line. Press **F3** to copy the remainder of the line. Press [Enter].

List the file. Key the text in bold type below after "semester." on line 18. At the * command prompt, key **18** and press [Enter] to make line 18 current. Press **F3** to copy the line and then add the text shown in bold to the line. Press [Enter] to return to the * prompt. Key **19i** to insert new lines at line 19. Press [Enter] to start inserting the six new lines.

- the coming fall semester. **I would also**   [Enter]
- **appreciate a list of graduation requirements.**   [Enter]
- **A college education has long been one of my**   [Enter]
- **goals. I will, no doubt, need counseling**   [Enter]
- **since I do not know what I would like to do**   [Enter]
- **when I graduate. Please recommend a career**   [Enter]
- **counselor for me to see.**   [Enter]
- **[Ctrl-Z]**   [Enter]

List the file. Insert two more blank lines for your signature by keying **28i** at the * prompt and pressing [Enter] three times (once to go to the text area, twice to add two lines). Press Ctrl-Z and [Enter] to exit from the insert mode.

List the file again. Divide the second paragraph into two paragraphs. First insert a line above the line that begins "goals." Key "**goals**." on this line and press [Enter] twice. Exit the insert mode on the second blank line.

List the file. Next edit the first line of the new paragraph. Press **F4** and the uppercase letter **I** to delete the word "goals." Press **F3** to complete the revised line. Press [Enter] to return to the * prompt.

List the file to proofread it. The revised file should look like the following:.

```
 1:     Your Name
 2:     Your Street Address
 3:     City, State  Zip
 4:
 5:
 6:     Trabuco Valley College
 7:     1311 Alicia Allyson Avenue
 8:     Orland Park, IL  60464
 9:
10:     Dear Ladies and Gentlemen:
11:
12:     I hope to enroll in and attend your college
13:     this fall.  My brother attends now and he is very
14:     pleased with the classes, particularly those
15:     in the computer department.
16:
17:     Please send me the schedule of classes for
18:     the coming fall semester.  I would also
19:     appreciate a list of graduation requirements.
20:     A college education has long been one of my
21:     goals.
22:
23:     I will, no doubt, need counseling
24:     since I do not know what I would like to do
25:     when I graduate.  Please recommend a career
26:     counselor for me to see.
27:
28:     Thank you,
29:
30:
31:     Your Name
```

Notice that the file is now longer than 23 lines (a screenful). When you use the L command alone, EDLIN displays the current line with the 11 lines before it and the 11 lines after it. To display the entire file in two passes, list the file with the following two commands:

- ***1,10L**   [Enter]
- ***11L**   [Enter]

This enables you to see the entire file. You can use other line number combinations to accomplish this, of course.

When you are satisfied with your letter, press **E** to exit and save the file. Then use the COPY or TYPE command to print the letter.

Your introduction to the first of the two text editors is completed. Test your comprehension of the material by completing the Self-Check Quiz and Assignment before going on to the next chapter on EDIT.

CHAPTER 8 SELF-CHECK QUIZ

True/False (Write T if the statement is true, F is the statement is false.)

_____ 1. EDLIN can be used to edit files created with COPY CON.

_____ 2. EDLIN recognizes commands keyed in uppercase or lowercase letters.

_____ 3. The EDLIN command can be keyed either before or after the line number(s).

_____ 4. EDLIN line numbers can be displayed with the TYPE command.

_____ 5. EDLIN, EDIT, and COPY CON create files in ASCII format.

Multiple Choice (Circle the correct answer.)

6. Which EDLIN command would you use to insert a line at line 6?

    a.   i6   c.   6
    b.   5i   d.   6i

7. Which EDLIN command would you use to remove line 10?

    a.   r10   c.   10d
    b.   10r   d.   d10

8. Which EDLIN command would you use to revise line 4?

    a. 4   c.   4*
    b. 4c   d.   4r

9. Which function key would you use to copy all characters up to the letter keyed?

    a.   F1   c.   F2
    b.   F3   d.   F4

10. If you were editing the line
    1:*Employer: Ace Computers
    and pressed F4, A, and F3, what would the result be?

    a.   Employer   c.   Employer: A
    b.   Ace Computers   d.   A

ASSIGNMENT

To practice using the commands in this chapter, complete the following steps. Check off each step when you understand its operation, or mark the step with a question mark if it is not clear. Write the commands or keystrokes in the space provided.

   1. Create a new EDLIN file named WINNERS.TXT on your TREE DISK in the COMM subdirectory. Input the following text:

     Mr. and Mrs. John Brown
     111 Main Street
     San Diego, CA 92706

     Dear Mr. and Mrs. Brown:

     Today you have been declared the winners of the lottery sponsored by the Main Street Camera Store.

     Your winnings will be announced later in the week but I can assure you that you will be very happy with the amount of your check.

     Please bring the lottery ticket to the counter when you come and we will be happy to help you carry your winnings home or to the bank.

     Sincerely,

     Your friendly sales clerk,

   2. Print a copy of the file.

_____

   3. Revise the file as follows:

     Add your name under the "friendly sales clerk," line.

_____

   4. Change the name and address in the letter to your name and address.

_____

5. Change the salutation to CONGRATULATIONS! Save and exit the file.

_____

6. Print the revised letter.

_____

7. List only the first 15 lines of the letter. Print the screen showing the command line.

_____

8. Delete the last paragraph. Print the screen showing the command line.

_____

9. Revise the letter again and add the date at the top of the letter and the following paragraph at the end of the second paragraph.

   As you know, as the sellers of your lottery ticket we are entitled to a percentage of your winnings. Thank you for purchasing the winning ticket from our store.

_____

10. Save and print the file.

_____

9

AN INTRODUCTION TO EDIT, THE DOS TEXT EDITOR

OBJECTIVES

When you have completed the activities and assignment in this chapter, you will be able to:

1. Use EDIT to create, revise, and save text files.

2. Open and use EDIT menus and dialog boxes.

3. Select, insert, delete, copy, cut, and paste text.

4. Find and change words and phrases.

5. Print text files.

6. Look up information in EDIT HELP screens.

THE DOS EDITOR

The DOS Editor is a full-screen text editor. It is a simple text editing program that allows users to easily create, revise, and print short documents. The Editor can be used in the Shell or started at the DOS prompt with the command EDIT. The Editor can be used to revise all text files created with COPY CON and with other text editors such as EDLIN, E, and Notepad.

The EDIT command requires access to the QBASIC program that is bundled with DOS as well as EDIT.COM. EDIT utilizes the part of the QBASIC code that is used for editing and writing BASIC programs. You will not be aware that you are using QBASIC and you do not need to know any programming to work with EDIT. EDIT also requires access to EDIT.HLP, a file containing help information for the Editor.

Although the Editor is much more flexible than the older methods of creating and revising text files, COPY CON and EDLIN, it still lacks the power of a true word processor. For example, you cannot set margins or custom tabs, control line spacing, or spell check. The Editor does not have the word-wrap capability found in a true word processing program. Nevertheless, EDIT is extremely useful when you need to create a short document in ASCII or to write or revise a batch file. Batch files are the subject of Chapter 10.

INSTALLING THE MOUSE

As you learned in Chapter 1, the mouse is an excellent input device. When working with EDIT, you may choose to work with a mouse or the keyboard.

Depending on the way the computer has been set up, the mouse may or may not be automatically installed when you boot your computer. If the mouse is not active, install it by keying at the DOS prompt:

MOUSE   (Assuming MOUSE is the appropriate driver name for
                     the mouse device.)

DOS will display a message verifying that the mouse has been successfully installed.

Practice: Installing the Mouse

If necessary, install the mouse as follows:

■ **MOUSE**   [Enter]

Other than the verification of successful installation of the mouse, you will see no indication of the mouse on the screen.

USING EDIT

Since EDIT is an external command, you will either need to change the directory to the DOS subdirectory or have the path set to the DOS files in order to use EDIT. The command to load EDIT is:

C:\>EDIT

Note: EDIT is not available in PC-DOS 6.1.

Practice: Loading EDIT

Use the TREE DISK diskette in this exercise. Access the COMM directory on the disk in drive A to work from with the EDIT program. To start the Editor, key the following from the DOS prompt:

■ **EDIT**   [Enter]

USING THE MOUSE

When the mouse is installed on your computer and you are in the EDIT program, move the mouse to see if it is active. You should see a small rectangle move on the screen when you move the mouse. This is the mouse pointer.

The **scroll bars**, scroll arrows, and scroll boxes are used to scroll the screen with the mouse (see Figure 9-1). There are several actions you will use with the mouse.

They are:

- Point   Move the mouse to move the small rectangle or arrow that moves on the screen when you move the mouse. The mouse is used to point at objects such as scroll bars, menu names, icons, or other objects on the screen.

- Click   Press and release a mouse button, usually the left button.

- Double-click   Click the mouse button twice and quickly release.

- Drag   Hold down the mouse button and move the mouse pointer to a different place.

You will work with only the left button on the mouse in EDIT.

Features of the EDIT Screen

If you do not specify a file name after EDIT, the first screen you see is empty except for a dialog box asking if you want to see the "Survival Guide" or go directly into the EDIT program. The Survival Guide is the Help menu for EDIT (see Figure 9-1). At this point, press Esc to clear the dialog box and go to the EDIT screen.

You will see a blank editing area with a **menu bar** above it listing five options: File, Edit, Search, Options, and Help. The document title appears at

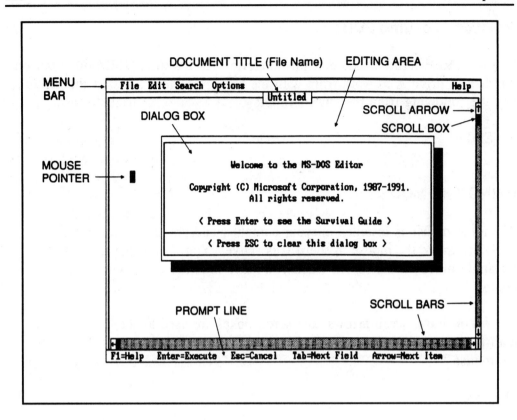

Figure 9-1. EDIT screen.

the top center of the editing screen. At this time the document is "Untitled."
At the bottom of the screen there is a **prompt line**. This line provides help by
reminding you of the keystrokes you may want to use next. Its contents
change as you perform different operations.

Practice: Creating a File Using EDIT

To provide practice in creating files in specific directories, create the following
file in the COMM directory. You should be at the EDIT screen. Press Esc to
clear the full-screen display and start your document by keying the following
text on one line:

■ **I am creating this file to test the features of the new DOS editor.**

Revise the line as follows:

■ Insert the word **text** in front of the words "file" and "editor" as follows:

   Press the left arrow key enough times to position the cursor under the "e"
   in "editor," key the word **text** and press the spacebar once to create a
   space.

You can also position the cursor with the mouse by moving the mouse pointer to the place where you want the cursor to be and clicking (pressing) the left button.

■ Next, hold down the Ctrl key and tap the left arrow key (Ctrl-Left) to move the cursor one word to the left. Continue to press Ctrl-Left until the cursor is on the "f" in "file." (If you go too far, use the Ctrl and the right arrow keys (Ctrl-Right) to move one word to the right.) Key the word **text** and press the spacebar once to create a space. The sentence should now read:

```
I am creating this text file to test the features of
the new DOS text editor.
```

■ Delete the word "new" in the sentence. Use Ctrl-Right or the mouse to position the cursor under the "n" in "new." Press the Del key four times (once for each character in the word and the following space).

The sentence now reads:

```
I am creating this text file to test the features of
the DOS text editor.
```

Practice: Saving and Exiting from EDIT

You have keyed text and made minor revisions. Now save the file. Notice the message in the prompt line at the bottom of the screen:

```
Press ALT to activate menus
```

Five menu names are listed in the menu bar across the top of the screen: File, Edit, Search, Options, and Help. Pressing the Alt key and the first character of the menu name (F, E, S, O, or H) will open that menu. Try this by pressing

■ **Alt**

The File menu name is highlighted or selected. (See Figure 9-2.) Use the right arrow key to move the highlight and select the other options in the menu bar. The initial letters of the menu names become bright white as you move from one option to another.

To save the file, open the File menu by pressing **F**. (Press **Alt** first if the menu initial letters are no

Figure 9-2. File menu.

longer bright white.) You can also open the menu with the mouse by pointing at the File menu name and clicking the left button.

A **menu** contains a list of command options. The options available in the File menu are shown in Figure 9-2. "New" is highlighted. Use the down arrow key to move the highlight down through the options. Watch the prompt line at the bottom of the screen for a brief explanation of what each option in the menu does.

Notice that several of the options have an ellipse (...) following them, such as "Save As..." If a menu option has an ellipse, a **dialog box** will display when the command is chosen. A dialog box allows you to key additional information or make other choices required by the command.

Two options exist for saving a file, Save and Save As. When the file is Untitled, you can use either option. The different color (or bold) letter indicates the keyboard letter that activates the option. To activate the Save option, key **S**; to activate the Save As option, key

■ **A**

With the mouse, click the left button anywhere on the Save As option. The Save As dialog box is displayed. Press **F1** to see a Help screen that identifies the parts of the dialog box. Press **Esc** to remove the Help screen.

Below "File Name:" the current directory A:\COMM is shown. Since this is where you want the file to be stored, you can simply key the file name at the blinking cursor. Key

■ **DOS6A.TXT**   [Enter]

The file is written to disk and the dialog box is removed. Notice that the file name DOS6A.TXT has replaced Untitled at the top of the screen. It is wise to form the habit of backing up all of your work; start by backing up this document on the CLASS diskette. Press the following keys

■ **Alt F A**

Watch this key combination, choose the File menu and Save As. Exchange the diskettes in drive A and use the same name you used previously. Note that the DOS6A.TXT file goes in the root directory of the destination diskette.

You have completed your first EDIT document. To exit from EDIT, open the File menu and select Exit. Use the mouse or these keystrokes:

■ **Alt F X**

If you had not saved the file, you would be prompted to do so before exiting EDIT.

SELECTING, COPYING, CUTTING, AND PASTING TEXT

If you are not familiar with word processing, selecting, copying, cutting, and pasting text into new locations may be new to you. The following descriptions explain each of these operations briefly. See Figure 9-3.

Selecting Text: Before text can be copied, cut, or deleted, you must **select** it. In EDIT and most other editing software, text is selected by using keystroke combinations or a mouse. You will learn the keystrokes for selecting text in EDIT. When text is selected, it appears in reverse video or the opposite color from the surrounding text.

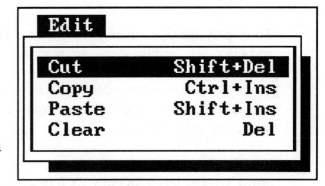

Figure 9-3. Edit menu.

Copying Text: When you use the EDIT **Copy** command to copy text, a duplicate of the selected text is placed in a memory buffer. The copied text replaces any other text that might have been placed in the buffer by an earlier Copy or Cut command. The selected text on the screen does not change.

Cutting Text: When you use the EDIT **Cut** command, the selected text is placed in the memory buffer, replacing any other text that might be there. The selected text is removed from the screen.

When you remove text from the screen with the Delete key or the EDIT Clear command, it does not go into the memory buffer.

Pasting Text: When you use the EDIT **Paste** command, whatever text is in the memory buffer is inserted at the location of the cursor. Always position the cursor where you want the text to appear before using the Paste command. Multiple copies of the text in the buffer can be pasted by repeating the Paste command.

To move text, use the Cut and Paste commands; to duplicate text, use the Copy and Paste commands.

Practice: **Revising a Text File**

Practice using the Cut, Copy, and Paste commands by revising the text file DOS6A.TXT now. Be sure you are in the COMM directory. Reload the file by keying EDIT DOS6A.TXT at the prompt, or you can select the file from a list displayed in EDIT. Try that method now. At the DOS prompt, key

■ **A:\COMM>EDIT**   [Enter]

At the EDIT opening screen press Esc. To open an existing file, open the File menu and select Open. Use the mouse or these keystrokes:

■ **Alt F O**

To display the Open dialog box with the mouse, point at File in the menu bar and click. In the File menu, point at Open and click.

In the Open dialog box, check the pathname under File Name:. If it is not A:\COMM, tab to the Dirs/Drives box, use the arrow keys to select the correct drive, and press [Enter].

Key the file name in the File Name box, or tab to the file list and use the arrow keys to select DOS6A.TXT from the list. When the file name is highlighted, press [Enter] to open the file.

You can open the file with the mouse by double-clicking on its name. (A double click is two rapid clicks of the left button. The second click is the equivalent of pressing [Enter].)

A file in another drive or directory can be opened by keying its filespec (drive, pathname, and file name) in the File Name box and pressing [Enter].

You should recognize the file you created earlier. Move the cursor to the second line. Key two more lines of text; at the end of each line, you must press [Enter]. Remember that EDIT is only an editing program, not a word processing program. It does not word-wrap at the right margin (that is, automatically move down to the next line).   Key the following text on two lines:

■ **I will now learn other methods for editing and manipulating text.**[Enter]
■ **Before DOS 5.0 I used a different method: EDLIN.**   [Enter]

Your file should now resemble the following:

```
I am creating this text file to test the features of
the DOS text editor.
```

```
I will now learn other methods for editing and
manipulating text.
Before DOS 5.0 I used a different method:   EDLIN.
```

Save the file as DOS6B.TXT in the COMM directory with these keystrokes:

■ **Alt F A DOS6B.TXT**   [Enter]

Practice: Cutting and Pasting Text

Let's improve on the text in the third sentence by moving "EDLIN" to the right of "used." To do this use the Cut and Paste commands in the Edit menu.

Move the cursor under the space before the word "EDLIN."   Hold down the Shift key and press the right arrow key 6 times to select or "block" EDLIN (without the period). To select a block of text with the mouse, click where you want the block to begin, hold down the left mouse button, and drag the mouse to where you want the block to end.

Next open the Edit menu. Press **Alt E** for Edit, or point and click with the mouse.

The options available in the Edit menu are shown in Figure 9-3. Use the down arrow key to select each option and watch the prompt line for a brief description of what it does.

Key **T** or click on the Cut option.   Notice that the highlighted text on the screen disappeared. It was moved to the memory buffer, waiting for your next action.

Move the cursor to the space between "used" and "a." Then open the Edit menu and select Paste with these keystrokes:

■ **Alt E P**

or open the menu and click on the Paste option with the mouse.

The block of text you cut will be inserted or pasted in the line which now reads:

```
Before DOS 5.0 I used EDLIN a different method:
```

At this point you will need to place the cursor on the space following EDLIN and insert a "," and then move the cursor under the ":" and press **Del** enough times to delete the ":" and the spaces in front of the period. The sentence should now read:

```
Before DOS 5.0 I used EDLIN, a different method.
```

Practice: Copying Text

To complete the last sentence, copy the phrase "for editing and manipulating text" from the second line and place it after "a different method" and before the period (.) in the third line.

Select the block of text by placing your cursor under the "f" in the word "for." Hold down the Shift key and use the right arrow key to highlight the phrase "for editing and manipulating text" up to the period.   (Or use the mouse and highlight the phrase by dragging the mouse.)

Open the Edit menu and select Copy with these keystrokes:

- **Alt E C**

Position the cursor on the period at the end of the sentence in the third line. Paste the copied phrase from the memory buffer with these keystrokes:

- **Alt E P**

or click on the Paste option with the mouse.

You will need to place the cursor on the "f" in "for" and press the spacebar once for appropriate spacing. If any line extends beyond the right edge of the screen, press the End key to view the right end of the line. To scroll back to the left, press the Home key.

If any lines are too long, shorten them by moving the cursor to the beginning of the word of the text you would like to move to the next line and press [Enter].

The text should now read:

```
I am creating this text file to test the features of
the DOS text editor.
I will now learn other methods for editing and
manipulating text.
Before DOS 5.0 I used EDLIN, a different method for
editing and manipulating text.
```

Save the file as DOS6C.TXT with these keystrokes:

■ **Alt F A DOS6C.TXT**   [Enter]

PRINTING A FILE

With the EDIT **Print** command you are able to print the current file directly from EDIT. Open the file menu and select Print with these keystrokes:

Alt F P

The Print dialog box is displayed. Note that you can choose to print "Selected Text Only" or the "Complete Document." If you had selected a block of text in the file, you could print that portion of the file with the first option. At this time you want to print the complete document. The dot within the parentheses shows that Complete Document is selected. Press [Enter] to begin printing.

Since the document is saved, you can elect to exit the EDIT program or continue with the next activity.

Practice: Printing a File

With the file DOS6C.TXT on the screen, print the file using the mouse or the following keystrokes:

■ **Alt F P**

USING THE SEARCH MENU

In this activity, you will use the Search menu (see Figure 9-4) to find words in a text file. EDIT's search function provides several alternative methods of finding or finding and changing text. You can find one or more characters or a whole word. The Search menu allows you to find, repeat the previous find, and change.

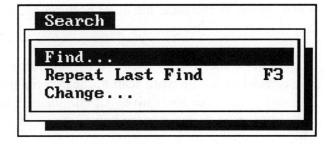

Figure 9-4. Search menu.

Practice: Using the Search Menu

If necessary, load the last file, DOS6C.TXT, into EDIT by keying this command line:

■   A:\COMM>**EDIT DOS6C.TXT**   [Enter]

When you enter the file name as a parameter to the EDIT command, EDIT loads the file and it appears in the opening screen.

Open the Search menu by pressing **Alt S**. "Find..." is highlighted. Use the down arrow to select each option and read the description in the prompt line.

Press [Enter] to select Find. In the dialog box, key the word **text**, and press [Enter]. The cursor moves to an occurrence of the word "text."

Open the Search menu and select Repeat Last Find (or press **F3**); the cursor moves to the next occurrence of "text." Press **F3** repeatedly and you will see that the cursor moves in a circle from occurrence to occurrence of the word "text."

Now try something different. Open the Search menu and press [Enter] to select Find. In the Find dialog box, key "**to**" and press [Enter]. Press **F3** repeatedly until the cursor stops at "to" in the word "editor." Press the Home key to move the cursor back to the beginning of the line.

Access the Find dialog box again and key "to" as the word to find. This time, press Tab twice to move the cursor to [ ] Whole Word.

Press the spacebar to activate this option. An X will appear within the brackets.

Press [Enter], then **F3**. Notice that now the cursor ignores the "to" in editor and stops only at the word "to" where it appears in the text. When you want to search for a word and not for a combination of letters, select the **Whole Word** option to eliminate the other occurrences.

> **Note:** If the word is followed by punctuation, as in "text". it will not be found in a whole-word search. Search for the whole word "text" to verify this. An alternative that eliminates letter combinations in many instances is to key a space before the word in the Find What: entry.

Your final task is to find words and change them to other words. This is similar to the "search and replace" function of many word processors. To find and change words, access the Change option in the Search menu by keying

■   **Alt S**

Press down arrow to select Change.

In the Find What: box, key

■ **editing and manipulating**

Press Tab. In the Change To: box, key

■ **finding and changing**   [Enter]

You will next see the Change dialog box with options to Change, Skip, Cancel, or Help. With the cursor on Change, press [Enter] to confirm the change. The next occurrence of "editing and manipulating" was changed. If, however, the phrase extended over two lines, EDIT would not replace the phrase.

You can specify whether the search should be case-sensitive—that is, match upper- and lowercase letters in a word or phrase. Since you did not select Match Upper/Lowercase in the Search or Change dialog box, you can key all lowercase or a mixture of upper- and lowercase and the results will be the same. Save the file as DOS6D.TXT.

USING HELP

Figure 9-5. HELP menu.

You have used many keystroke combinations for moving the cursor and selecting text. Can you remember them all? The Help screens in EDIT will provide reminders when you are working on a file. See Figure 9-5.

Practice: **The Help Menu**

To access the Help menu, press

■ **Alt H**

Use the down arrow key to select each command option, and read the prompt line at the bottom of the screen for a brief description of what each option does.

Nice work on EDIT! Test your knowledge of the information by completing the Self-Check Quiz and Assignment.

CHAPTER 9 SELF-CHECK QUIZ

True/False (Write T if the statement is true, F if the statement is false.)

_____ 1. EDIT is an external command and must have access to the EDIT.COM and QBASIC.EXE files.

_____ 2. It is possible to open a menu by pressing the Ctrl key and then the highlighted initial letter for that menu.

_____ 3. To copy selected text in EDIT, press Alt E C or Ctrl-Ins.

_____ 4. HELP is available only when you first load EDIT.

_____ 5. The function keys operate in EDIT just as they do at the DOS prompt.

Multiple Choice (Circle the correct answer.)

6. Which combination of operations is used to move selected text?

   a. copy and paste   c. cut and paste
   b. delete and paste   d. clear and paste

7. To view text that extends beyond the 80-character display screen, use the following key(s):

   a. Alt - Right   c. Shift - PgUp
   b. End   d. Tab

8. If Whole Word and Match Upper/Lowercase are selected, which of the following will be found when the Find What: entry is "Ton"?

   a. Ton and ton.   c. Ton and ton
   b. Ton and Tone   d. Ton

9. If you want to copy selected text in order to paste it, use these keystrokes:

   a. Alt E or Shift - Del   c. Alt E C or Ctrl - Ins
   b. Alt C T or Alt - Ins   d. Alt E T or [Shift - Del

10. To open the Find dialog box, use these keystrokes:

   a. Alt E C   c. Alt S C
   b. Alt S F   d. Alt C F

ASSIGNMENT

To practice using the commands in this chapter, complete the following steps.
Check off each step when you understand its operation, or mark the step with a
question mark if it is not clear. Write the commands or keystrokes in the
space provided.

1. Install the mouse, if necessary.

    _____

2. Access the COMM directory and EDIT.

    _____

3. Key and print the following text:

    Selecting Text: Before text can be copied, cut, or deleted, you must select
    it. In EDIT and most other editing software, text is selected by using
    keystroke combinations or a mouse. You will learn the keystrokes for
    selecting text in EDIT. When text is selected, it appears in reverse video or
    the opposite colors from the surrounding text.

    _____

4. Remove (cut) the text at the beginning of the second sentence, "In EDIT
    and most other editing software,".

    _____

5. Capitalize the "t" in text which will now begin the second sentence.

    _____

6. Add the following to the beginning of the paragraph after "Selecting Text"
    and before the colon ":" **in a file created with EDIT.** Adjust the lines
    appropriately for even printing.

    _____

7. Save the file as SELECT.TXT and print the file.

    _____

8. Create a letter that you might send to a friend who would like to attend college with you. Tell her or him about your interesting classes in Computer Science. Save the file as LEARN.TXT. Print the file.

9. Retrieve the file LEARN.TXT and make the following change:

Using the Change feature of the Search menu, change the words "Computer Science" to "Technical Computer Sciences."

10. Print the file.

AN INTRODUCTION TO BATCH FILES

OBJECTIVES

When you have completed the activities and assignment in this chapter, you will be able to:

1. Describe the contents and functions of batch files.

2. Create a batch file.

3. Run a batch file.

4. Use the batch file commands REM, PAUSE, and ECHO.

5. Create a simple AUTOEXEC.BAT file and describe its function.

6. Create a simple CONFIG.SYS file and describe its function.

7. Create a custom menu system.

CREATING SIMPLE BATCH FILES

Batch files are special text files containing a sequence of DOS commands that are performed together to accomplish a task. These user-developed command files must have the extension BAT in order for the system to recognize them as executable files. When you key the filename minus the extension, DOS executes the sequence of commands contained in the file.

Batch files are useful because they enable you to store all the steps required for a complex DOS procedure. Also, you can repeat the execution of the steps innumerable times without rekeying the commands each time. This saves time and avoids errors that might occur when rekeying.

If you display the DOS directory, you will notice that most of the files in the directory have the extension COM or EXE. From your experience with DOS external commands, you know that you can "execute" files like LABEL or FORMAT without keying the extension. In fact, any file from any DOS-compatible software that has either the COM or EXE extension is an executable file and can be loaded into memory and "run" by keying the filename. For example, to load and run WordPerfect, you key WP, which executes the file WP.EXE to start the WordPerfect program. Batch files work similarly in that you do not have to key the extension.

Batch files are useful because they enable you to store all the steps required for a complex DOS procedure. Also, you can repeat the execution of the steps innumerable times without rekeying the commands each time. This saves time and avoids errors that might occur when rekeying.

An example of a batch file is when you set the search path to the DOS external command files and change the default prompt to show the current drive and directory. To continue with this example, rather than keying the PATH and PROMPT commands each time you boot the computer, you can put the two command lines in a batch file named P.BAT. Here P stands for "path" and "prompt."

```
PATH C:\DOS
PROMPT $P$G
```

Then, by entering the filename P, you can execute the P.BAT file. If the disk storing the batch file is not in the default drive, you must also enter the drive designator so that DOS will know where to look for the batch file. When you key

```
A:\>P
```

the DOS commands are executed to set the new search path and to change the default prompt to display the current drive and directory. Note that it was not necessary to key the extension for P.BAT to be executed.

Note that the filename P could be any legal filename. However, the *extension must be BAT*. This extension tells the system that the file is a batch file and to load it and perform the DOS commands contained within the file in the sequence listed.

DOS command files are executed in the following order: COM, EXE, and then BAT files. When you key a command such as COPYIT at the DOS prompt, DOS first looks for an internal command with that name and, if one is found, executes the command. If it does not find such an internal command, DOS next looks in the current directory for a file named COPYIT.COM, then for COPYIT.EXE, and finally for COPYIT.BAT. If you gave your batch file the same name as a file with the extension COM or EXE, the batch file would never be executed inasmuch as DOS would always execute the DOS COM or EXE command first *if* there is a COM or EXE file with that filename in the directory.

Like other text files, batch files can be created with EDLIN, EDIT, E or the COPY CON technique. Use the COPY CON technique for short files. If you make an error, you can rekey the file or correct it with a text editor. For longer batch files, you may prefer to start with EDLIN, EDIT, or E. If you use a word processor, you must save the file as a DOS text file.

Practice: Creating and Running a Batch File

First insert the TREE DISK diskette and create a BAT subdirectory. Change to that directory by keying:

- **A:\>MD BAT**   [Enter]

- **A:\>CD BAT**   [Enter]

Now create the batch file described above that will set the search path and change the prompt. Use COPY CON or any text editor. Include the BAT directory you created in the search path so that DOS can find the executable batch files you will place there.

- **A:\BAT>COPY CON P.BAT**   [Enter]
- **PATH C:\DOS;A:\BAT**   [Enter]
- **PROMPT PG**   [Enter]
- **[F6]**   [Enter]

To run P.BAT, ensure you are in the BAT directory. Once you have run the P.BAT file, since you set the path to the BAT directory, DOS should have no problem finding the location where P.BAT is stored. Simply key the filename **P** and press [Enter]. If DOS displays a "Bad command or file name" message, make certain that you stored P.BAT in the BAT directory and that you have set the search path.

After you run the file, check the current search path by entering the command

- **A:\>PATH**   [Enter]

The path to the DOS and BAT directories is displayed:

    A:\>PATH C:\DOS;A:\BAT

When there are multiple subdirectories in a path statement, each is separated with a semicolon. The semicolon serves only to separate the subdirectories. It is practical to list the subdirectories in the order that you most commonly used their files. Some software, in the installation process, will insert the subdirectory in which its files are located first in the path statement.

Create a second batch file in the BAT directory. Since you just used the batch file P.BAT to set your path, DOS should have no trouble finding the external command files necessary to locate the text editing program files.

The next batch file is one that you might use with a data file that you revise often. It checks to see if the file is in the COMM directory on the disk in the default drive, tells you when the file was last revised, and displays the contents of the latest version. Create the following batch file in the BAT directory:

- **A:\BAT>COPY CON** (or other text editor) **AUTOCHK.BAT**   [Enter]

When the display screen appears, key the following:

- **CLS**   [Enter]
- **DIR \COMM\DOS6D.TXT**   [Enter]
- **TYPE \COMM\DOS6D.TXT**   [Enter]

Save the file as **AUTOCHK.BAT** and exit the text editor.

Because the file has a BAT extension, you are able to key the filename AUTOCHK without the extension BAT at the DOS prompt and the system will load and run the file and execute the commands it contains. To run the file, key:

- **A:BAT\>AUTOCHK**   [Enter]

You see the screen cleared as DOS executes the CLS command. Next the directory listing for the file DOS6D.TXT in the COMM subdirectory is displayed, verifying that the file is there and showing the date and time when it was last revised. Finally the contents of the file are displayed.

You can rerun AUTOCHK as many times as you wish. If DOS6D.TXT were a file that you revised frequently, this batch file would enable you to call it up for review quickly and easily.

Now you will create a batch file that can be used to obtain a printed copy of the root directory, to see how much free space remains on the disk, and to determine if the disk has any bad or lost sectors.

Create AUTODIR.BAT in the BAT subdirectory. Key the following at the DOS prompt:

- **A:\BAT>COPY CON AUTODIR.BAT**   [Enter]
- **CLS**   [Enter]
- **CD **   [Enter]
- **DIR /W**   [Enter]
- **DIR /W > PRN**   [Enter]

■ **CHKDSK**   [Enter]

Save the file and exit the text editor. The AUTODIR.BAT file directs the
system to clear the screen, to change to the root directory, to display and print
a wide version of the directory, and to check the disk. In this batch file you
have used one external command, CHKDSK. It is essential to have access to
the DOS commands. The path command in the P.BAT file should take care of
this.

To run the file, key:

■ **A:\BAT>AUTODIR**   [Enter]

Again, keying the BAT extension is unnecessary. Following the sequence of
commands listed in the file, DOS clears the screen, changes to the root
directory, displays and prints the root directory in wide form, checks the disk,
and displays the results. This information does seem to fly by on the screen.
Read on for help in correcting this.

BATCH FILE COMMANDS: REM, PAUSE, and ECHO

Special DOS internal commands are used in batch files. Several of these are
used to give information or instructions about the batch file. Others give the
user control over the execution of commands or base the execution on specific
conditions. Often batch files are used by several people. Documentation
within the file can help everyone know what the file does and how to use it.
The REM (remark) command is used to include useful information in the batch
file without affecting the execution of other commands.

Another batch file command that can be used to provide information to the
user performs a second function that is even more important. The PAUSE
command will halt execution of the batch commands until a key is pressed.
When a batch file is run, the screen display of commands and other data can
scroll by so quickly that it is difficult, if not impossible, to read what is shown.

The PAUSE command will temporarily halt the display of information, freezing
the screen until the user is ready to proceed. The prompt "Press a key
to continue. . ." appears at the cursor location. You can take any
amount of time you wish to read the screen before pressing a key. The
PAUSE command can include a prompt to give the user instructions, as you
will see in the following activities.

Have you noticed that DOS commands in the batch files you have created so
far appear on the screen when the file is run? Batch files often perform tasks
where you want the DOS command and its results displayed; at other times the
display would be less confusing if the command itself did not appear on the

screen. When this is the case, the command display can be turned off so that only the results of the command appear on the screen.

The ECHO ON and ECHO OFF commands are used to turn the display of the commands on and off. With ECHO ON, the commands appear when the system processes them as the batch file is running. With ECHO OFF, commands that are processed do not appear on the screen; only their results are displayed.

If the ECHO command is followed by any wording other than ON or OFF, the wording is displayed as a comment similar to a REM command remark. One important thing to remember is that the default for ECHO is the ON condition. When a batch file starts running, ECHO is always ON, and commands in the file will be echoed or displayed on the screen. When a batch file finishes running, the system automatically returns to the ECHO ON condition, even though ECHO may have been turned off with an ECHO OFF command within the batch file.

Practice: Using REM, PAUSE, and ECHO

REM

Retrieve the AUTODIR.BAT file to add a REM line in the file to clarify its use. From the BAT directory key:

- **A:\BAT>EDIT (or EDLIN) AUTODIR.BAT**   [Enter]

  Insert a blank line at the end of the first line (CLS)   [Enter]
  On the blank line you have created, key:

- **REM This file displays and prints the**   [Enter]
- **REM root directory and checks the disk.**   [Enter]

Save the file under the same name and exit the text editor.

Run the AUTODIR batch file to be sure that it runs as before but now has two lines of explanation added.

PAUSE

As with the REM command, the PAUSE command can be used to add documentation to the file with no effect on the execution of the program, except for halting execution until you are ready to proceed. After keying the PAUSE command, space once and then key the information you wish to add on the same line.

To demonstrate how PAUSE works, add a PAUSE command to the AUTODIR.BAT file. Retrieve the file again by keying

- **A:\BAT>EDIT (or EDLIN) AUTODIR.BAT**   [Enter]

After the line DIR /W, insert a line by pressing [Enter] and add the following statement into the blank line you have created:

- **PAUSE If the printer is not on, turn it on now.**   [Enter]

Save the file under the same name and exit the text editor.

Run the AUTODIR file. When DOS encounters the PAUSE command, the system halts execution of the file to give you a chance to read the directory and turn on the printer. The system will not continue until a key is pressed.

ECHO

To see how ECHO works, create a new batch file named EX.BAT to experiment with the ECHO ON and ECHO OFF commands. Key the following:

- **A:\BAT>COPY CON EX.BAT (or EDIT or EDLIN EX.BAT)**   [Enter]
- **ECHO OFF**   [Enter]
- **ECHO Echo is OFF now.**   [Enter]
- **TIME**   [Enter]
- **ECHO ON**   [Enter]
- **ECHO Will this ECHO line display?**   [Enter]
- **TIME**   [Enter]

Save the file as **EX.BAT** and exit the editor.

Run EX.BAT by keying the filename **EX** and pressing [Enter]. (It will be necessary to press [Enter] for each time prompt.)

Since the default for ECHO is on, you will see the first command ECHO OFF. However, after that point you will not see the command itself, only the results of the command. Notice the difference in how the ECHO and TIME commands are displayed the first time, when ECHO is off, and the second time, when ECHO is on.

To prevent the ECHO OFF command from displaying on the first line as it did with EX.BAT, key an @ symbol at the beginning of the line as in the following:

    @ECHO OFF

To further experiment with the ECHO ON and ECHO OFF commands as well as the @ symbol, create the TRIAL.BAT file. Key the following:

- **A:\BAT>EDIT TRIAL.BAT**   [Enter]
- **@ECHO OFF**   [Enter]
- **ECHO Echo is OFF now.**   [Enter]
- **TIME**   [Enter]
- **REM Will this REM line display?**   [Enter]
- **PAUSE Will this PAUSE line display?**   [Enter]
- **ECHO Will this ECHO line display?**   [Enter]

Save the file as **TRIAL.BAT** and exit the text editor.

Run the file. Again, you will have to press [Enter] each time the system stops for the time prompt. After ECHO is turned off at the beginning of the file with the @ECHO OFF command, the commands themselves are not displayed—only the results appear as each command is executed in sequence. The information displayed by DOS for the TRIAL.BAT file looks similar to the following:

```
ECHO is OFF now.
Current time is (current time)
Enter new time:
Press any key to continue ...

Will this ECHO line display?
```

Note that the results for the TIME and PAUSE commands show, but not the commands TIME and PAUSE. The REM command and its text do not show at all with ECHO OFF. With ECHO OFF the ECHO command does not display. However, the text Will this ECHO line display? definitely does show. Only the statements following an ECHO command are displayed when preceded by ECHO OFF or @ECHO OFF.

With ECHO OFF, you can see that remark (REM) statements are useful for including reminders about the file itself—information that need not be displayed to the user. ECHO is preferable for displaying messages to the user, since the command ECHO is not displayed.

THE AUTOEXEC.BAT FILE

A special batch file with the reserved name of AUTOEXEC.BAT will load specific files and set special defaults when you boot the computer. For example, AUTOEXEC.BAT can cause DOS to display a custom prompt of your design, or change a color monitor screen to your favorite hue, or load a software program for you each time you turn on or warm-boot the computer.

These and other customized setups are made possible by storing commands in the AUTOEXEC.BAT file.

Whenever the computer is booted, the system looks for and loads COMMAND.COM; then the system checks to see if there is a file named AUTOEXEC.BAT in the root directory of the disk used for booting—the floppy disk in drive A or the hard disk. If it finds an AUTOEXEC.BAT file in the root directory, the system automatically executes the commands in the file.

The AUTOEXEC.BAT file is similar to other batch files in that it contains a series of DOS commands. It is keyed using a text editor and must be stored in ASCII format as you have done with all batch files.

Practice: Creating an AUTOEXEC.BAT File

Write an AUTOEXEC.BAT file on the CLASS diskette to execute some of the commands you have learned so far. This AUTOEXEC.BAT file will set a search path for DOS, modify the DOS prompt to show the current drive and directory, install the DOSKEY program, install a mouse driver, list the root directory and pause to let you read the directory, and finally clear the screen. Key the following:

- **A:\>EDIT** (or **EDLIN**) **A:AUTOEXEC.BAT**   [Enter]
- **@ECHO OFF**   [Enter]
- **PATH C:\DOS** (Or to your DOS files)   [Enter]
- **PROMPT PG**   [Enter]
- **MOUSE**   [Enter]
- **DOSKEY**   [Enter]
- **DIR **   [Enter]
- **PAUSE**   [Enter]
- **CLS**   [Enter]

Save the file as **AUTOEXEC.BAT** and exit the text editor.

Now run the file by either keying the name, **AUTOEXEC,** and pressing [Enter], or by rebooting the computer. AUTOEXEC.BAT will execute the following:

Turn the display of commands off.
Set the path to the DOS files.
Set the prompt to show the current directory.
Install the mouse.
Install DOSKEY.
Display a wide directory of the root directory of the disk that booted the computer.
Pause the display so you will have time to read the directory.
Clear the screen.

Note that in order for the system to run the AUTOEXEC.BAT file as part of the boot process, DOS must find it and the system files required for booting in the root directory. In other words, the disk on which you store the AUTOEXEC.BAT file must also have the system files IBMBIO.COM and IBMDOS.COM (or their MS-DOS equivalents) and COMMAND.COM in the root directory. You placed the system files there when you formatted with the /S switch.

To the AUTOEXEC.BAT file you have created you could add many other commands including one to start an application program, such as WordPerfect, after the CLS command.

CONFIG.SYS

Like AUTOEXEC.BAT, the CONFIG.SYS file is a user-created and modified text file that customizes system operation. Like AUTOEXEC.BAT, CONFIG.SYS also has a reserved name and must be in the root directory of the boot disk. When you boot the computer, the CONFIG.SYS file gives DOS any special instructions you need for configuring the system. For example, some application software has specific requirements that must be put in the CONFIG.SYS file in order for them to run successfully. When the computer is booted, the CONFIG.SYS file is run before COMMAND.COM or AUTOEXEC.BAT and, therefore, before the application software is loaded. Consequently, CONFIG.SYS ensures that the requirements of the software program are met.

The following is a typical CONFIG.SYS file:

```
FILES=20
BUFFERS=20
DEVICE=C:\DOS\ANSI.SYS
LASTDRIVE=J
SHELL=COMMAND.COM /P /E:512
```

Note that none of these commands are DOS internal or external commands. When CONFIG.SYS is run, DOS has not been fully loaded and only CONFIG.SYS commands can be used. The following is a brief description of each of the commands used in the above-listed CONFIG.SYS file:

The **FILES=** command tells DOS how many files can be open at one time, in this example 20. Otherwise, the default number of eight, with five dedicated to the standard input and output devices, such as the keyboard. This leaves only three for program files. Some software requires that additional files be open. The number can be as high as 255. For each file over eight, the memory requirement for the system increases by 64 bytes.

The **BUFFERS=** command tells DOS how much buffer space to reserve in memory for temporary storage of data it reads from the disk. Each buffer takes 528 bytes of memory. The default is 15 for a system with 640K of memory. Generally, there should be as many buffers as files.

The **DEVICE=** command tells DOS where to find and load drivers, which are system (SYS) files that control special devices, such as a mouse.

The **LASTDRIVE=** instruction gives the drive name of the last local drive you want DOS to recognize and is used for standalone and networked computers.

The **SHELL=** instruction tells DOS to use COMMAND.COM as the shell or umbrella program, to make it the permanent shell (/P), and to set the size of the environment (/E) to 512 bytes. The environment is a segment of memory set aside to store special instructions, such as the search path and any special prompt you specify.

Practice: Creating a CONFIG.SYS File

Use EDIT or other text editor to create the following CONFIG.SYS file in the root directory of your CLASS disk.

- **A:\>EDIT CONFIG.SYS**   [Enter]
- **FILES=20**   [Enter]
- **BUFFERS=20**   [Enter]
- **DEVICE=C:\DOS\ANSI.SYS**   [Enter]
- **SHELL=COMMAND.COM /P /E:512**   [Enter]

Save the file as **CONFIG.SYS** and exit the text editor.

After you have saved the CONFIG.SYS file in the root directory, you must reboot the computer so that DOS will reconfigure the computer according to the CONFIG.SYS file instructions. There will be no apparent effect on the computer. However, the system will have these specified capabilities.

CUSTOM MENUS

Many users find it helpful to boot the computer and see a menu on the screen. A menu usually displays a number or letter-coded list of the various software options available on the computer. The user keys a number or letter to load and use the desired software package.

A custom menu system can be set up by creating a text file that is displayed by the AUTOEXEC.BAT file and a set of batch files to start each software program. Here is one way a custom menu system can work:

1. When you boot the computer, the system reads and executes the AUTOEXEC.BAT file.

2. Within the AUTOEXEC.BAT file there is a TYPE command to display a text file that shows the list of menu options.

3. You select from these options and key the letter or number representing your selection. Each option you choose has a corresponding batch file with a matching filename (A.BAT, B.BAT, 1.BAT, 2.BAT, etc.). When you key the letter or number for your choice, which is the filename of the related batch file, the batch file executes.

4. The batch file contains commands for starting the software application you have chosen.

In this activity you will create a custom menu of the type just described. Rather than setting up an application software menu on a hard disk, you will create a more modest, but equally useful, project on your floppy disk in drive A. You will set up a menu and batch files for using DOS commands such as FORMAT, DISKCOPY, DIR, and CHKDSK. The same principles apply when you set up an application software menu system on your hard disk.

Practice: Creating a Custom Menu

On your CLASS diskette, create a custom menu system of the type just described. The first step in creating the custom menu is to modify the AUTOEXEC.BAT file by adding the line in bold at the end of the AUTOEXEC.BAT file. It is also important to add the BAT directory on the CLASS disk to the path statement so that the 1.BAT, 2.BAT, 3.BAT, and 4.BAT files can be found.

```
        @ECHO OFF
        PATH C:\DOS (Or to your DOS files);A:\BAT
        PROMPT $P$G
        MOUSE
        DOSKEY
        DIR \
        PAUSE
        CLS
 ■    TYPE TEXT\MENU.TXT                                      [Enter]
```

Now use a text editor to create a text file named MENU.TXT on the disk in drive A. You could place the MENU.TXT file in the root directory of drive A; however, for practice in working with paths and subdirectories, store it with other text files in the TEXT directory or in the CLASS disk in drive A. If you have no TEXT directory, it will be necessary for you to create one in which to

store MENU.TXT. MENU.TXT is a *text* file that will be displayed with the
TYPE command.

Key the following:

- **A:\TEXT>EDIT** (or other text editor) **MENU.TXT**   [Enter]
- ∎   [Enter]
- ∎   [Enter]
- **DISK OPERATING SYSTEM UTILITY MENU**   [Enter]
- **CREATED BY (YOUR NAME)**   [Enter]
-   [Enter]
- **1. Check the volume label on the disk.**   [Enter]
- **2. Check the version of DOS.**   [Enter]
- **3. List files on a data disk.**   [Enter]
- **4. Check a data disk.**   [Enter]

- **Enter your choice at the DOS prompt**   [Enter]

Save the file as **MENU.TXT**.

In order for the system to execute these commands when you select 1, 2, 3, or
4 from the menu, you must have a batch file for each option. For example,
when you want the VOL command to be executed, you will need a file named
1.BAT.   VER requires 2.BAT, DIR requires 3.BAT, and CHKDSK requires
4.BAT. When you key 1, 2, 3, or 4, the system will run the appropriate batch
file, since the number is the filename. Of course, the search path must be set
to the BAT and DOS directories.

Create batch files that will carry out each of the numbered functions above.
Store the files in the BAT directory. Adapt the command parameters if
necessary to accommodate the drive configuration on the computer where the
menu will be used. Key the batch file for option 1 on the menu as follows:

- **A:\BAT>EDIT 1.BAT**   [Enter]
- **@ECHO OFF**   [Enter]
- **CLS**   [Enter]
- **VOL A:**   [Enter]
- **PAUSE**   [Enter]
- **CLS**   [Enter]
- **TYPE \TEXT\MENU.TXT**   [Enter]

Save the file as **1.BAT** with the SAVE AS command and do **not** exit the text
editor.

With the file still on display, cursor to the command line that reads VOL A:.
Change that line to read as follows:

■ **VER**   [Enter]

Save this file as **2.BAT** with the SAVE AS command and do **not** exit the text editor.

With the file still on display, now the title reading 2.BAT, cursor to the command line for VER and change the line to read as follows:

■ **DIR A:\ /P**   [Enter]

Again, use the SAVE AS command to save the file as **3.BAT**. Do **not** exit the text editor. The file will still be displayed, but the title will now read 3.BAT. Cursor to the command line DIR A:\ /P and change it to read as follows:

■ **CHKDSK A:**

Save the file as **4.BAT** and exit the text editor. Reboot the computer with this disk in drive A or key AUTOEXEC. The AUTOEXEC.BAT file executes and displays the menu. Does it work for you? If not, go back and troubleshoot the files to find your errors. Try each menu option.

Very nice work on batch files! Check your comprehension of the concepts presented in this chapter by completing the Self-Check Quiz and Assignment.

CHAPTER 10 SELF-CHECK QUIZ

True/False (Write T if the statement is true, F if the statement is false.)

_____ 1.   It is not necessary to key the file extension to run a batch file.

_____ 2.   The REM command is used to remove lines from a batch file.

_____ 3.   After the PAUSE command halts the system operation, it will automatically restart in a few seconds.

_____ 4.   The ECHO command gives you a choice of displaying or not displaying the commands when a batch file is run.

_____ 5.   The CONFIG.SYS file must be in the root directory.

Multiple Choice (Circle the correct answer.)

6. Following an ECHO OFF statement, which of these lines in a batch file will display the instruction "Select one" when the file is run?

    a. PAUSE Select one   c. Select one
    b. ECHO Select one   d. REM Select one

7. Which of these commands should appear before the others in an AUTOEXEC.BAT file?

    a. PATH C:\DOS   c. DIR /P
    b. CHKDSK   d. ECHO OFF

8. Which command would you use in a batch file to display the directory of all backup (BAK) files on the disk in drive A?

    a. A:DIR*.BAK   c. REM DIR*.BAK FILES
    b. DIR A:*.BAK /S   d. PAUSE DIR A:*.BAK

9. Which of the following is not a legal batch file name?

    a. ERASEA.BAT   c. COPY.BAT
    b. REPEAT.BAT   d. &25_$220.BAT

10. Which of the following lines might appear in a CONFIG.SYS file?

    a. PROMPT PG   c. FILES=20
    b. PATH C:\DOS   d. CLS

ASSIGNMENT

To practice using the commands in this chapter, complete the following steps. Check off each step when you understand its operation, or mark the step with a question mark if it is not clear. Write the commands or keystrokes in the space provided.

1. Insert the TREE DISK diskette, create and print a batch file using a text editor, name it LOOKAT.BAT, and store it in the BAT subdirectory. Use DOS commands to accomplish the following in the batch file:

   a. Leave ECHO ON for trouble shooting purposes.
   b. Clear the screen.
   c. Explain the purpose of the batch file with a REM statement.
   d. Display a directory of the BAT subdirectory.
   e. Display a directory listing for AUTODIR.BAT.
   f. Display the AUTODIR.BAT file using the TYPE command.

   a. _____

   b. _____

   c. _____

   d. _____

   e. _____

   f. _____

2. Clear the screen and run the LOOKAT.BAT file. Print the screen or run the file with echo printing toggled on.

   _____

3. The batch file may have scrolled past you on the screen so that you could not read certain data. Place a PAUSE command where appropriate.

   _____

4. Add a REM statement explaining the purpose of the file.

   _____

5. Clear the screen and run the LOOKAT.BAT file. Print the screen or run
   the file with echo printing toggled on.

   _____

6. If the commands in LOOKAT.BAT run properly, turn ECHO OFF.

   _____

7. Print a directory of the BAT directory.

   _____

8. Use the TYPE command to print a copy of the LOOKAT.BAT file.

   _____

9. Create a simple AUTOEXEC.BAT file in the root directory on TREE DISK
   that will do the following:

   a. Turn ECHO OFF.
   b. Clear the screen.
   c. Display the root directory of drive C.
   d. Print the directory of drive A sorted by date, latest date first.
   e. Access a text editor such as EDLIN or EDIT.

   a. _____

   b. _____

   c. _____

   d. _____

   e. _____

10. Run the AUTOEXEC.BAT file with echo printing on. If you do not have
    echo print capability, print the screen. Print a copy of the
    AUTOEXEC.BAT file.

    _____

INDEX

A

Aborting DOS Commands, 41-42
Adapter Card, 3
Allocation Unit, 43, 88
Alternate (Alt) Key, 5
ANSI.SYS, 190
APPEND, 73-74
ASCII Codes, 10
AUTOEXEC.BAT, 188-190

B

Backslash, 115
BAK Extension, 155-156
Batch Files, 181-189
Booting the System, 12
    Cold, 12
    Warm, 13
Break Key, 41-42
Bytes, 10

C

Canceling a line, 22
CD or CHDIR, 116-118
CHKDSK, 103-105
CLS (Clearing the screen), 24
Cluster, 43, 88,
    See also Allocation Unit
Cold Boot, 12
Combing Files, 73-74
COMMAND.COM, 14, 23, 46
COMP (Comparing Disks) 99-101
Comparing Files, 74-76
CONFIG.SYS, 190-191
Control (Ctrl) key
    Ctrl-C or Ctrl-Break, 41-42
    Ctrl-PrtSc or Ctrl-P, 24-25, 57
    Ctrl-Z or F6, 54, 152
COPY, 63-70
    combining files, 71-73
    to a different disk, 65
    to a different subdirectory, 128-129
    to the Hard Drive, 67-68, 121
    to the same disk, 64
    used with wildcards, 69-70

CPU, 3

CPU, 3
Current Drive, 16
Custom Menu, 192-194

D

DATE, 14
Default Directory, 16, 51, 116
DEFRAG, 106
DEL, 86-87
Deletion Tracking (Deletion-Tracking File), 89
DELTREE, 135-136
Device names, 26, 30
DIR, 27-34
    searching directories for
    selected file(s), 28
    sorted, 32
    switches
        /P, 29
        /W, 30
Disk drives, 3, 7
Disk Operating System (DOS), 1-2
DISKCOMP, 99-101
DISKCOPY, 96-98
DOS Editing Keys, 79-81
    See also Function Keys
DOS Prompt, 13
DOSKEY, 53
Drive Prompts, 23

E

Echo, 187-188
Echo Printing, 57
    See Printing
EDIT, 166-177
EDLIN, 145-160
End-of-File marker, 75
ERASE, 86-87
    See DEL
Error Messages, 16
Extensions, (File Name), 25
External commands, 14, 23, 0

F

FAT (See File Allocation Tab), 43, 88
FC, 99-101
    See COMP
File Allocation Table, 43, 88
File Names, 25
    extension, 26
Floppy Disks, 38, (Illus.), 39
FORMAT, 42-48,
Fragmented Files, 103
Function Keys, 7

G

Gigabytes (GB) 10

H

HELP, 35
Hidden files, 46, 103

I

IBM PC-DOS, 2
Internal Commands, 1, 23, 40

J

K

Keyboard, 5-6
Kilobytes (K or KB), 10

L

LABEL, 49
Labeling a disk, 49

M

MD MKDIR, 113
Megabytes (MB) 10
Memory
    Random-access memory (RAM), 4-5
    Read-only memory (ROM), 4-5
Menu (Custom), 192-194
Microsoft MS DOS, 2
MIRROR, 89

Monitor, 4, 7, 12
Mother Board, 3-4
Mouse, 3
MOVE, 78-79
MS/PC DOS, 2

N

Non-Contiguous Files, 105
    See Fragmented Files

O

Operating System, 2

P

PATH, 41, 114-115
PAUSE, 186-187
    See Batch File Commands
PC-DOS, 2
Permanent Data Storage, 9
Print, 23, 57-58
    Copy command to print, 58
    Directory listings, 22
    Echo Print, 57
    Print Screen, 24-25, 57
    Type command to print, 58
Printer, 3, 11-12
Program Extensions, 26
Prompt, 18
    PROMPT PG, 17-18

Q

QBASIC, 165

R

RAM, 5
RD or RMDIR, 132-133
REM, 185-186
Removing Directories, 132-133
REN or Renaming files, 76-77
    Using wildcards, 77-78
Reset button, 13
ROM, 104-105
Root Directory, 112

S

SCANDISK, 105-106
Sector, 42
Search PATH, 40-41
        See also PATH
Self-booting, 46
Sentry, 91
        See UNDELETE
Software, 11
Subdirectory, 111-135
Subdirectory Marker, 131-132
Subdirectory
        Move (Rename), 136
System unit, 3, 4, 12

T

Text files
        Creating, 53-56
        Displaying contents, 56
Things to Remember, 21
TIME, 15
TREE, 134-135
TYPE, 56

U

Unconditional FORMAT, 48
UNDELETE, 87-94
UNFORMAT, 95

V

Version (VER), 34
Versions of DOS, 2
VOL (Volume label), 49

W

Warm Boot, 12
Wildcards, 32-34
Write-Protect, 39

X

XCOPY, 137-138

SILVER EDITION

Teacher's Edition with Tests

Mosaic 1

READING

Brenda Wegmann

Miki Knezevic

Teacher's Edition by Robyn Brinks

Mosaic 1 Reading Teacher's Edition with Tests, Silver Edition

Published by McGraw-Hill ESL/ELT, a business unit of The McGraw-Hill Companies, Inc. 1221 Avenue of the Americas, New York, NY 10020. Copyright © 2007 by The McGraw-Hill Companies, Inc. All rights reserved. No part of this publication may be reproduced or distributed in any form or by any means, or stored in a database or retrieval system, without the prior written consent of The McGraw-Hill Companies, Inc., including, but not limited to, in any network or other electronic storage or transmission, or broadcast for distance learning.

ISBN 13: 978-0-07-328394-4 (Teacher's Edition)
ISBN 10: 0-07-328394-0 (Teacher's Edition)
2 3 4 5 6 7 8 9 10 EUS 11 10 09 08 07

Editorial director: Erik Gundersen
Series editor: Valerie Kelemen
Developmental editor: Mary Sutton-Paul
Production manager: Juanita Thompson
Production coordinator: Vanessa Nuttry
Cover designer: Robin Locke Monda
Interior designer: Nesbitt Graphics, Inc.

Cover photo: David Samuel Robbins/CORBIS

www.esl-elt.mcgraw-hill.com

The **McGraw·Hill** Companies

Table of Contents

Introduction

Welcome to the Teacher's Edition iv
The Interactions/Mosaic Silver Edition Program v
Best Practices vii

Student Book Teaching Notes and Answer Keys

Chapter **1**   New Challenges 2

Chapter **2**   Teamwork and Competition 16

Chapter **3**   Gender and Relationships 28

Chapter **4**   Health and Leisure 38

Chapter **5**   High Tech, Low Teach 48

Chapter **6**   Money Matters 60

Chapter **7**   Remarkable Individuals 70

Chapter **8**   Creativity 82

Chapter **9**   Human Behavior 92

Chapter **10**   Crime and Punishment 102

Black Line Masters . . . . BLM 1
Black Line Master Answer Keys . . . . BLM 27

Chapter Tests T1
Chapter Test Answer Keys T41

Placement Test T43
Placement Test Answer Keys T54

Welcome to the Teacher's Edition

The Teacher's Edition of *Interactions/Mosaic* Silver Edition provides support and flexibility to teachers using the *Interactions/Mosaic* Silver Edition 18-book academic skills series. The Teacher's Edition provides step-by-step guidance for implementing each activity in the Student Book. The Teacher's Edition also provides expansion activities with photocopiable masters of select expansion activities, identification of activities that support a Best Practice, valuable notes on content, answer keys, audioscripts, end-of-chapter tests, and placement tests. Each chapter in the Teacher's Edition begins with an overview of the content, vocabulary, and teaching goals in that chapter. Each chapter in the Student Book begins with an engaging photo and related discussion questions that strengthen the educational experience and connect students to the topic.

■ **Procedural Notes**

The procedural notes are useful for both experienced and new teachers. Experienced teachers can use the bulleted, step-by step procedural notes as a quick guide and refresher before class, while newer or substitute teachers can use the notes as a more extensive guide to assist them in the classroom. The procedural notes guide teachers through each strategy and activity; describe what materials teachers might need for an activity; and help teachers provide context for the activities.

■ **Answer Keys**

Answer keys are provided for all activities that have definite answers. For items that have multiple correct answers, various possible answers are provided. The answer key follows the procedural note for the relevant activity. Answer keys are also provided for the Chapter Tests and the Placement Tests.

■ **Expansion Activities**

A number of expansion activities with procedural notes are included in each chapter. These activities offer teachers creative ideas for reinforcing the chapter content while appealing to different learning styles. Activities include games, conversation practice, presentations, and projects. These expansion activities often allow students to practice integrated language skills, not just the skills that the student book focuses on. Some of the expansion activities include photocopiable black line masters included in the back of the book.

■ **Content Notes**

Where appropriate, content notes are included in the Teacher's Edition. These are notes that might illuminate or enhance a learning point in the activity and might help teachers answer student questions about the content. These notes are provided at the logical point of use, but teachers can decide if and when to use the information in class.

■ **Chapter Tests**

Each chapter includes a chapter test that was designed to test the vocabulary, reading, writing, grammar, and/or listening strategies taught in the chapter, depending on the language skill strand being used. Teachers can simply copy and distribute the tests, then use the answer keys found in the Teacher's Edition. The purpose of the chapter tests is not only to assess students' understanding of material covered in the chapter but also to give students an idea of how they are doing and what they need to work on. Each chapter test has four parts with items totaling 100 points. Item types include multiple choice, fill-in-the blank, and true/false. Audioscripts are provided when used.

■ **Black Line Masters (Photocopiable Masters)**

Each chapter includes a number of expansion activities with black line masters, or master worksheets, that teachers can copy and distribute. These activities and black line masters are optional. They can help reinforce and expand on chapter material in an engaging way. Activities include games;

conversation practice; working with manipulatives such as sentence strips; projects; and presentations. Procedural notes and answer keys (when applicable) are provided in the Teacher's Edition.

■ **Placement Tests**

Each of the four language skill strands has a placement test designed to help assess in which level the student belongs. Each test has been constructed to be given in under an hour. Be sure to go over the directions and answer any questions before the test begins. Students are instructed not to ask questions once the test begins. Following each placement test, you'll find a scoring placement key that suggests the appropriate book to be used based on the number of items answered correctly. Teachers should use judgment in placing students and selecting texts.

The Interactions/Mosaic Silver Edition Program

Interactions/Mosaic Silver Edition is a fully-integrated, 18-book academic skills series. Language proficiencies are articulated from the beginning through advance levels <u>within</u> each of the four language skill strands. Chapter themes articulate <u>across</u> the four skill strands to systematically recycle content, vocabulary, and grammar.

■ **Reading Strand**

Reading skills and strategies are strategically presented and practiced through a variety of themes and reading genres in the five Reading books. Pre-reading, reading, and post-reading activities include strategies and activities that aid comprehension, build vocabulary, and prepare students for academic success. Each chapter includes at least two readings that center around the same theme, allowing students to deepen their understanding of a topic and command of vocabulary related to that topic. Readings include magazine articles, textbook passages, essays, letters, and website articles. They explore, and guide the student to explore, stimulating topics. Vocabulary is presented before each reading and is built on throughout the chapter. High-frequency words and words from the Academic Word List are focused on and pointed out with asterisks (*) in each chapter's Self-Assessment Log.

■ **Listening/Speaking Strand**

A variety of listening input, including lectures, academic discussions, and conversations help students explore stimulating topics in the five Listening/Speaking books. Activities associated with the listening input, such as pre-listening tasks, systematically guide students through strategies and critical thinking skills that help prepare them for academic achievement. In the Interactions books, the activities are coupled with instructional photos featuring a cast of engaging, multi-ethnic students participating in North American college life. Across the strand, lectures and dialogues are broken down into manageable parts giving students an opportunity to predict, identify main ideas, and effectively manage lengthy input. Questions, guided discussion activities, and structured pair and group work stimulate interest and interaction among students, often culminating in organizing their information and ideas in a graphic organizer, writing, and/or making a presentation to the class. Pronunciation is highlighted in every chapter, an aid to improving both listening comprehension and speaking fluency. Enhanced focus on vocabulary building is developed throughout and a list of target words for each chapter is provided so students can interact meaningfully with the material. Finally, Online Learning Center features MP3 files from the Student Book audio program for students to download onto portable digital audio players.

■ **Writing Strand**

Activities in each of the four Writing books are systematically structured to culminate in a *Writing Product* task. Activities build on key elements of writing from sentence development to writing single paragraphs, articles, narratives, and essays of multiple lengths and genres. Connections between writing and grammar tie the writing skill in focus with the grammar structures needed to develop each writing skill. Academic themes, activities, writing topics, vocabulary development, and critical thinking strategies prepare students for university life. Instructional photos are used to strengthen engagement and the educational experience. Explicit pre-writing questions and discussions activate prior knowledge, help organize ideas and information, and create a foundation for the writing product. Each chapter includes a self-evaluation rubric which supports the learner as he or she builds confidence and autonomy in academic writing. Finally, the Writing Articulation Chart helps teachers see the progression of writing strategies both in terms of mechanics and writing genres.

■ **Grammar Strand**

Questions and topical quotes in the four Grammar books, coupled with instructional photos stimulate interest, activate prior knowledge, and launch the topic of each chapter. Engaging academic topics provide context for the grammar and stimulate interest in content as well as grammar. A variety of activity types, including individual, pair, and group work, allow students to build grammar skills and use the grammar they are learning in activities that cultivate critical thinking skills. Students can refer to grammar charts to review or learn the form and function of each grammar point. These charts are numbered sequentially, formatted consistently, and indexed systematically, providing lifelong reference value for students.

■ **Focus on Testing for the TOEFL® iBT**

The all-new TOEFL® iBT *Focus on Testing* sections prepare students for success on the TOEFL® iBT by presenting and practicing specific strategies for each language skill area. The Focus on Testing sections are introduced in Interactions 1 and are included in all subsequent levels of the Reading, Listening/Speaking, and Writing strands. These strategies focus on what The Educational Testing Service (ETS) has identified as the target skills in each language skill area. For example, "reading for basic comprehension" (identifying the main idea, understanding pronoun reference) is a target reading skill and is presented and practiced in one or more *Focus on Testing* sections. In addition, this and other target skills are presented and practiced in chapter components outside the *Focus on Testing* sections and have special relevance to the TOEFL® iBT. For example, note-taking is an important test-taking strategy, particularly in the listening section of the TOEFL® iBT, and is included in activities within each of the Listening/Speaking books. All but two of the *Interactions/Mosaic* titles have a *Focus on Testing* section. Although *Interactions Access Reading* and *Interaction Access Listening/Speaking* don't include these sections because of their level, they do present and develop skills that will prepare students for the TOEFL® iBT.

■ **Best Practices**

In each chapter of this Teacher's Edition, you'll find Best Practices boxes that highlight a particular activity and show how this activity is tied to a particular Best Practice. The Interactions/Mosaic Silver Edition team of writers, editors, and teacher consultants has identified the following six interconnected Best Practices.

---

* TOEFL is a registered trademark of Educational Testing Services (ETS). This publication is not endorsed or approved by ETS.

Best Practices

Each chapter identifies at least six different activities that support six Best Practices, principles that contribute to excellent language teaching and learning. Identifying Best Practices helps teachers to see, and make explicit for students, how a particular activity will aid the learning process.

Making Use of Academic Content

Materials and tasks based on academic content and experiences give learning real purpose. Students explore real world issues, discuss academic topics, and study content-based and thematic materials.

Organizing Information

Students learn to organize thoughts and notes through a variety of graphic organizers that accommodate diverse learning and thinking styles.

Scaffolding Instruction

A scaffold is a physical structure that facilitates construction of a building. Similarly, scaffolding instruction is a tool used to facilitate language learning in the form of predictable and flexible tasks. Some examples include oral or written modeling by the teacher or students, placing information in a larger framework, and reinterpretation.

Activating Prior Knowledge

Students can better understand new spoken or written material when they connect to the content. Activating prior knowledge allows students to tap into what they already know, building on this knowledge, and stirring a curiosity for more knowledge.

Interacting with Others

Activities that promote human interaction in pair work, small group work, and whole class activities present opportunities for real world contact and real world use of language.

Cultivating Critical Thinking

Strategies for critical thinking are taught explicitly. Students learn tools that promote critical thinking skills crucial to success in the academic world.

1

New Challenges

In this chapter, students will read about customs and attitudes in English-speaking countries. In the first reading, they will learn about the different first impressions people have about the United States, including its size, climate, and speech. Students will work with classmates to learn more about U.S. customs and compare those to customs from other countries. After reading about "comfort zones," students will think about what questions are considered polite and rate social acceptance in a continuum. Students will then learn to find the main idea of the paragraphs as they read about Canada. The new vocabulary, reading strategies, and topics will encourage students to think critically about the challenges associated with different customs in a variety of countries.

Chapter Opener

❑ Direct students' attention to the photo and ask questions. *Who are the people in this picture? How do they feel?*

❑ Put students into small groups to discuss the **Connecting to the Topic** section. (The photo is of the winner of a track race.)

❑ Read the Chinese proverb aloud and ask students what they think it means.

❑ Guide the conversation towards learning a second language by posing questions such as *Why are you studying English? Have you experienced any difficulties while learning English?*

❑ Put students in pairs and ask them to list any difficulties they have experienced while learning English.

❑ Call on students to share their ideas with the class.

❝ A person who can not tolerate small difficulties can never accomplish great things. **❞**

—Chinese proverb

Chapter Overview

Reading Skills and Strategies

Reading without knowing every word

Recalling information

Analyzing paragraphs for the main idea and its development

Finding the implied main idea of a paragraph

Checking reading comprehension by evaluating statements as true or false.

Critical Thinking Skills

Interpreting cultural differences

Ranking phrases for social acceptance (on a continuum)

Synthesizing a group discussion and reporting on it

Expressing an opinion

Synthesizing Internet content: taking notes and presenting results

Supporting your ideas with details in writing

Vocabulary Building

Understanding the meaning of words from context

Analyzing suffixes

Making new words by adding suffixes

Getting compound words (with and without hyphens)

Getting the meaning of words from context and structure

Analyzing the prefixes *non-* and *anti-*

Focusing on words from the Academic Word List

Focus on Testing

Analyzing points of contrast on tests

Vocabulary

Nouns			Adjectives	
attitudes*	informality	stigma	acceptable	mysterious
brevity*	inhabitants	style*	anti-American	observant
chores	lawmen	symbol*	blunt	occasional
displays*	makeup	uprisings	comfortable	outgoing
driver	melting pot	vastness	continental	personal
environment*	moderation		desirable	powerful
formality	movement	**Verbs**	do-it-yourself	restless
gardener	nationalities	assume*	endless	
heritage	newcomer	contrasts*	French-style	**Adverb**
humidity	non-Canadians	refusing	household	thoroughly
imagination	responsibility	removed*	leisure	
	scheme*		menial	
	settlement		mountainous	

*These words are from the Academic Word List. For more information on this list, see www.vuw.ac.nz/lals/research/awl.

First Impressions

Before You Read

Strategy

Reading without Knowing Every Word

- Read the information in the Strategy Box and explain as needed.

- Ask students to look over the article quickly. Have them call out words that are new to them.

- Compile a list on the board. Tell students it is not necessary to know every word to understand an article.

1   Reading Without Knowing Every Word

Best Practice

Making Use of Academic Content

This activity will help students read and understand without knowing every word. By skimming the article for headings and main ideas and skipping over unknown words, students will increase their reading fluency and be prepared to handle the types of readings they will encounter in academic textbooks.

- Have students read the Introduction and answer the questions.

- Tell them to pay attention to the words in bold blue type.

- Put students in pairs to discuss the answers.

- Call on pairs to share their answers with the class.

ANSWER KEY

Answers will vary.

Read

- Have students read the passage silently within a time limit (10 minutes).

- Tell them to underline any words or phrases that are new or that they don't understand.

- Remind them **not** to use a dictionary during this part of the lesson.

- Tell students to complete Activity 2, **Recalling Information,** when they finish the passage.

- When the time limit is up, go back to the questions from the **Introduction** and ask students if their answers were correct.

After You Read

2   Recalling Information

- Read the first statement. Ask a student to explain why the answer is *T*.

- Continue with the rest of the statements. Make corrections when necessary.

- For *F* answers, ask student volunteers to write correct statements on the board.

ANSWER KEY

1. T 2. F 3. F 4. F 5. T 6. T 7. F 8. T 9. F

Corrected False Statements: Possible answers.

2. Its continental climate is one of extremes.

3. Americans are restless. They like to be active.

4. Americans are blunt, but not rude.

7. Americans prefer family privacy and do not often have servants. They like to do things themselves.

9. Americans are noticeably informal.

Content Notes

■ Today, more than 75% of American homes are equipped with air conditioners. In Florida, one of the hottest states in the country, more than 85% of homes have air conditioning.

■ Greenland Ranch, California, holds the record for the highest temperature ever observed and recorded in the United States. On July 10, 1913, it was 134 degrees Fahrenheit (56.6 degrees Celsius).

■ Americans tend to be informal. For example, Americans wear casual clothes to school and sometimes to work. It is common for college students to greet professors by their first names. Nevertheless, Americans are polite and courteous. Casual and impolite are not synonyms!

Strategy

Analyzing Paragraphs for the Main Idea and Its Development

■ Read the information in the Strategy Box and explain as needed.

■ Ask students to find an example of a main idea in the reading.

■ Write a few of the questions they have about the reading on the board.

3 Analyzing Paragraphs for the Main Idea and its Development

❑ Read the directions and put students in small groups to answer the questions.

❑ Have one student from each group present their answers.

ANSWER KEY

Possible answers

1. Yes.

2. 1

3. 2

4. Exclamation point; Houses interest Americans greatly

Strategy

Understanding the Meaning of Words from Context

■ Read the information in the Strategy Box and explain as needed.

■ Tell students that it is possible to figure out the meaning of a word without using a dictionary.

■ Tell students to find one word that they underlined in the reading and figure out the meaning from the context.

■ Call on a few students to tell which words they chose and their meanings.

4 Understanding the Meaning of Words from Context

❑ Read the directions and explain as needed.

❑ Model the activity by doing the first item as a class. Have students find the word *blunt* in the reading and look at its context.

❑ Ask them if they agree with the circled answer.

❑ Ask the students to work in pairs to guess the meanings of the rest of the words.

❑ Discuss the answers as a class. Check for comprehension by posing questions such as: *In your own words, what does "leisure" mean? What are some chores you have to do every day? What is another word for "assume"?*

ANSWER KEY

1. b 2. c 3. a 4. a 5. c 6. b 7. b 8. b 9. a

EXPANSION ACTIVITY

- The aim of this activity is to give students additional practice with the new vocabulary.

- Tell students they will write a vocabulary quiz for the class.

- Have students choose three words from Activity 4.

- For each word, ask them to write three sentences using the word in context. Tell them to make sure the context adequately conveys the meaning of the word.

- Have each student write one of their sentences on the board and draw a blank line to show where the vocabulary word should go.

- Have students copy the sentences from the board and fill in the blanks with the correct words based on the context provided by the sentence.

Analyzing Suffixes

- ❑ Read the information in the instruction box and explain as needed.

- ❑ Ask students to think of a word that ends with one of the suffixes in the box.

- ❑ Compile a word list on the board.

- **5** Analyzing Suffixes

- ❑ Give the class 5 minutes to study the meanings of the suffixes.

- ❑ After the time is up, tell students to complete the activity on their own.

- ❑ Call on students to share their answers.

- ❑ Make corrections and answer questions as needed.

- ❑ Explain how the suffix changes the part of speech of the word.

ANSWER KEY

1. affordable 2. seasonal 3. applicant 4. teacher
5. cordiality 6. harmless

6 **Making New Words by Adding Suffixes**

- ❑ Read the directions and explain as needed.

- ❑ Remind students they can look back at the reading to find the answers.

- ❑ Call on students to share their answers.

- ❑ Make corrections and address any questions.

ANSWER KEY

1. settler 2. gardener 3. driver 4. comfortable
5. formality 6. informality 7. inhabitants
8. acceptable 9. occasional 10. desirable
11. personal 12. responsibility 13. restless
14. continental 15. brevity 16. nationalities

Strategy

Understanding Compound Words

- Read the information in the Strategy Box and explain as needed.

- Ask students to think of other compound words. Answers will vary.

- Compile a list on the board.

7 **Understanding Compound Words**

- ❑ Ask students to complete this activity on their own.

❏ Review the correct answers as a class.

❏ Check comprehension by asking students to use the words in new sentences.

ANSWER KEY

Possible answers: *Compound Words with Hyphens:* 1. music that is soft and easy to listen to 2. list of things that must be done 3. books that teach people how to help themselves 4. someone who is always doing good things for others; *Compound Words without Hyphens:* 1. A train trip that continues through the night 2. used by many people 3. ways of saying goodbye 4. areas by the sea 5. the home or house

Best Practice

Cultivating Critical Thinking

In the following Expansion Activity, students use their critical thinking skills by analyzing the patterns of words and applying what they have already learned about compound words.

 EXPANSION ACTIVITY

■ The aim of this activity is to provide additional practice with compound words.

■ Copy and hand out the Black Line Master, **Compound Words** (BLM 1).

■ Read the instructions and explain the example. Model how to create additional compound words.

■ When students complete the worksheet, review the answers and make corrections.

■ Begin a list of new words on the board.

Pronunciation Note

■ If you have two nouns that form a compound word, usually the first word is stressed. For example, *keyboard, boyfriend*

ANSWER KEY

1. bedroom 2. blackberry 3. friendship
4. sweetheart 5. basketball 6. mailbox 7. wildlife
8. wristwatch 9. armchair 10. sunlight
Creating new words Column: Answers will vary.

8 Around the Globe

Best Practice

Interacting with Others

In Activity 8, students interact in pairs to study the photos and answer questions. By participating in pair work and listening to and expressing opinions, students are able to practice authentic conversation based on the topics presented in the reading.

❏ Put students in pairs and tell them to look at the photos in Sections A, B, and C.

❏ Read the captions below the photos aloud.

❏ Give each pair enough time to read the directions and answer the questions.

❏ Discuss the answers as a class.

Content Note

■ Some typical physical greetings in the U.S. depend on the relationship between the people. Friends will wave or nod their heads if they don't use a verbal "hello". Handshakes are common for people who have never met before, are acquaintances, or are business colleagues. Many Americans greet family or close friends with hugs and kisses on the cheek. Many visitors to the United States are surprised to learn Americans use "How are you?" as a greeting. It is a question, but they often do not expect an answer. Referring back to the reading, this greeting that Americans offer as they walk by should not be taken as being rude. It is the same as saying "Good Morning."

9 Asking Personal Questions

❑ Read the directions and explain as necessary.

❑ Look at the photo and read the questions below.

❑ Ask students to think about which questions would be impolite in their culture(s).

ANSWER KEY

Answers will vary.

Best Practice

Cultivating Critical Thinking

The following Expansion Activity involves a collaborative role-play activity. The dialogues require students to synthesize and apply what they learned in the reading and apply it to a new situation.

EXPANSION ACTIVITY

■ The aim of this activity is to provide practice with differentiating between polite and impolite questions through dialogue practice.

■ Tell pairs of students to develop a list of four things that are considered impolite in American culture.

■ Have each pair write a 4–6 line dialogue in which Student 1 greets Student 2, Student 2 responds, Student 1 poses one of the impolite questions, and Student 2 responds appropriately.

■ Tell students to practice their dialogues and reverse roles.

■ Set aside time for students to read their dialogues to the class.

10 Politeness

Best Practice

Activating Prior Knowledge

Activities such as this require students to connect their own ideas and prior knowledge with new topics presented in the chapter. In this case, students are asked to discuss a list of questions and decide whether or not they would be polite in the U.S. This activity gets students to activate experiences they have had, and the language and vocabulary they have learned.

❑ Read the directions and explain as necessary.

❑ Have students complete the activity independently.

❑ Go over the answers as a class.

ANSWER KEY

1. Polite 2. Impolite 3. Polite 4. Impolite
5. Polite 6. Impolite 7. Polite 8. Impolite

11 Talking About Preferences

❑ Read the directions and explain as necessary.

❑ Put students in small groups to discuss the questions.

❑ Call on students to share their answers.

Strategy

Using a Continuum

- Read the information in the Strategy Box and explain as needed.

- Ask students to think of other topics that could be rated on a continuum.

- Compile a list on the board.

12 Using a Continuum: Rating Social Acceptance

Best Practice

Organizing Information

Activities such as this teach students how to organize and rate information using a graphic organizer (a continuum.) In this case, students are rating actions according to degrees of acceptability based on the information from the reading passage and their own opinions and prior knowledge.

- ❏ Read the situation and list of actions as a class.

- ❏ As a class, place the first three actions on the continuum in the Strategy Box.

- ❏ Encourage discussion until a majority of the class agrees on where to place each item.

- ❏ Put students in small groups to finish Continuum 1.

- ❏ Repeat the process for Continuum 2 and have the groups complete the activity for another culture they are familiar with.

- ❏ Have groups compare answers for Continuum 1 and 2.

My Country (excerpts)

Before You Read

1 **Getting the Meaning of Words from Context and Structure**

❏ Read the directions and explain as necessary.

❏ Remind students to use what they learned about suffixes and compound words in Part 1.

❏ Go over the answers.

ANSWER KEY

1. stretching out in all directions 2. large size
3. looks around 4. character 5. similar
6. wetness 7. has just arrived 8. small battles
9. sheriffs and policemen 10. shy 11. in the
French way

Read

Strategy

Finding the Implied Main Idea of a Paragraph

■ Read the information in the Strategy Box and explain as needed.

■ Make sure students understand the definition of "implied." Ask: *Has someone ever tried to tell you something without using exact words? Has a teacher helped you figure out an answer by giving an example instead of telling you the exact answer?*

2 **Reading an Article: Finding Implied Main Ideas**

Best Practice

Activating Prior Knowledge

The questions in Activity 2 get students to activate their prior knowledge about Canadians and Americans and the difference between them. This type of activity will help students relate their own ideas about the two cultures with the information presented in the reading.

❏ Read the Introduction and discuss the answers to the questions as a class.

❏ Have students read the first five paragraphs of the article and choose the best main idea from the choices provided.

❏ Go over the answers.

ANSWER KEY

1. B 2. C 3. B 4. A 5. C

After You Read

3 **Checking your Comprehension**

❏ Read the directions and ask students to work independently.

❏ Have students mark each statement as T or F and correct the false statements.

❏ Go over the answers and write the corrected false statements on the board.

ANSWER KEY

1. F, Most inhabit cities 2. T 3. F, Canada can get very hot. 4. F, The history of Canada is not as bloody or violent as the United States'. 5. T
6. F, The "wild" west was not part of Canadian history. In Canada, law came first, settlement followed. 7. F, Outward displays of emotion are

not their style. Americans are far more outgoing.
8. T 9. F, Canadians are not anti-American. 10. F,
The buildings are designed in international styles.
and the brand names in the supermarkets are all
familiar.

Content Note

- The reading discusses Quebec's separatist movement. Separatists support Quebec's becoming its own state and having its own constitution. They believe that the people of Quebec (called *Québécois*) will be better able to handle their own economic, social, and cultural development.

Best Practice

Organizing Information

Activities such as the following Expansion Activity help students organize information from the reading passage so that they are better able to compare and contrast the topics and recall information from them.

 EXPANSION ACTIVITY

- The aim of this activity is to practice comparing and contrasting two topics using a Venn diagram.

- Copy and hand out the Black Line Master, **Canada / United States** Venn Diagram (BLM 2).

- Model a Venn diagram on the board and explain how using a Venn diagram will make it easier to compare and contrast two topics.

- Direct students' attention to the article "My Country" on pages 18–21. Elicit one thing Canada and the United States have in common. e.g. *Both countries have hot temperatures in the summer.*

- Have students complete the Venn diagram and then compare diagrams with a partner.

- Call on students to share their diagrams with the class.

Strategy

Analyzing the Prefixes *non-* and *anti-*

- Read the information in the Strategy Box and explain as needed.

- Ask students to give examples of words they know with those prefixes.

- Compile a list of their examples on the board.

4 Analyzing the Prefixes *non-* and *anti-*

- ❑ Review the article "My Country" and have students find the examples *non-Canadians* and *anti-American*.

- ❑ Discuss their meanings.

- ❑ Have students write definitions for the words and phrases listed in Activity 4 on page 22.

- ❑ Go over the answers.

ANSWER KEY

Possible answers: 1. people who are not residents 2. pills that stop anxiety 3. a protest against a war 4. a group of people who do not use violence 5. people who are not German 6. people who are not Mexican 7. someone who is against communism 8. people who do not vote 9. laws that are against monopolies 10. not a payment

5 Analyzing Four More Suffixes

- ❑ Read the suffixes and definitions.

- ❑ Have students complete this activity on their own.

❑ Review correct answers as a class

❑ Check comprehension by asking students to use the words in new sentences.

ANSWER KEY

1. decoration 2. harmful 3. government
4. glorious

6 Making New Words by Adding Suffixes

❑ Read the directions.

❑ Model the activity by doing item 1 as a class.

❑ Ask students to complete the rest of the activity.

❑ Go over the answers.

ANSWER KEY

1. environment 2. imagination 3. powerful
4. moderation 5. settlement 6. movement
7. mountainous 8. mysterious

7 Focusing on Words from the Academic Word List

❑ Direct students' attention to the words in the box.

❑ Tell students to complete this activity on their own.

❑ Review correct answers as a class.

❑ Check comprehension by asking students to use the words in new sentences.

ANSWER KEY

1. scheme 2. symbol 3. contrasts 4. symbol
5. attitudes 6. displays 7. style 8. removed

8 Guided Academic Conversation

Best Practice

Scaffolding Instruction

This activity requires students to draw on the information they have learned in Chapter 1. When students use their prior knowledge as a scaffold, they can better understand and organize new ideas about the topics.

❑ Divide the class into groups of three.

❑ Ask groups to discuss three of the four topics, giving each member of the group a chance to respond.

❑ Tell groups to choose one student from their group to share their ideas with the class.

Focus on Testing   TOEFL® iBT

Analyzing Points of Contrast on Tests

■ Read the instructions in the Focus on Testing box and explain as needed.

■ Give students time to complete the practice activities.

■ Go over the answers.

ANSWER KEY

	Canadian	American
1. freedom rather than order		X
2. the neat and clean Mountie	X	
3. order instead of freedom	X	
4. sheriffs elected by vote		X
5. keeping peace with guns		X

6. lawmen appointed from above	X	
7. settlement before law		X
8. law before settlement	X	
9. lawmen in scarlet coats	X	
10. the "wild" west		X

9 **What Do You Think?**

❑ Read or ask a volunteer to read the paragraph aloud.

❑ Divide students into small groups to discuss the questions that follow.

1 Making Connections

> ### Best Practice
>
> **Scaffolding instruction**
> Activities such as this will enable students to link recently acquired knowledge with new information they gather from their research.

- ❑ Put students in pairs or have them work independently.

- ❑ Tell them they will look up information on an English-speaking country.

- ❑ Allow the students to choose one of the questions that interests them. Instruct them to look at websites on the Internet.

- ❑ Have each student or pair report their findings to the class.

Responding in Writing

Writing Tip: Using Details to Support Your Ideas

- ❑ Have students read the Writing Tip.

- ❑ Ask for other examples of details and what they illustrate to be sure students understand the point.

2 Writing a Paragraph Using Details

- ❑ Read the directions and the steps and explain them as necessary

- ❑ Circulate around the class to check on their progress.

- ❑ Remind students to check spelling, grammar and vocabulary and to make their paragraphs as correct, clear, and interesting as they can.

Self-Assessment Log

- ❏ Encourage students to maintain a self-assessment log.

- ❏ Allow class time so students can check the strategies and vocabulary they learned in the chapter.

- ❏ Address any questions and review strategies as needed.

2

Teamwork and Competition

In this chapter, students will focus on teamwork and competition in the areas of sports and business. In the first reading, they will read about soccer player David Beckham, as he describes the teamwork and competition he experienced when he moved from England to Spain. Students will then explore teamwork and competition in the context of business in Part 2 as they read about Kim Ssang Su, a Korean businessman, and his globally competitive company. New vocabulary, reading strategies, and critical thinking will be brought together as students learn test-taking strategies in Part 3.

Chapter Opener

❑ Direct student's attention to the photo and ask questions: *What kinds of teams are there? Can you be on a team in business? How are business teams the same as sports teams?*

❑ Read the English proverb aloud and ask students what they think it means.

❑ Put students in groups and ask them to list the teams they have been a part of and discuss the pros and cons to being on a team.

❑ Put students in groups and have them discuss the questions in the **Connecting to the Topic** section. (The photo is of David Beckham and Juan Carlos Valeron fighting for the ball during their Spanish League Soccer (football) match in Madrid on October 3, 2004. In this photo, David Beckham is playing for Real Madrid and Juan Carlos Valeron is playing for Deportivo de la Coruna.)

❑ Call on groups to recount their discussions with the whole class.

❝ Two heads are better than one. ❞

—English proverb

Chapter Overview

Reading Skills and Strategies

Reading without knowing every word

Scanning for numbers

Selecting the main idea of an article

Critical Thinking Skills

Using a graphic organizer (chain of events diagram) to identify the sequence of events

Recognizing implied feelings

Taking a stand for or against a proposal

Synthesizing Internet content: taking notes and presenting results

Choosing adjectives to describe people in writing

Vocabulary Building

Figuring out idiomatic expressions and specialized terms

Learning sports-related vocabulary

Understanding metaphors

Using compound adjectives

Inferring the meanings of words for synonyms or antonyms

Focusing on words from the Academic Word List

Focus on Testing

Using strategies to correctly answer multiple choice questions

Vocabulary

Nouns	Verbs	Adjectives	Idioms and Expressions	
CEO	ascends	chilly	be our night	left wing
factories	barks	ear-numbing	bracing myself	midfield
global brands	cavorts	flat-screen	chested	miss out
goals*	chant	high-speed	cross it	(the) near post
innovation*	croon	knee-deep	cut in	spurring on
job*	duplicate	leading-edge	didn't (don't) really have	took (take) a
mountainside	issuing*	low-cost	a clue	knock or two
net profits	jumped	low-end	feel at home	took (take) me off
oldie	perceived*	nondescript	get the drift	touch
revenues*	rallying	odd^	go for goal	twist in the pit of
stratosphere	sliced	snow-covered	goalkeeper	my stomach
testing ground	stoop	tireless	in a comfort zone	whisked off
turnaround	storms	vicious	kick-off	
vigor	underestimate*			
V.P.				

*These words are from the Academic Word List. For more information on this list, see www.vuw.ac.nz/lals/research/awl.

Beckham: An Autobiography

Before You Read

Strategy

Figuring Out Idiomatic Expressions and Specialized Terms

- Read the information in the Strategy Box and explain as needed.

- Ask students to find an example of an idiomatic expression or specialized term from the reading passage.

- Write a list of the idioms they find on the board.

1 Getting the Meaning of Idiomatic Expressions from Context

- ❏ Read the directions and explain as needed.

- ❏ Model the activity and try to figure out what it means from its context: by reading the first idiom and **Hint**.

- ❏ Ask a student to guess the meaning of *took a knock or two* from the **Hint**. Tell students to fill in the correct answer.

- ❏ Ask students to guess the meanings of the rest of the idioms and expressions.

- ❏ Discuss the answers as a class. Check for comprehension by having students describe a situation in which they might hear the idiom or expression in use. Give students an example, tell students about a time that you *took a knock or two*, such as having a difficult time at a new job or moving to a new city or country.

ANSWER KEY

1. C   2. A   3. D   4. B   5. D   6. C   7. A   8. D   9. B

2 Getting the Meaning of Specialized Terms from Context

- ❏ Read the directions and explain as needed.

- ❏ Make sure students understand the completed example.

- ❏ Discuss the answers as a class. Check for comprehension by posing questions such as: *What sports have a "kick-off"? What sports have a "left wing"?*

ANSWER KEY

1. e   2. j   3. g   4. c   5. d   6. l   7. k   8. i   9. h   10. b
11. a   12. f

Read 🎧

3 Reading Without Knowing Every Word

- ❏ Read the directions and explain as needed.

Content Notes

- ■ Football (or soccer) is the most popular sport in the world today. The first World Cup involved 13 teams and was held in Uruguay in 1930. 32 teams competed in the 2006 World Cup in Germany. To date, the most goals scored in a game is 12 in a World Cup game between Austria and Switzerland in 1954. The final score was Austria 7, Switzerland 5. The first player to ever miss a penalty kick was Valdemar de Brito of Brazil in 1934.

- ■ In the United States, baseball is so popular that it is called "America's National Pastime."

- ■ At the end of the baseball season, there is a round of playoffs in which the best teams of each league compete until the winning team from each league is determined. The two league champions compete in what is called the World Series. The first team to win four of seven games in the World Series becomes the World Series champion.

READING TIP: LEARNING SPORTS-RELATED TERMS

- Direct students' attention to the Reading Tip in the margin and explain as needed.

- Ask students if they are familiar with any sports-related terms in English.

- Tell students to skim the reading passage for sports-related terms in the reading.

- Tell them to choose one and say what they think it means based on its context.

- Read the Introduction or ask a volunteer(s) to read it aloud.

- Discuss the question as a class.

- Have students read the passage silently within a time limit (suggested time limit: 10 minutes).

After You Read

 EXPANSION ACTIVITY

- The aim of this activity is to give students additional practice with sports-related idioms.

- Make copies of the Black Line Master, "Idiom Puzzles" (BLM 3) and cut the words so each is its own "piece."

- Place the pieces in envelopes and prepare enough envelopes for each pair to have one. Note: The idioms are divided into two sections: idioms from the reading about David Beckham, and baseball idioms. To begin, you may wish to have students work on the soccer

idioms alone, and then later the baseball idioms. You may want to spend some time before the activity brainstorming baseball-related idioms as a class. To make the activity more challenging, combine both sets of idioms together.

- Put students in pairs.

- Direct students to close their books and complete this activity without looking back at the reading.

- Explain that they need to put the words together to complete the idioms.

- Call on pairs to read the idioms they put together.

- Write the correct idioms on the board and review the definitions if necessary.

Strategy

Using a Graphic Organizer to Follow the Sequence of Events

- Read the information in the Strategy Box and explain as needed.

- Ask students to recount/recall the first two events that Beckham describes in the reading.

4 Finding the Sequence of Events

- ❑ Read the directions and explain as needed.

- ❑ Ask students to read the list of key events and complete the chain of events diagram.

ANSWER KEY

Beginning: First Event D F C G B A End: Last Event E

Best Practice

Organizing Information

Activities such as the chain of events diagram and the sequencing table in the following Expansion Activity will help students organize information from the reading passage so that they are better able to recall the order of events. By having students focus on the order in which things happened, they will not only be able to remember ideas from the reading but also think about them in a logical way.

 EXPANSION ACTIVITY

■ The aim of this activity is to provide students with additional practice with chain of events diagrams.

■ Copy and hand out the Black Line Master **Chain of Events Diagram: A Selection from My Autobiography** (BLM 4).

■ Tell students that they will now have an opportunity to fill out a chain of events diagram based on an event in their own autobiographies. Ask them to take a few minutes to think of an important event in their own lives, for example getting married, moving to a new country, an accident, etc. and some of the events that occurred during that time.

■ Ask them to choose four of the events and write them in the diagram in the correct order. When they have completed their charts, have students share their diagrams in pairs or small groups.

5 Guided Academic Conversation: The Inside Story

❏ Put students in pairs.

❏ Ask students to follow the five steps listed in the activity.

❏ After they have completed the activity, have them compare their lists with those of other classmates.

ANSWER KEY

Answers will vary.

6 Practicing Speaking by Doing Tasks

Best Practice

Interacting with Others

Activities such as this will help students increase their speaking ability and confidence. By creating a presentation together, students practice explaining their ideas clearly, and understanding those of their partners.

❏ Put students in pairs. Read the three role-play situations.

❏ Ask students to choose one of the role-plays and write a dialogue for it.

❏ Encourage them to incorporate vocabulary and idioms from the reading.

❏ Allow time for students to perform their role plays for the class.

7 What Do You Think?

❏ Have students read the paragraph and discuss the questions that follow.

Content Notes

■ The Olympic Games have been the cause of many controversies throughout history. One of the most famous events happened in 1972 when eleven Israeli athletes were kidnapped and killed. The movie, *Munich*, made in 2005, details this event. *Munich* was directed by Steven Spielberg and was nominated for the Academy Award for Best Picture.

- Another well-known film detailing a controversial Olympic event was *Chariots of Fire*. It was made in 1981 and won the Academy Award for Best Picture. *Chariots of Fire* is an English film detailing the true story of two competing British track athletes.

Outward Bound

Before You Read

1 **Using the Context to Infer the Meanings of Words**

Best Practice

Cultivating Critical Thinking

This type of activity teaches students how to infer the meanings of new words and phrases from their contexts. It also gets them to realize what they may already know about the context and vocabulary.

- ❑ Draw student's attention to the *Language Tip* in the margin.

- ❑ Read the directions and explain as needed.

- ❑ Read the first sentence aloud and ask students to guess the meaning of *CEO* based on the context. Ask the students to complete the rest of the activity.

- ❑ Discuss the answers as a class. Check for comprehension: *What's another word for "CEO." What is V.P. an abbreviation for?*

ANSWER KEY

1. C 2. A 3. D 4. B 5. C 6. C 7. D 8. A

Strategy

Scanning

- ■ Read the information in the Strategy Box and explain as needed.

- ■ Ask students to scan a paragraph from the reading and say a number that they found. Their answers will vary.

- ■ Write a list on the board of the numbers called out.

2 **Scanning for Numbers**

- ❑ Read the directions and ask students to work individually.

- ❑ Give students 5 minutes to complete the activity.

- ❑ Ask volunteers to give their answers.

ANSWER KEY

1. 59 2. 35 3. 17 billion, 556 million 4. 36.4 billion 5. 84% 6. 1996 7. 4.7 billion 8. 7:00

Read 🎧

- ❑ Introduce the reading about Kim Ssang Su by reading the introduction aloud or having a volunteer read it.

- ❑ Discuss the questions as a class.

- ❑ Set a time limit for students to read the passage (10 minutes).

After You Read

3 **Selecting the Main Idea**

- ❑ Draw students' attention to the Reading Tip in the margin and remind students of what they learned about main ideas in Chapter 1.

- ❑ Read the directions and list of possible main ideas.

- ❑ Ask students why this statement is better than the other two.

ANSWER KEY

2

Strategy

Understanding Metaphors

- Read the information in the Strategy Box and explain as needed.

- Ask students to find an example of a metaphor in the reading.

- Write a list on the board of the metaphors they find.

4 Understanding Metaphors

- ❏ Read the directions and explain as needed.

- ❏ Have students complete the activity on their own or with a partner.

- ❏ Go over the answers.

ANSWER KEY

Answers will vary. Possible answers:

1. Usage: "Great people! Great company!" he barks. Metaphor: The way Kim shouts is being compared to the barking of a dog.

2. Usage: Revenues jumped 18% last year; Metaphor: The way revenues rose is being compared to something that jumps.

3. Usage: "Great company! Great company!" they chant back. Metaphor: The way the employees respond is being compared to religious chanting.

4. Usage: Kim... cavorts in a mosh pit. Metaphor: The way Kim jumps around is being compared to leaping and prancing.

5. Usage: Kim sliced costs. Metaphor: The way Kim decreased costs is being compared to slicing a piece of cheese with a knife.

6. Usage: He storms about LG's factories and offices; Metaphor: The way Kim visits his factories is being compared to a storm.

Grammar Note

- Another way to compare two things is to use similes. Similes are different from metaphors because they contain the words "like" or "as" and compare two objects. A metaphor does not have the words "like" or "as" and states that one thing is something else. For example, "That boy eats like a pig" is a simile, but "That boy is a pig" is a metaphor. Similarly, "Her legs are like sticks." is a simile, whereas the sentence "Her legs are sticks." means her legs are skinny but is a metaphor because it actually says her legs are another object.

Best Practice

Activating Prior Knowledge

Activities such as this Expansion Activity get students to activate and build on the information they have already learned. Using a topic students are comfortable with enables students to more easily apply new concepts. The following Expansion Activity activates prior knowledge by connecting the familiar topic of friends and family with the new concepts of metaphors and similes.

EXPANSION ACTIVITY

- The aim of this activity is to practice similes and metaphors.

- Tell students they will practice writing their own similes and metaphors.

- Ask students to tell any common similes they know in English or common idioms from their native languages.

- Give examples such as *big as a house, quiet as a mouse, his/her face is as red as a beet, cold as ice, black as night, sleeps like a baby, grows like a weed*, etc.

- Tell students to look at the underlined verbs in

activity 4 and think of some new metaphors using the same verbs.

- Have students think about people they know and write sentences using similes to describe their friends and family.

- Ask volunteers to read their sentences.

USING COMPOUND ADJECTIVES

- Read the information in the instruction box and explain as needed.

- Work with students to define *leading-edge gadget*.

---

5 **Using Compound Adjectives**

- Read the directions and review the scanning strategy taught earlier in this chapter on page 42.

- Ask the students to match the compound adjectives in the left column with the nouns they modify in the right column.

- Have students give their answers.

ANSWER KEY

1. e 2. c 3. a 4. g 5. d 6. b 7. f

Grammar Notes

- Usually when a compound word is an adjective, it is hyphenated. The compound adjective is placed before the noun in common English word order. If the words are placed after the noun, they are not hyphenated.

- **Hint**: If the words can be separated and retain their meaning, no hyphen is necessary. If the words need to be together to retain the meaning, a hyphen is required.

- Compare:
The three-year-old child was excited. (When

each word in the compound adjective is used alone in the sentence, the sentence doesn't make sense—"The three child...; The year child...; The old child.... Therefore, hyphens are needed when the three are combined.

---

6 **Inferring Meaning: Same or Opposite?**

- Define *synonym* and *antonym*. Remind students that a synonym is a word with a similar definition and an antonym is a word with the opposite (or almost opposite) meaning.

- Read the directions and model the first item.

- Ask students to answer the rest of the questions.

- Go over the answers.

ANSWER KEY

1. Antonym 2. Synonym 3. Antonym 4. Synonym
5. Synonym 6. Antonym 7. Synonym 8. Antonym
9. Antonym 10. Synonym 11. Antonym
12. Antonym 13. Synonym 14. Synonym
15. Antonym

---

7 **Focusing on Words from the Academic Word List**

- Read the directions and explain as necessary.

- Tell students to complete this activity on their own.

- Set a time limit of 5 minutes.

- Review correct answers as a class.

- Check comprehension by asking students to use words in new sentences.

ANSWER KEY

1. odd 2. job 3. underestimate 4. innovation
5. issuing 6. goals 7. perceived

EXPANSION ACTIVITY

- The aim of this activity is to provide further practice with new vocabulary.

- Tell students they will write a vocabulary quiz for the class.

- Have students choose three words from Activity 7.

- For each word, ask them to write a sentence using the word in context. Tell them to make sure the context adequately conveys the word's meaning. Each student will write three sentences.

- Have each student write one of their sentences on the board and draw a blank where the missing vocabulary word should go.

- Have students copy the sentences from the board and fill in the blanks. They should be able to choose the correct vocabulary word based on the context of the sentence.

☐ Put students in groups of three.

☐ Ask them to discuss three of the four topics.

☐ Tell students to focus on the topic they agree on and write a statement detailing their opinion.

☐ Have each group share their opinion statement with the class.

☐ Assign the writing of the opinion statement as homework, or, for variety, as a journal entry.

8 Guided Academic Conversation

Best Practice

Interacting with Others

Activities such as this get students to generate new ideas with the help of their peers and practice expressing their ideas and comprehending and respecting those of others. This type of interaction builds listening and speaking fluency, which is essential to academic success.

1 End-of-Chapter Debate

- ❑ Write the word *Competition* on one side of the board and *Teamwork* on the other.

- ❑ Have students choose to stand beside the word they think is more important.

Best Practice

Organizing Information

Graphic organizers such as T-charts help students organize information in a way that compares and contrasts the topics. By having the class focus on the columns of a T-chart (as in the following Expansion Activity), students will be able to remember ideas from the readings in this chapter. This type of tool is helpful for organizing information in a broad range of academic contexts.

 EXPANSION ACTIVITY

- ■ The aim of this activity is to have students practice using a T-chart to organize their ideas for a debate.

- ■ Copy and hand out the Black Line Master, **Competition/Teamwork T-Chart** (BLM 5).

- ■ Model a T-chart on the board and explain how using a diagram will make it easier to prepare for a debate because the information is organized.

- ■ Group students by the categories they chose in Activity 1, or, to make the activity more challenging, group them by the category opposite to the one they support.

- ■ With their group, they should fill in half of the T-chart with reasons why they support that concept and the other half of the T-chart with reasons why the other concept should not be supported.

- ■ Each group should then write their points on the board and be prepared to discuss their reasoning.

- ■ Discuss which half of the T-chart has more pros and which half has more cons.

2 Making Connections

Best Practice

Scaffolding Instruction

Activities such as this will enable students to link recently acquired knowledge with even newer information they gather from their research.

- ❑ Tell students they will look up information on one of the people they have read about.

- ❑ Have them choose one of the topics to research.

- ❑ Have students share their findings with the class or in small groups.

Responding in Writing

WRITING TIP: DESCRIBING PEOPLE BY USING ADJECTIVES

- ■ Read the *Writing Tip* and explain as necessary.

- ■ Point out the example and ask volunteers to describe someone using adjectives and examples.

3 Writing and Using Adjectives

Best Practice

Making Use of Academic Content

Brainstorming and developing a paragraph is a concept students will see often throughout their academic careers. Using real-world examples like David Beckham and Kim Ssang Su makes use of topics and tasks found in academic textbooks.

- ❑ Read the directions and go over each of the steps explaining as necessary.

- ❑ Tell students to work on their own.

❑ Circulate around the class to check on the progress of each student and offer help as needed.

Vocabulary Note

■ Certain suffixes form adjectives; *-y*, *-ful*, *-ing*, *-ive*, and *-able* are common. Examples include *happy, funny, beautiful, fruitful, hard-working, exciting, innovative, knowledgeable*, and *capable*. It may help students expand their vocabularies if they know they can add a suffix to a word to make it an adjective.

Focus on Testing

General Testing Practice

■ Read the information in the Focus on Testing box and explain as needed.

■ Have students complete the practice activity.

■ Go over the answers.

ANSWER KEY

1. C 2. C 3. B 4. D 5. C 6. A 7. A 8. B 9. D
10. D

Self-Assessment Log

❑ Encourage students to maintain a self-assessment log.

❑ Allow class time so students can check the strategies and vocabulary they learned in the chapter.

❑ Address any questions and review strategies as needed.

3

Gender and Relationships

In this chapter, students will focus on personal relationships and families. In the first reading, they will read about the timely concern of child care: the care of children in families with two working parents. Students will learn how this issue is handled in the United States and will examine statistics detailing who is considered "family." In Part 2, students will read about a Russian business that exports "mail-order" brides. New vocabulary, reading strategies, and critical thinking will be brought together as students learn test-taking techniques in Part 3.

Chapter Opener

- ❑ Direct student's attention to the photo and ask questions. *How would you describe this family? Where are they?*

- ❑ Put students in small groups to discuss the questions in the **Connecting to the Topic** section. (The photo is of a family sitting at a table outside with a notebook.)

- ❑ Call on students to share their answers.

- ❑ Read the Swedish proverb aloud and ask students what they think it means.

- ❑ Call on groups to recount their discussions with the whole class.

❝ A life without love is as bleak as a year without summertime. **❞**

—Swedish proverb

Chapter Overview

Reading Skills and Strategies

Skimming for the general idea

Recalling information

Reading a chart for information

Scanning for facts

Distinguishing between general and specific statements

Selecting the main idea

Critical Thinking Skills

Presenting ideas effectively in a group

Summarizing a group opinion

Comparing past and present generations

Synthesizing Internet content: taking notes and presenting results

Summarizing by listing key points in writing

Vocabulary Building

Matching words to their definitions

Identifying antonyms

Focusing on words from the Academic Word List

Reviewing vocabulary through pantomime

Focus on Testing

Answering vocabulary questions

Vocabulary

Nouns		**Adjectives**	**Adverb**
attitude*	job sharing	advantageous	radically*
blended family	nanny	fictitious	
breadwinner	palace	intolerant	**Idiom**
cottage	requirements*	invalid	(be) in touch
couple*	torrent	legal*	
criteria*	trend*	medical*	
exporter*	trickle	self-employed	
extended families		stay-at-home (mom)	
flex time	**Verbs**	valid*	
glass ceiling	flourishing	well-to-do	
guarantee*	obtain*		
househusband	portrayed		
immediate family	registered*		
	requires*		

*These words are from the Academic Word List. For more information on this list, see www.vuw.ac.nz/lals/research/awl.

Who's Taking Care of the Children

Before You Read

Strategy

Skimming for the General Idea

- Read the information in the Strategy box and explain as needed.

- Define "general idea" and compare it to the definition for "main idea."

1 **Skimming for the General Idea**

- ❏ Read the directions and explain as necessary.

- ❏ Ask students to choose the best general idea. Tell students to be prepared to discuss their choices.

- ❏ Discuss the answers as a class.

ANSWER KEY

2; Explanations will vary.

Read

- ❏ Read the Introduction aloud or ask a volunteer to read it.

- ❏ Discuss the questions as a class.

- ❏ Have students read the passage silently within a time limit (10 minutes).

Content Notes

- According to the U.S. Department of Labor report "Changes in Women's Work Participation", only one of every three women worked in 1950. This was approximately 33% of the workforce. Three

of every five women worked in 1998 making up almost 60% of the workforce

- In more modern times, 63% of women aged 16–24 work whereas only 43% worked in 1950. The largest age group of women workers is 35–44. In 1950, approximately 39% of women aged 35–44 worked. By 2000, approximately 77% of women aged 35–44 worked.

After You Read

2 **Matching Words to Their Definitions**

- ❏ Read the directions and explain as needed.

- ❏ Model the activity by reading the first word "glass ceiling" and asking students to scan the reading for it and try to determine its meaning from context.

- ❏ Have students complete the activity independently.

- ❏ Go over the answers.

- ❏ Check for comprehension by posing questions, such as *Do you think "job sharing" is a good idea? Who are members of your "extended family"? Who are members of your "immediate family"?*

ANSWER KEY

1. c 2. i 3. e 4. g 5. n 6. h 7. b 8. j 9. k 10. l
11. f 12. d 13. a 14. m

3 **Recalling Information**

- ❏ Read the directions and explain as needed.

- ❏ Go over the answers.

ANSWER KEY

1. 70 2. stay-at-home mom 3. immediate
4. larger cities 5. more 6. 20 7. some

❑ Put students in pairs.

❑ Read the directions and have students follow the steps listed in the Strategy Box.

❑ Discuss the answers as a class.

Best Practice

Making Use of Academic Content

Charts are an integral part of academic readings, authentic business reports, and newspaper and magazine articles. Giving students examples of charts provides authentic context. The ability to read and understand charts can be applied in broader academic and business contexts.

ANSWER KEY

1. with a grandparent 2. with other nonrelative
3. 12-17, Answers will vary. 4. 12–17;
5. Answers will vary. 6. Answers will vary.

 EXPANSION ACTIVITY

■ The aim of this activity is to have students practice reading charts for specific information by completing an information gap activity.

■ Copy and distribute the Black Line Master, **Information Gap: Population Charts** (BLM 6).

■ Put students in pairs and distribute the charts so that one student has a copy of the Student A chart and one has a copy of the Student B chart.

■ Tell students to ask their partner questions in order to complete their charts.

■ Once they have finished, have them discuss any of the information they feel is particularly interesting or surprising.

■ Call on students to share their thoughts with the class.

Strategy

Reading a Chart for Information

■ Read the information in the Strategy Box and explain as needed.

■ Remind students how to skim and scan for information.

■ Consider bringing in a local newspaper or a textbook with examples.

4 Reading a Chart for Information

Best Practice

Cultivating Critical Thinking

In Activity 4 and the Expansion Activity that follows, students are asked to read charts and answer questions by skimming for the general idea, and scanning for specific information. Students must read through all the information in the chart to find the information they need to answer the questions. This type of activity promotes critical thinking as well as applying the reading strategy.

5 Guided Academic Conversation: Presenting Your Ideas

Best Practice

Interacting with Others

Discussion activities such as this provide students with opportunities to practice their fluency while expressing and explaining their opinions to their classmates.

Working in pairs and small groups also allows for a lot of speaking time for each individual student.

❏ Put students in pairs.

❏ Read the directions and steps and explain as needed.

❏ Combine pairs into groups of four for steps 3 and 4.

❏ Call on students to share their group's opinions.

6 What Do You Think?

Best Practice

Cultivating Critical Thinking

Activities such as this will help students develop the ability to synthesize information from the reading and combine it with their own ideas. This will enable them to better express their opinions about the topic in a clear and logical way.

❏ Read the directions and explain as needed.

Content Notes

■ Prospective parents who want to adopt may be childless or already have other children.

■ Adoptive parents are not required to own their own homes or have high incomes because it is most important that they offer the children stability, commitment, and family values; all things money cannot buy.

■ Although rules and laws vary state by state, in the United States some adoption agencies consider only couples who have been married one to three years and are between the ages of 25 and 40. Often, agencies will require one parent to not work or work from home for six months after the adoption.

70 Brides for 7 Foreigners

Before You Read

1 Scanning for Facts

- ❏ Read the directions and explain as needed.

- ❏ Model the activity by reading the first item and having students find the correct answer, *23*, in the article.

- ❏ Go over the answers.

ANSWER KEY

1. 23 2. Yaroslav the Wise 3. 100 4. 10 5. 5
6. United States, Germany, and Britain 7. 1,200

Read 🎧

- ❏ Introduce the article by reading or having a volunteer read the Introduction aloud.

- ❏ Discuss the questions as a class.

- ❏ Ask students to read the passage. Set a time limit (10 minutes).

Best Practice

Organizing Information

Activities such as the following Expansion Activity will help students organize their ideas about the topic of the reading passage. By completing the KWL chart, student are required to draw on their prior knowledge of the topic, outline the specific information they would like to find out, and take notes on new information in an organized way. This type of activity can help students recall the information later in written and oral activities.

REPRODUCIBLE | EXPANSION ACTIVITY

- ■ The aim of this activity is to get students to organize their ideas before, during and after the reading passage.

- ■ Before having students read the passage, copy and hand out Black Line Master **KWL Chart** (BLM 7).

- ■ Explain that a KWL chart will help students remember and organize what they read. K stands for "What I KNOW". Students should write down information that they already know about the topic. Be sure they understand that there are no wrong answers. W stands for "What I WANT to Know" and students should fill this in with questions about the topic that they do not know the answer for but would like to learn about. L stands for "What I LEARNED" and is filled in after reading. Encourage use of this chart for textbook readings. Tell students to think about the questions in the Introduction box and to look at the title of the passage.

- ■ Tell students fill in the first two columns of the KWL chart based on the title and information in the Introduction box.

- ■ Then have the students read the passage.

- ■ Upon completion, students should fill in the third column of the chart. This column will be notes from the reading.

- ■ Compare charts.

Vocabulary Note

- ■ The word *milieu* may be unfamiliar to students. Prepare to define it as "setting" or "environment". "Women must be successful in their professional *milieu*" means they should be successful at their jobs.

After You Read

DISTINGUISHING BETWEEN GENERAL AND SPECIFIC STATEMENTS

- Read the information in the instruction note and explain as needed.

- Define "general" statements and "specific" statements and make sure students are clear on the difference.

- Ask for volunteers to write general and specific statements on the board.

2 Distinguishing Between General and Specific Statements

- ❑ Read the directions and have students complete the activity on their own.

- ❑ Go over the answers.

ANSWER KEY

Column 1, Specific

Column 2, General

1. b 2. e 3. a 4. d 5. c

3 Selecting the Main Idea

Best Practice

Making Use of Academic Content

Reading articles from authentic sources (such as the article "70 Brides for 7 Foreigners," from the *World Press Review*) and identifying the main idea helps students prepare for the type of readings and reading tasks they will encounter in their academic studies.

- ❑ Review the definition for "main idea."

- ❑ Read the directions and have students choose which statement best expresses the main idea of the reading passage.

- ❑ Ask them to think about why their choice is better than the others.

- ❑ Put students in pairs or small groups and have them compare and explain their answers.

- ❑ Take a vote at the end of the allotted time to see which statement was selected most often.

ANSWER KEY

2

IDENTIFYING ANTONYMS

- Read the information in the instruction note and explain as needed.

- Go over the examples provided, and ask students if they can think of any other examples of antonyms.

4 Recalling Antonyms

- ❑ Read the directions and do the first item as a class.

- ❑ Have students complete the activity on their own.

- ❑ Go over the answers.

ANSWER KEY

1. advantageous 2. exporter 3. fictitious
4. flourishing 5. legal 6. intolerant 7. cottage
8. trickle 9. invalid 10. well-to-do

EXPANSION ACTIVITY

- The aim of this activity is to practice synonyms and antonyms.

- Tell students they will practice synonyms and antonyms. Review synonyms from Chapter 2 if necessary.

- Divide the class into two teams. Assign one team as the *Synonym Team* and the other as the *Antonym Team*.
- Tell students that for each word you call out, the *Synonym Team* has to write down as many synonyms for the word as they can while the *Antonym Team* writes words meaning the opposite. Whichever team thinks of the most correct words gets a point.
- As the game progresses, shorten the amount of time teams have to make their lists.

Grammar Note

- Remind students that often a prefix can be added to a word to give it the opposite meaning. Some of these prefixes are *un-, in-, dis-, il-, ir-, im-* and *non-*. Examples include *unhappy, incorrect, dishonest, illegible, irregular, impolite, nonathletic*. Warn students that this rule does not always apply. For example, the antonym for easy is not *uneasy*.

REPRODUCIBLE **EXPANSION ACTIVITY**

- The aim of this activity is to provide practice with prefixes.
- Copy and hand out the Black Line Master, **Prefix Categorizing** (BLM 8).
- Teach the information in the Vocabulary Note above.
- Ask students to put the root words under the correct prefix for that word.
- Go over the answers.
- If time permits, have students define the words and say whether or not the prefix makes it an antonym.

5 Focusing on Words from the Academic Word List

- Read the directions and explain as needed.

- Have students complete this activity on their own.
- Go over the answers as a class.
- Check comprehension by asking students to use words in new sentences.

ANSWER KEY

1. requires 2. guarantee 3. attitude 4. requires
5. obtain 6. legal 7. registers 8. couple
9. medical 10. requirements

6 Choosing Points for Discussion

- Put students in small groups and tell them to discuss three of the questions presented in the activity.
- Tell students they should be prepared to report on their group's opinions.
- Allow enough time for each group to present their opinions.

7 Reading Personal Ads

- Read the directions and explain as needed.
- Put students in small groups and have them discuss the questions.

8 Looking Back at the Past

Best Practice

Activating Prior Knowledge

Activities such as this one, which has students compare two paragraphs and answer questions encourages students to draw on their own experiences and previously learned vocabulary.

- Put students in pairs and direct their attention to the two wedding photos as you read the directions and the questions for each frame.
- Go over the answers as a class.

ANSWER KEY

Answers will vary.

Focus on Testing

Answering Vocabulary Questions on Tests

- Read the information in the Focus on Testing box and explain as needed.

- Have students complete the practice section.

- Discuss the answers as a class.

ANSWER KEY

1. A 2. D 3. B 4. C 5. B 6. A 7. D 8. B

1   Vocabulary Review Pantomime

❏ Write "Actions speak louder than words." on the board and discuss the meaning.

❏ Define "pantomime" and give examples. Pantomime an activity like *driving a car* or *talking on a cell phone*. Ask a volunteer to pantomime *eating or drinking something hot*.

❏ Put students in small groups.

❏ Read the directions and explain as needed.

EXPANSION ACTIVITY

■ The aim of this activity is to provide more practice with new vocabulary items through pantomiming.

■ After students practice their pantomimes, turn the activity into a game.

■ Each group is now a team. Give teams 10 minutes to create a list of actions that they will pantomime for the other groups.

■ Team members perform their pantomimes.

■ Whichever group correctly guesses the word or phrase first, gets a point.

■ The team with the most points after all of the performances wins.

■ Consider small prizes like pencils or notepads.

2   Making Connections

Best Practice

Scaffolding Instruction

Activities such as this will enable students to link recently acquired knowledge with even newer information that they gather from research. By compiling the strategies, vocabulary, and notes from the chapter, students will be able to write concise summaries.

❏ Go over the topics, and explain as needed.

❏ Tell students to choose one of the topics and research it on their own.

❏ If you have access to a computer lab, you can do this as a lab activity. If not, you can assign it for homework.

❏ Schedule time during the next class for students to report their findings.

Responding in Writing

WRITING TIP: WRITING DOWN THE KEY POINTS IN A SUMMARY

■ Read the Writing Tip and explain as needed.

■ Make sure students understand the terms "summary" and "key ideas".

■ Ask students to tell you which reading from the chapter they liked better. Explain that this is an opinion and thus does not belong in a summary.

3   Writing a Summary

❏ Read the directions and steps and explain as needed.

❏ Move about the room and offer help to students as they write.

❏ If time permits, put students in small groups to read their summaries and decide which one is the best (short, clear, complete, and interesting).

❏ Assign revisions as homework.

Self-Assessment Log

❏ Encourage students to maintain a self-assessment log.

❏ Allow class time so students can check the strategies and vocabulary they learned in the chapter.

❏ Tell students to find definitions in the chapter for any words they did not check.

Chapter 4

Health and Leisure

In this chapter, students will read about different diets from around the world. In the first reading, they will learn about how what we eat affects us. The second reading explores the notion of ecotourism through the observations of Deborah McLaren, a journalist and director of an international nonprofit program. It also examines the effects that tourists have on the places they visit.

Chapter Opener

- ❏ Direct student's attention to the photo and ask questions. *Who are the people in the photo? Where are they?*

- ❏ Put students in small groups to discuss the questions in the **Connecting to the Topic** section. (The photo is of an elderly man and a young boy in a garden. They are holding a carrot.)

- ❏ Read the Irish proverb aloud and ask students what they think it means.

- ❏ Put this sentence on the board: *An apple a day keeps the doctor away.* Ask students: *How is this American proverb similar to the Irish one? How is it different?*

- ❏ Put students in pairs and ask them to help each other think of proverbs (or other common pieces of advice) from their cultures that address simple ways to maintain good health.

- ❏ Call on pairs to report on their discussions to the whole class.

❝ A good laugh and a long sleep are the best cures in the doctor's book. ❞

—Irish proverb

Chapter Overview

Reading Skills and Strategies

Using headings to preview a reading passage

Recalling information

Paraphrasing main ideas

Understanding and analyzing points of view

Distinguishing between fact and opinion

Reading charts for specific information

Critical Thinking Skills

Using a graphic organizer (a continuum) to rank items

Taking a stand by agreeing or disagreeing

Analyzing points of view

Using a Venn diagram to compare answers from an interview

Reaching a group consensus and writing an opinion statement

Synthesizing Internet content: taking notes and presenting results

Structuring an argument to support an opinion in writing

Vocabulary Building

Getting the meaning from context

Recognizing synonyms

Scanning for vocabulary

Focusing on words from the Academic Word List

Focus on Testing

Analyzing compound words on vocabulary tests

Vocabulary

Nouns		Adjectives	Adverbs
affluence	monounsaturates	affluent	hence*
bargaining	natural resources*	annoyed	virtually*
begging	peasant	demanding	
benefit*	prosperity	eclectic	
cancer	requests	elite	
communities*	stinginess	enchanted	
compensation*	subculture	inappropriate*	
cuisine	tourists	indigenous	
diet	treats	inexpensive	
ecotourism		peasant	
fiber	**Verbs**	physical*	
frontiers	acquiring*	taboo	
grain	bargained	up-front	
heart disease	distinguish		
hippies	flock		
legumes	found (find)		
locals	prevent		

*These words are from the Academic Word List. For more information on this list, see www.vuw.ac.nz/lals/research/awl.

Eat Like a Peasant, *Feel* Like a King

Before You Read

Strategy

Using Headings to Preview

- Read the information in the Strategy Box and explain as needed.

- Ask students to flip through the chapter quickly and look at the headings. Call on volunteers to tell one of the headings they found. Write a couple of examples on the board and ask students whether they are meant to grab the reader's attention or provide the main idea.

1 Using Headings to Preview

- ❑ Read the directions and explain as needed.

- ❑ Have students identify the headings from the article and write them down.

- ❑ Go over the answers.

ANSWER KEY

1. Early Diets: Nuts and Plants, Why Socrates Loved Olive Oil 2. Early Diets: Nuts and Plants 3. Answers will vary.

2 Getting Meaning from Context

- ❑ Read the directions and explain as needed.

- ❑ Model the activity. Read the first question under *Getting Meaning from Context*. Ask a student to guess the meaning of the word *peasant* through its relation to the word *king*. Tell students to write the correct answer.

- ❑ Have students complete the activity independently.

- ❑ Go over the answers.

ANSWER KEY

Possible answers

It's the traditional cuisine of poor, agrarian countries.

If you eat a simple diet, you will feel great.

Read

Best Practice

Activating Prior Knowledge

Activities such as this will help students activate their prior knowledge about the topic of the reading passage. In this case, students are asked to think about and discuss what they already know about healthy eating habits and the diets of different cultures.

- ❑ Read the Introduction aloud or have a volunteer read it.

- ❑ Discuss the questions and any comments.

- ❑ Have students read the passage silently within a time limit (10 minutes).

Content Notes

- ■ Vegetarianism became popular in the United States in the 1960s, but it has been around for quite some time. Ancient Hindus and Buddhists, as well as followers of the Greek philosopher Pythagoras and Christian monks of the Renaissance era, have all been known to avoid eating the meat of other creatures for spiritual reasons.

- ■ Veganism is a term that was coined in 1944 by those who were frustrated, for various ethical reasons, by vegetarians who drank milk and ate other dairy products.

Consequently, it refers to a lifestyle in which no foods derived from animals are consumed and no products, like fur or leather, made from animals are used.

- The Slow Food Movement was started in Italy, in 1986, by Carlo Petrini. He became concerned that the same processed and fast foods sold the world over would kill many of the existing food traditions. Currently, the nonprofit organization Slow Food USA supports and celebrates American practices like Cajun cooking, the growing of heirloom varieties of fruits and vegetables, the organic raising of animal breeds, and handcrafting wine and beer.

- The Raw Foods Movement was inspired by the notion that our bodies are more suited for the digestion of raw, uncooked foods, as those our ancestors ate before the discovery of fire. It has become popular in recent years.

After You Read

3 Recalling Information

- ❏ Read the directions and explain as needed.
- ❏ Model the activity by completing the first item as a class.
- ❏ Have students complete the activity independently.
- ❏ Go over the answers.

ANSWER KEY

1. d 2. e 3. a 4. c 5. b

Strategy

Paraphrasing Main Ideas

- Read the information in the Strategy Box and explain as needed.

- Make sure students understand the difference between quoting directly and paraphrasing.

4 Paraphrasing Main Ideas

- ❏ Read the directions and explain as needed.
- ❏ Circulate among the groups and help students as needed
- ❏ Go over the answers.

ANSWER KEY

Answers may vary. Possible answers

1. (title) A sure way to feel healthy and energetic is by eating simple foods free of sugar and fat.
2. When people begin to make more money or gain exposure to different lifestyles they abandon traditional diets. Often this may lead to new illnesses.

Strategy

Recognizing Synonyms

- Read the information in the Strategy Box and explain as needed.

- Ask students to think of a pair of synonyms they know.

- Compile a short list on the board.

5 Recognizing Synonyms

- ❏ Read the directions and explain as needed
- ❏ Have students complete the activity on their own.
- ❏ Go over the answers.
- ❏ Check comprehension by asking students to use the words in new sentences.

ANSWER KEY

1. c 2. f 3. a 4. e 5. b 6. d

Strategy

Organizing Information Using a Continuum

- Read the information in the Strategy Box and explain as needed.

- Draw a sample of a continuum on the board.

- Ask students to think of things that can be rated on a continuum.

- Write their ideas on the board.

6 Ranking Foods on a Continuum

Best Practice

Organizing Information

Activities such as this will help students organize information from the reading passage so that they are better able to synthesize and recall it later. By placing common food items on the numbered list, or continuum, students will be able to remember ideas and details from the reading more easily.

- ❏ Put students in pairs.

- ❏ Read the directions and explain as needed.

- ❏ Ask students for adjectives that describe the foods listed in the vocabulary box (*fattening, natural, processed, etc.*) and write them on the board.

- ❏ Have students complete the activity in pairs, using the adjectives to discuss where each food item should be listed.

- ❏ Have students compare their answers.

EXPANSION ACTIVITY

- ▪ The aim of this activity is to have students create a continuum themselves based on their personal likes and dislikes of certain foods.

- ▪ Tell students they will practice organizing different foods on a continuum.

- ▪ Designate one end of the room as the "Dislike Very Much" side and the other as the "Like Very Much" side. Explain that all points in between vary from the two extremes.

- ▪ Tell students you will call out a food item and they need to line up along the continuum as to how much they like or dislike that food.

- ▪ For variation, have students state why they placed themselves where they did on the continuum.

- ▪ Discuss how the items on a continuum are not always equally distributed.

7 Take a Stand: Agree or Disagree?

Best Practice

Scaffolding Instruction

When students use their prior knowledge as a scaffold, they can better organize the new concepts presented to them. This activity will help students connect what they have already learned about healthy and unhealthy eating habits to the topics they choose to defend in their debates.

- ❏ Put students in small groups.

- ❏ Read the directions and explain as necessary.

- ❏ Remind students to be prepared to report their positions to the class.

8 Guided Academic Conversation

Best Practice

Interacting with Others

Activities such as this encourage collaborative interaction and authentic conversations. In this case, students are working together to create a TV add or a menu for a healthy restaurant.

❑ Read the directions and tasks.

❑ Put students in small groups and ask each group to choose one task.

❑ Have groups that chose #1 read their scripts to the rest of the class. Have groups that chose #2 present their menus.

Focus on Testing TOEFL® iBT

Analyzing Compound Words

■ Read the information in the Focus on Testing box and explain as needed.

■ Review the compound nouns studied in Chapter 1.

■ Give students time to complete the practice activities.

■ Go over the answers.

ANSWER KEY

1. B 2. D 3. C 4. D 5. C 6. C

9 **What Do You Think?**

❑ Read or ask a volunteer to read the paragraph aloud.

❑ Put students in small groups to discuss the questions that follow.

10 **Discussing Information from a Chart**

Best Practice

Cultivating Critical Thinking

Activity 10 provides an opportunity for students to reinterpret data from the chart, synthesize it, and apply it when answering the questions that follow. This type of activity requires students to process the

information they have read and express their own ideas and opinions about it.

❑ Ask students to look at the chart.

❑ Discuss the answers that follow as a class.

ANSWER KEY

1. Possible answers: Blood pressure drops, carbon monoxide level drops, chance of heart attack increases, circulation improves, lung function increases up to 30%.

Here Come the Tourists!

Before You Read

Strategy

Understanding Point of View

- Read the information in the Strategy Box and explain as needed.

- Tell students the next reading is about tourism and that they should try to pay attention to the writer's point of view.

1   Skimming for the Point of View

- Read the directions and explain as needed.

- Have students skim the reading on pages 93–94.

- Ask students which of the three points of view they think is expressed in the article.

ANSWER KEY

2

2   Analyzing the Point of View

- Put students in pairs.

- Read the directions and explain as needed.

3   Getting the Meaning of Words from Context

- Read the directions and model the activity by doing the first item as a class.

- Make sure students understand why "C" is the correct answer.

- Have students complete the activity.

- Go over answers.

ANSWER KEY

1. C   2. D   3. A, B   4. D   5. B   6. C , B   7. C , B

Read

- Read the Introduction aloud or ask a volunteer to read it. Explain as needed.

- Discuss the questions as a class.

Content Note

- The mission of the Rethinking Tourism project is to teach people about tourism and create a network of groups who support indigenous peoples. The projects aims to battle the environmental, cultural, social, and economic impacts of tourism that affect communities worldwide.

After You Read

Strategy

Distinguishing Between Fact and Opinion

- Read the information in the Strategy Box and explain as needed.

- Ask students to give examples of facts and opinions.

4   Distinguishing Between Fact and Opinion

- Read the directions and explain as needed.

- Make sure students understand the difference between *fact* and *opinion* statements.

- Have students complete the activity independently.

ANSWER KEY

1. F 2. F 3. O 4. O 5. O 6. F 7. F 8. O 9. F 10. F

 EXPANSION ACTIVITY

- The aim of this activity is to have students practice organize information according to whether it is a fact or an opinion.

- Copy and hand out Black Line Master **Fact and Opinion Organizer** (BLM 9).

- Explain that this chart will help them distinguish between facts and opinions and help them remember details from the reading.

- Assign students a letter: A, B, C, or D. Depending on their letter, that is the paragraph they should use to fill in their Fact and Opinion Organizer.

- After about 10 minutes, have students with the same paragraph assignment work together and compare answers.

5 **Scanning for Vocabulary**

- ❑ Read the directions and explain as needed.

- ❑ Tell students to complete this activity on their own.

- ❑ Review correct answers as a class.

- ❑ Check comprehension by asking students to use the words in new sentences.

ANSWER KEY

1. natural resources 2. enchanted
3. inappropriate 4. taboo 5. acquiring
6. flock 7. inexpensive 8. hippie 9. virtually
10. bargaining

6 **Focusing on Words from the Academic Word List**

- ❑ Read the directions and explain as needed.

- ❑ Tell students to complete this activity on their own.

- ❑ Go over the answers as a class.

- ❑ Check comprehension by asking students to use the words in new sentences.

ANSWER KEY

1. compensation 2. benefit 3. communities
4. physical 5. hence 6. found 7. acquiring

Strategy

Using a Venn Diagram to Compare and Contrast

- Read the information in the Strategy Box and explain as needed.

- Tell students to think of two items or ideas that they could compare in a Venn diagram. Answers will vary.

7 **Comparing and Contrasting with a Venn Diagram**

Best Practice

Organizing Information

Activities such as this will help students organize information from the reading passage so that they are better able to recall important information and talk about it in a logical way. In this case, students are using a Venn diagram to compare and contrast the attitudes and actions of tourists and locals.

- ❑ Read the directions and explain as needed.

❑ Have students scan the article to complete a Venn diagram that compares and contrasts tourists and locals.

❑ Put students in pairs to compare their diagrams.

❑ Go over the answers and have students be prepared to explain their choices.

ANSWER KEY

Possible answers: *Circle A*: annoyed, eager for adventure, believe they can contribute, take pictures, give away tokens *Circle B*: enchanted, skilled, playful, up-front, demanding, don't believe tourists can contribute, hate pictures, beg *Middle part C*: think money can help

 EXPANSION ACTIVITY

■ The aim of this activity is to have students compare and contrast their own travel experiences using a Venn diagram.

■ Photocopy and hand out the Black Line Master, **Venn Diagram: Comparing Travel Experiences** (BLM 10).

■ Ask students to take a couple of minutes to think about a place they have visited, preferably a place that is outside of their country.

■ Put students in pairs and tell them to share their travel experiences and impressions of the place they visited; the people who live there, their attitude towards tourists, and the impact they felt tourism had on the place and culture they visited. Tell them to use the questions above the Venn diagram on the Black Line master as a guide.

■ Tell students to fill out the differences and similarities between the two places based on their conversations.

■ Have each pair present their findings to the class.

8 Guided Academic Conversations

Best Practice

Making Use of Academic Content

Activities such as this will help students develop the ability to separate the ideas presented in the reading from their own ideas about it before they write an opinion statement. Coming to a consensus and writing an opinion statement is an assignment students may encounter in other academic classes.

❑ Put students in small groups. Read the directions and explain as needed.

❑ Have students discuss the first topic along with two others.

❑ Remind them they need to try to reach a group consensus on each topic.

❑ Call on groups to share their opinion statements.

9 Reading Charts

❑ Read the directions and explain as needed.

❑ Put students in small groups to discuss the charts and the questions that follow.

❑ Go over the answers as a class.

ANSWER KEY

1. They are the most popular tourist destinations, Europe, Answers will vary 2. Chart 1 lists the top 10 countries according to number of tourists that visit, Chart 2 lists the top ten countries based on the money the earn from tourism 3. The amount of vacation days people living in that country have each year, 29, answers will vary

1   End-of-Chapter Game Show

- ❑ Read the directions and explain as needed.
- ❑ Divide the class into two teams.
- ❑ Use the board to keep score.

EXPANSION ACTIVITY

- ■ The aim of this activity is to have students practice arguing the opposing side of a debate question.

- ■ Add a surprise bonus round to Activity 1 in which each team is asked to argue an opposing side of a debate question. This question should build on the factual knowledge the game show has already quizzed students on, but enable them to create a more sophisticated analysis.

- ■ Sample questions: *Are there more advantages or disadvantages to globalization? Can technology be used to protect culture instead of erase it?*

- ■ Have a small group of students serve as judges and give points for every valid argument. Whichever team has more points, wins.

2   Making Connections

- ❑ Read the directions and explain as needed.
- ❑ Tell them they will look up information on self-improvement fads inspired by international influences on American health and leisure activities.
- ❑ Allow students to choose their topics. Instruct them to look at websites on the Internet.
- ❑ Have students report their findings to the class.

ANSWER KEY

Answers will vary.

Responding in Writing

3   Writing a Paragraph that Expresses Your Opinion

- ❑ Draw students' attention to the Writing Tip and explain as needed.
- ❑ Put students in pairs.
- ❑ Go over the steps and directions and explain as needed.
- ❑ Circulate around the class to check on the progress of each pair.

Self-Assessment Log

- ❑ Encourage students to maintain a self-assessment log.
- ❑ Allow class time so students can check the strategies and vocabulary they learned in the chapter.
- ❑ Tell students to find definitions in the chapter for any words they did not check.

5

High Tech, Low Tech

In this chapter, students will focus on different types of technology. In the first reading, they will read about hybrid cars and discuss air pollution. Students will learn how to skim for the general ideas and specialized terms. In Part 2, students will read about "leapfroggers," communities which use information and communication technology that help them move from being agricultural economies to information ones. New vocabulary, reading strategies, and critical thinking will be brought together as students create a study outline, perform interviews, and incorporate ideas in speech and writing.

Chapter Opener

- ❏ Have students look at the photo and ask questions: *Who is the man in the photo? What do you think his occupation is?*

- ❏ Put students in groups and have them discuss the questions in the **Connecting to the Topic** section. (The photo is of a man at the beach. He is sitting under an umbrella with his laptop.)

- ❏ Read the quote aloud and ask students what they think it means.

- ❏ Lead the class in discussion and guide the conversation towards technology.

- ❏ Ask students: *What kinds of tools do we have today? What kinds of tools existed in Henry David Thoreau's time? Do you think that Thoreau liked technology?*

❝ Men [and women] have become tools of their tools. **❞**

—Henry David Thoreau, U.S. philosopher
and writer (1817–1862)

Chapter Overview

Reading Skills and Strategies

Skimming for the general idea

Scanning for definitions of key terms

Identifying the pattern of organization in a reading passage

Outlining the specific details from a reading passage

Analyzing the main point (thesis) of an article

Critical Thinking Skills

Filling out a chart for comparison

Comparing opinions

Choosing a favorite theme-related item and researching it

Creating a study outline

Interviewing and using a graphic organizer (Venn diagram) to compare answers

Synthesizing Internet content: taking notes and presenting results

Selecting strong examples to support a point of view in writing

Vocabulary Building

Inferring the meaning of expressions from context and vocabulary

Inferring the meanings of specialized terms

Understanding compound words

Analyzing compound adjectives with hyphens

Focusing on words from the Academic Word List

Focus on Testing

Using a computer effectively on tests

Vocabulary

Nouns

benefits*
best-case scenario
braking
components*
computers*
craftsmen
data*
economy*
exhaust (from a car)
four-cylinder engine
fuel tank
gas pump
generator
global warming
greenhouse effect
hybrid car

landmarks
leapfroggers
locomotives
marketplace
mileage
network*
propulsion power
rpm (rotations per minute)
scenario*
speeds
tailpipe emissions
telecenters (also spelled telecentres)
transmission*
vehicle*

Verbs

charge (batteries)
download
upload

Preposition

via*

Adjectives

efficient
English-speaking
global*
grassroots
handmade
Internet-enabled
Internet-linked
interwoven

knowledge-based
large-scale
medical*
parallel*
service-based
shocked
tech-savvy
twofold
well-educated
widespread*

Expression

on the block

*These words are from the Academic Word List. For more information on this list, see www.vuw.ac.nz/lals/research/awl.

How Hybrid Cars Work

Content Notes

- Henry David Thoreau probably used a pen and ink to write. The typewriter was not invented until 1873, 11 years after Thoreau's death.

- Even if the typewriter had existed, Thoreau would not have used one. Thoreau tried to champion nature and fought against materialism. His most famous book is *Walden*, which he wrote in 1854. In *Walden*, he describes the time he spent living alone with nature.

Before You Read

1 Skimming for the General Idea

- ❏ Direct students' attention to the Reading Tip in the margin. Review skimming if necessary.

- ❏ Read the directions and explain as needed. Remind students not to look up words in their dictionaries.

- ❏ Ask students to choose the best general idea.

- ❏ Go over the answers.

ANSWER KEY

b

Strategy

Scanning for Definitions of Key Terms

- Read the information in the Strategy Box and explain as needed.

- Tell students to take a minute to scan the article and pick one word that is new to them.

- Tell them to quickly scan the article to see if the definition is provided.

2 Scanning for Definitions of Key Terms

- ❏ Read the directions.

- ❏ Ask students to complete the activity on their own.

- ❏ Go over the answers.

ANSWER KEY

1. it combines two or more sources of power
2. a cross between a gasoline-powered car and an electric car

Strategy

Inferring Meaning

- Read the information in the Strategy Box and explain as needed.

- Define the difference between "words" and "expressions." Point out that "educated guess" is a synonym for "inference."

3 Inferring the Meaning of Expressions from Context and Vocabulary

- ❏ Read the directions and explain as needed. Ask students to select the best answer.

- ❏ Have students complete the activity independently.

- ❏ Discuss the answers as a class.

ANSWER KEY

1. C 2. A 3. C 4. A 5. B 6. A 7. B 8. B 9. A

Read

Best Practice

Best Practice

Activating Prior Knowledge

This Introduction to the reading and the questions that accompany it, give students an opportunity to activate their prior knowledge. In this case, students are asked about their thoughts on air pollution and the perfect car. The discussion questions require students to activate their knowledge on these two topics along with any related vocabulary they have acquired.

❑ Read the Introduction box aloud, or ask a volunteer to read it.

❑ Discuss the questions and any comments.

❑ Have students read "How Hybrid Cars Work" silently within a time limit (10 minutes).

Strategy

Learning Specialized Terms

■ Read the information in the Strategy Box and explain as needed.

■ Tell students to look back at the reading and choose one specialized term for this topic.

■ Compile a list on the board.

4 **Inferring the Meaning of Specialized Terms**

❑ Read the directions and model the activity by completing the first item as a class.

❑ Have students complete the activity independently.

❑ Go over the answers as a class.

ANSWER KEY

1. d 2. n 3. g 4. i 5. h 6. l 7. m 8. b 9. j 10. e
11. a 12. c 13. k 14. f

Best Practice

Scaffolding Instruction

When students use their prior knowledge as a scaffold, they are better able to organize their ideas about new concepts. The following Expansion Activity requires students to apply what they have already learned about the topic and about distinguishing between facts and opinions in order to complete and discuss the "Fact and Opinion Chart". In this case, students are dealing with facts and opinions about different types of cars.

 EXPANSION ACTIVITY

■ The aim of this activity is to practice organizing facts and opinions about the reading topic.

■ Copy and hand out Black Line Master **Fact and Opinion Chart** (BLM 11).

■ Tell students that completing a Fact and Opinion Chart, a type of graphic organizer, will help them separate ideas in the reading from their own thoughts. Define *fact* and *opinion* to make sure students are clear on the difference. Provide examples to clarify as needed, for example, "Exhaust causes the greenhouse effect." (fact) and "SUVs, sports utility vehicles, are unnecessary." (opinion).

■ Have students write five facts from the article, "How Hybrid Cars Work" in the "Fact" column of the chart. Then ask them to write their own opinion about each of the facts.

■ Allow time for students to share their facts and opinions.

ANSWER KEY

Answers will vary.

Strategy

Using a Graphic Organizer Chart for Comparison

- Read the information in the Strategy Box and explain as needed.
- Go over how to create a chart.
- Refer to the chart in Activity 5 as an example.

5 Filling Out a Chart for Comparison

Best Practice

Organizing Information

Activities such as this will help students organize information from the reading passage so that they are better able to comprehend it and recall it later. In this case, students are completing a chart according to the qualities of different types of cars.

- ❏ Put students in pairs.
- ❏ Read the directions and explain as needed.
- ❏ Have students complete the chart in pairs.
- ❏ Discuss the answers as a class.

ANSWER KEY

Quality	Gasoline Car	Electric Car	Parallel Hybrid	Series Hybrid
Has a fuel tank	X		X	
Has batteries to store energy		X	X	X
Can operate at speeds of up to 8,000 rpm			X	X
Has a range of 50–100 miles		X		
Runs only on electricity		X		

Has a generator				X
Has a four-cylinder engine	X			
Has both a four-cylinder engine and an electric motor.		X	X	X
Has a four-cylinder engine in the trunk (back) area		X		

Best Practice

Cultivating Critical Thinking

Activities such as the following Expansion Activity, "Automobile Survey," require students to use their critical thinking skills to synthesize the information they gather by interviewing a partner and reporting their findings in a clear and logical way.

 REPRODUCIBLE **EXPANSION ACTIVITY**

- The aim of this activity is to have students gather information through interviews and report on their findings.
- Copy and hand out Black Line Master, **Automobile Survey** (BLM 12).
- Have students interview five classmates using the chart provided in the Black Line Master to record their classmates' responses.
- Afterwards, have students report their findings. For example, *Four of the five students I interviewed chose their car based on the price.*

6 Talking It Over

❏ Put students in pairs. Read the instructions and explain as needed.

❏ Have students discuss the questions with their partners.

❏ After they finish, have students compare their answers with those of another pair.

7 Researching a Gadget

Vocabulary Note

■ If students aren't familiar with the technological gadgets named in this activity, allow time for them to do research on the Web. They should search image banks and online encyclopedias for pictures and descriptions.

❏ Read the directions and explain as needed.

❏ If your school has a computer lab, schedule class time for students to do Internet research. Otherwise, assign this activity as homework.

❏ Schedule time for students to present their gadgets to the class.

Leapfrogging the Technology Gap

Before You Read

Strategy

Identifying the Pattern of Organization in a Reading

- Read the information in the Strategy Box and explain as needed.
- Ask students to name professions in which writing has a structure.
- Review main points and specific details.

1 Identifying the Pattern of Organization

- ❏ Read the directions and answer the questions in the direction line as a class.
- ❏ Read the rest of the directions together and then have students complete the activity independently.
- ❏ Go over the answers as a class.

ANSWER KEY

Pattern 3.

2 Outlining the Specific Details

- ❏ Read the directions and explain as needed.
- ❏ Ask students to scan the article and identify the examples.
- ❏ Go over the answers.

ANSWER KEY

I. Rohib, Cambodia

II. Vietnam

III. Bangalore, India

IV. Bolivia

V. Nallavadu a village in Pondicherry, India

3 Analyzing the Main Point (Thesis) of an Article

- ❏ Define "thesis" as *an unproven opinion explained in detail and offered as a basis for discussion or argument.*
- ❏ Read the directions and explain as needed.
- ❏ Model the activity by completing the first item as a class. The two words making up the compound word are "leap" and "frog." The image of frogs jumping over wires represents an economy moving from being agricultural to information.
- ❏ Go over the answers.

ANSWER KEY

Possible answer: The image of the frog leaping over another represents how a community can go directly from being an agricultural to an information economy.

UNDERSTANDING COMPOUND WORDS

- Read the information in the instruction box and explain as needed.
- Ask students to call out compound words they think of. Answers will vary. Compile a list on the board.
- Review compound words on pages 11 and 88.

4 Understanding Compound Words

- ❏ Read the directions and explain as needed.
- ❏ Model the activity by completing the first item as a class.

❏ Go over the answers.

ANSWER KEY
1. A 2. C 3. B 4. B 5. A 6. C 7. A 8. C

Grammar Note
■ Most of the compound words in this activity are common and accepted as permanent. These "permanent" compounds can usually be found in the dictionary and they do not require hyphens.

EXPANSION ACTIVITY

■ The purpose of this activity is to have students increase their awareness of compound words and their meanings.

■ Ask students to choose an article on a topic that interests them and read it outside of class.

■ Tell them that as they read, they should look for compound words. They should break apart the words and/or use the context to help them figure out the meanings.

■ Tell them to write down the compound words along with a definition based on the context clues.

■ During the next class, put students in groups and have them teach each other the new compound words.

■ Call on students to present one or two of their new words to the class.

Read

❏ Read the Introduction aloud, or ask a volunteer to read it.

❏ Discuss the questions as a class.

❏ Have students read the passage within a time limit (10 minutes)

After You Read

Strategy

Creating a Study Outline
■ Read the information in the Strategy Box and explain as needed.

■ Review roman numerals if necessary.

■ Consider showing a sample of an outline to students.

Content Note
■ According the U.S. Bureau of Labor Statistics, there are over 396,000 computer programmers in the United States. Their average yearly salary is approximately $60,000. The state with the largest number of programmers is New Jersey.

5 Creating a Study Outline

Best Practice

Making Use of Academic Content
In Activity 5, students are creating an outline detailing the key topics and main ideas from the reading. This strategy will enable them to recall information later. Learning to create outlines is a strategy that students will find useful in a wide range of academic courses.

❏ Read the directions and have students complete the outline.

❏ Remind students that this is an independent activity.

❏ Go over the answers.

ANSWER KEY

I. Location: *Rohib, Cambodia*

   1. *Motorcycles are Internet-enabled. They carry information between remote villages and central computer hubs.*

II. Location: *Vietnam*

   1. *knowledge-based*

III. Location: Bangalore, India

   1. interlocking programming *shops*

   2. call *centers*

   3. *tech companies*

IV. Location: Bolivia

   1. *a rural radio station uses the Internet to research information*

V. Location: Nallavadu, a village in Pondicherry, India

   1. *village's telecentres*

   2. *used as a community alarm during the* tsunami *of 2004*

UNDERSTANDING COMPOUND ADJECTIVES

- Read the information in the instruction note and explain as needed.

- Ask students to take a minute to scan the reading and find examples of compound adjectives.

- Make a list on the board.

6 Analyzing Compound Adjectives with Hyphens

- ❏ Read the directions and explain as needed.

- ❏ Model the activity and do the first item as a class.

- ❏ Have students complete the activity independently.

- ❏ Go over the answers.

ANSWER KEY

Possible answers: 1. motorcycles that can access the Internet 2. an economy based on services rather than goods 3. factories that produce goods on a large scale, in large quantities 4. an economy that is based on information and/or knowledge 5. the best course of action possible 6. people who have a high-level of education; programmers who know a lot about technology; People who speak English 7. people with a high level of education, who know a lot about technology and speak English 8. a center where communication is connected to the Internet

7 Focusing on Words from the Academic Word List

- ❏ Read the directions and explain as needed.

- ❏ Have students complete the activity independently.

- ❏ Have students refer back to the reading passage to check their answers.

- ❏ Go over the answers as a class.

- ❏ Check comprehension by asking students to use words in new sentences.

ANSWER KEY

1. medical 2. economy 3. global 4. benefits 5. via 6. network 7. computers 8. vehicle 9. data 10. data 11. transmission

Talking It Over

8 Discussing Information Technology

- ❏ Put students in small groups to discuss the questions.

❑ After they have finished, have them compare
    their answers with those of another group.

❑ Call on students to share their answers.

9 What Do You Think?

❑ Put students in small groups.

❑ Ask them to read the short paragraph called
    "Using Cellular Phones" and discuss the
    answers that follow.

❑ Call on groups to share their answers with the
    class.

1 Guided Academic Conversation

- ❑ Direct students' attention to the *Culture Note* about *blogs* in the margin of page 123.

- ❑ Go over the directions and steps and explain as needed.

- ❑ Put students in pairs to complete the interviews.

EXPANSION ACTIVITY

- ▪ The purpose of this activity is to provide students with additional topic-related research practice.

- ▪ Photocopy and hand out the Black Line Master *Blog* **Research Chart** (BLM 13)

- ▪ Tell students that they are going to research a blog on a topic that interests them, such as a hobby, sport, place of interest, etc.

- ▪ Tell them they can type in "*blog search*" in the search engine to find *blogs* on various topics.

- ▪ Tell them to fill out the chart from the Black Line Master as they do their research.

- ▪ Allow time during the next class for students to present their *blogs*.

2 Making Connections

- ❑ Read the instructions and explain as needed.

- ❑ Tell students to select a topic to research on the Internet.

- ❑ If you have access to a computer lab, schedule this as a lab activity. Otherwise, assign it as homework.

Responding in Writing

SELECTING STRONG EXAMPLES TO SUPPORT YOUR POINT OF VIEW

- ▪ Read the Writing Tip and explain as needed.

- ▪ Ask students whether they feel technology has had a positive or negative impact on modern society.

- ▪ Ask students to think of a strong example to support their opinion.

3 Writing about Technology

- ❑ Go over the directions and the steps and explain as needed.

- ❑ Have students complete the writing task independently.

Focus on Testing

- ▪ Present the information in the Focus on Testing Box and explain as needed.

- ▪ Allow time for students to complete the practice activities.

- ▪ Go over the answers.

ANSWER KEY

1. mouse 2. adaptive 3. linear 4. table
5. directions 6. drag and drop
7. glossary 8. timer 9. notepaper

Self-Assessment Log

❑ Encourage students to maintain a self-assessment log.

❑ Allow class time so students can check the strategies and vocabulary they learned in the chapter.

❑ Tell students to find definitions in the chapter for any words they did not check.

6

Money Matters

In this chapter, students will focus on financial matters in both business and in personal situations. In the first reading, they will learn about a small business in Spain that grew into a global success. Students will learn how to scan for specific information and recognize word families. In Part 2, students will read a short story by William Somerset Maugham that focuses on the embarrassment that a lack of money can cause in a social situation. New vocabulary, reading strategies, and critical thinking will be brought together as students research, discuss, and diagram their ideas.

Chapter Opener

- ❏ Draw students' attention to the photograph and ask questions. *Look at the woman in the photo. Who do you think she is? What do you think she does for work?*

- ❏ Put students in groups and have them discuss the questions in the **Connecting to the Topic** section. (The photo is of a woman riding in the back of a limo with her poddle—surrounded by shopping bags.)

- ❏ Read the Arabic proverb aloud and ask students what they think it means.

- ❏ Ask students: *Does the Arabic proverb mean that it is okay to not have much money? How much money do you need to survive? How much money do you need to buy something you want?*

- ❏ Put students in groups and ask them to discuss any proverbs about money from their own culture.

❝ One coin in an empty moneybox makes more noise than when it is full. **❞**

—Arabic proverb

Chapter Overview

Reading Skills and Strategies

Scanning for specific information

Checking comprehension by answering multiple choice questions

Identifying the characters, setting, and conflict in a narrative

Predicting events in a narrative

Using a timeline to recall the series of events in a plot

Critical Thinking Skills

Comparing opinions

Synthesizing Internet Content: Taking notes and presenting results

Analyzing the actions and outcomes of a situation and presenting an alternative solution through a skit

Solving problems related to the theme

Using a cluster diagram to help organize ideas for a writing task

Vocabulary Building

Recognizing word families

Getting the meaning of words from context

Focusing on words from the Academic Word List

Focus on Testing

Reading between the lines on reading comprehension tests

Vocabulary

Nouns		Adjectives	Adverb
boom	pizzeria	affordable	absentmindedly
chain (as in a group of similar businesses)	projected sales	amicable	
	specialties	effusive	
convenience	untapped market	enormous*	
drama*		imposing*	
executive	**Verbs**	inadequate*	
franchises	anticipated*	inclined*	
globalization*	flattered	marketing	
growth markets	found* (find)	mortifying	
management	maturing*	multinational	
mentality*	modernizing	succulent	
outlets (as in individual businesses in a chain)	prospered	vindictive	
	startled		
	transform*		

*These words are from the Academic Word List. For more information on this list, see www.vuw.ac.nz/lals/research/awl.

Executive Takes Chance on Pizza, Transforms Spain

Before You Read

Strategy

Previewing a Reading

■ Read the information in the Strategy Box, and explain as needed.

■ Ask the students to look at the title and state what they think the general idea of the reading will be.

■ Answers may vary. Possible answers may include *Businessman starts pizza business, Executive opens pizzeria, New pizza restaurant in Spain*.

1 **Scanning for Specific Information**

❑ Read the directions and focus students' attention on the title again.

❑ Give students one minute to scan the reading.

❑ Have students answer the questions independently.

❑ Put students in small groups or pairs to compare answers.

ANSWER KEY

Possible answers: 1. Leopoldo Fernandez
2. decides to try something new 3. modernizes, adds convenience, Answers will vary.

Strategy

Recognizing Word Families

■ Read the information in the Strategy Box, and explain as needed.

■ Look at the examples *provided*, *combine*, *combined*, and *combination*.

■ Point out the word *transform* from Activity 1. Ask students if they know the noun form of the word (transformation).

2 **Recognizing Word Families**

❑ Read the directions, and explain as needed.

❑ Ask the students to fill in the related words from the reading.

❑ Go over the answers as a class.

ANSWER KEY

1. globalization 2. pizzeria 3. convenience
4. modernizing 5. management 6. prospered
7. specialties 8. affordable 9. mentality
10. maturing

Grammar Notes

Certain suffixes always make words the same part of speech. The suffixes -**ance/-ence**, -**hood**, -**ity**, -**ment**, -**ness**, -**ship**, and -**tion/-sion** all change words to nouns. The new words are in the same family but are different parts of speech.

■ -**ance/-ence** changes adjectives (and sometimes verbs) into nouns: *silent/silence, appear/appearance*

■ -**hood** changes nouns into other forms of nouns: *child/childhood*

■ -**ity** changes adjectives into nouns: *possible/possibility*

■ -**ment** changes verbs (and sometimes adjectives) into nouns: *enjoy/enjoyment, merry/merriment*

■ -**ness** changes adjectives into nouns: *open/openness* (noun).

■ -**ship** changes nouns into other forms of nouns: *friend/friendship*

■ **-tion/-sion** changes verbs into nouns: *describe/description, decide/decision*

Students should notice that sometimes other changes are made to the root word before the suffix is added.

Best Practice

Organizing Information

The following Expansion Activity gets students to use a cluster diagram to help them organize and build vocabulary. This activity requires students to reflect on what they have learned about word families and apply it as they complete their cluster diagrams.

 EXPANSION ACTIVITY

■ The aim of this activity is to have students practice noun suffixes.

■ Copy and hand out Black Line Master **Noun Suffix Clusters** (BLM 14).

■ Explain that students should fill each center circle with a common noun suffix. Ask them to think of suffixes that have not been covered in class, or use these suffixes: **-tion/-sion, -ment, -ity**. Write the suffixes on the board.

■ Allow enough time for students to complete each cluster by filling in the smaller circles with root words that take the noun suffix.

■ Go over answers and have students share clusters.

Read

❑ Read the Introduction aloud or ask a volunteer to read it.

❑ Discuss the questions as a class.

❑ Have students read the passage silently within a time limit (10 minutes).

Content Note

■ In the United States, Pizza Hut started small, just as TelePizza did. It has often been named the Best Pizza Chain in America as voted by consumers. Two brothers and their mother turned just $600 into the world's largest pizza company. They opened the first Pizza Hut in Wichita, Kansas.

After You Read

3 **Getting the Meaning of Words from Context**

❑ Read the directions and model the activity by doing the first item as a class.

❑ Have students complete the activity on their own.

❑ Discuss the answers as a class.

ANSWER KEY

1. promoting the buying and selling of products
2. used in and/or existing in many nations or countries 3. estimated sales 4. outlets 5. a company with many stores selling the same product 6. a quick and significant increase 7. a part of the business that has not been explored yet 8. chains that are owned by individuals 9. a market that has potential to grow

Best Practice

Scaffolding Instruction

The following Expansion Activity gets students to draw on what they learned from the reading passage and combine that with their own ideas and experiences in order to come up with a marketing plan. When students use their prior knowledge as a scaffold, they are better able to organize their ideas and apply them to new concepts.

EXPANSION ACTIVITY

- The aim of this activity is to have students create a mini marketing plan for their own pizza company.

- Tell students they will start their own pizzeria.

- Copy and hand out Black Line Master **Pizzeria Marketing Plan Outline** (BLM 15).

- Put students into small groups and tell them they've been given enough money to open their own restaurants.

- Allow them enough time to prepare a marketing presentation for the other groups. Consider bringing in a sample marketing plan from a local restaurant.

- Tell students their presentations should be approximately 5–10 minutes in length and include the name of their pizzeria, the kinds of pizza and services they will offer, menu costs, décor of the restaurant, and what makes them different from all the other pizzerias in town.

- Have each group present their marketing plan to the class.

4 Checking Your Comprehension

- ❏ Read the directions.

- ❏ Have students complete the activity on their own.

- ❏ Go over the answers as a class.

ANSWER KEY

1. B 2. C 3. A 4. C 5. B 6. C

5 Guided Academic Conversation: Globalization and How It Affects Us

Best Practice

Interacting with Others

Activities that involve group discussions give students an opportunity to practice expressing their ideas about different topics while increasing their listening and speaking fluency. In this case, students are discussing issues having to do with fast food, chain stores, and owning one's own business.

- ❏ Put students in small groups and read the directions.

- ❏ Have them discuss the issues in their groups.

- ❏ After they have finished, have each group join another group to compare their answers.

6 Making Connections

- ❏ Read the directions, and explain as needed.

- ❏ Have students look up "TelePizza" on the Internet or at the library.

- ❏ If your program has a computer lab, you can schedule class time for students to do Internet research, or you can assign this activity as homework.

- ❏ Ask students to answer the questions in the student book and prepare their answers in a 3–5 minute presentation.

- ❏ Schedule time for students to report their findings during the next class.

Focus on Testing TOEFL® iBT

Reading Between the Lines

- Read the information in the Focus on Testing box, and explain as needed.

- Have students work independently to read the passages and select the best answers.

- Go over the answers.

ANSWER KEY

1. C 2. D 3. B

7 What Do You Think?

❏ Put students in groups. Read the directions.

❏ Allow time for students to read the paragraph and answer the questions.

❏ Discuss the answers as a class.

The Luncheon

Before You Read

Strategy

Identifying the Setting, Characters, and Conflict in a Narrative

- Read the information in the Strategy Box, and explain as needed.

- Ask students to name the setting, characters, or plots in a favorite story.

1 **Identifying the Setting, Characters, and Conflict**

❏ Read the directions.

❏ Give students time to skim the first few paragraphs of the reading and answer the questions.

❏ Go over the answers.

ANSWER KEY

Possible answers: 1. in the 1930s, Paris
2. a writer, a woman
Woman: wealthy, forty, imposing, talkative
3. the restaurant is more expensive than main narrator can afford

2 **Getting the Meaning of Words from Context**

❏ Read the directions.

❏ Model the activity by looking at the first adjective and the answer.

❏ Have students finish the other questions.

❏ Go over the answers.

ANSWER KEY

1. B 2. A 3. B 4. A 5. C 6. A 7. C 8. B 9. B 10. C

Read

Strategy

Predicting Events in a Narrative

- Read the information in the Strategy Box, and explain as needed.

- Ask students to talk about movies they have seen or stories they have read which had endings that surprised them.

3 **Predicting Events in a Narrative**

❏ Read the directions.

❏ Have students make a prediction about the story based on the first few paragraphs they skimmed for Activity 2 (pages 139–141).

❏ List students' predictions on the board and revisit them after they have finished reading.

ANSWER KEY

Answers will vary.

REPRODUCIBLE **EXPANSION ACTIVITY**

- The aim of this activity is to have students practice making predictions about their own futures.

- Prepare note cards for the students from the Black Line Master **Futures** (BLM 16).

- Tell students they will now have a chance to predict their own futures.

- Hand out one index card to each student.

- Explain to students that they should predict where they think they will be in one year.

- Collect the cards and read them out loud.

- Distribute another set of cards but this time ask students to predict where they will be in 5 years. (You can vary this activity by changing the number of years.)

- Read the cards out loud without reading the students' names. Ask other students to guess whose prediction each is.

- Distribute the cards that ask them to predict where they will be in 10 years and repeat.

Introduction

- ❏ Now read the Introduction aloud or ask a student to read it.

- ❏ Discuss the questions in the Introduction as a class.

- ❏ Have students read the story within a time limit (15–20 minutes).

Vocabulary Note

- This is a lengthy reading with a great deal of vocabulary. Remind students they will not need to understand every word in order to understand the story. Although essential vocabulary is taught in the pre-reading, consider taking additional time after the reading to go over additional new vocabulary words.

Content Note

- The Latin Quarter is a historic Paris neighborhood. It is home to some of Paris' most famous monuments. The streets are narrow and it is this quarter where a tourist can find typical Parisian cafés, lots of students, bars, restaurants, and theaters.

EXPANSION ACTIVITY

- The aim of this activity is to give students additional practice with new vocabulary words.

- Distribute index cards or small pieces of paper to students.

- On the card or paper, students should write a word from the short story that is new to them. Let them know they should choose a word that has not been covered in class or in a previous activity.

- On the other side, students should write a definition of the unknown word based on its context.

- Collect the cards and go over them with the rest of the class.

- Encourage students to make a set of cards with words that are important to them.

After You Read

UNDERSTANDING THE PLOT: RECALLING THE SERIES OF EVENTS

- Read the information in the instruction note and explain as needed.

- Ensure that students understand the terms *plot*, *framework tale*, and *flashback*. Students should know that *plot* is the series of events, *framework tale* is a story inside another story, and *flashback* is a tool used to describe an event that happened before this point in the story.

---

4 Understanding the Plot: Recalling the Series of Events

❑ Point out the Reading Tip in the margin.

❑ Read the directions and have students complete the diagram.

❑ Have students complete the activity independently.

❑ Go over the answers.

ANSWER KEY

E, D, G, H, B, F, A, C

5 Focusing on Words from the Academic Word List

❑ Read the directions, and explain as needed.

❑ Tell students to complete this activity on their own.

❑ Have students refer back to the reading passage to check their answers.

❑ Go over the answers as a class.

❑ Check comprehension by asking students to use the words in new sentences.

ANSWER KEY

1. imposing 2. inclined 3. anticipated
4. enormous 5. drama 6. found 7. inadequate

Guided Academic Conversation

6 Creating a Skit

❑ Put students in pairs. If possible, pairs should be one female and one male.

❑ Have students read the question and write a dialogue to illustrate what the man might have said.

❑ Have each pair perform their skit for another pair.

❑ Discuss the various solutions as a class.

ANSWER KEY

Answers will vary.

7 Solving problems

Best Practice

Cultivating Critical Thinking

This type of discussion activity requires students to use critical thinking skills such as inferring meaning, hypothesizing, analyzing, and drawing conclusions.

❑ Put students into groups of four.

❑ Ask them to discuss the list of questions.

❑ Tell students that they will present the rule they develop in question 5 to the class.

❑ Have the class vote on which group developed the best rule.

1   Making Connections

- ❏ Read the paragraph in the box and the directions, and have students choose one of the topics to research on the Internet.

- ❏ If your program has a computer lab, you can schedule class time for students to do Internet research, or you can assign this activity as homework.

- ❏ Schedule time during the next class for presentations.

Responding in Writing

WRITING TIP: MAKING A CLUSTER DIAGRAM

- ■ Read the Writing Tip, and explain as needed.

- ■ Tell students to think of a successful entrepreneur, such as Bill Gates.

2   Using a Cluster Diagram to Organize Ideas and Write a Paragraph

Best Practice

Making Use of Academic Content

This activity requires students to go through the various steps of the process involved in writing a well-organized paragraph. By completing the steps in this activity, students practice some of the strategies that will help prepare them with the types of writing assignments they will encounter in a variety of academic contexts.

- ❏ Read the directions and the quotes, and go over the steps in the activity.

- ❏ Have students complete the activity on their own.

Self-Assessment Log

- ❏ Encourage students to maintain a self-assessment log.

- ❏ Allow class time so students can check and review the strategies and vocabulary they learned in the chapter.

- ❏ Tell students to find definitions in the chapter for any words they did not check.

7

Remarkable Individuals

In this chapter, students will focus on the qualities that make people remarkable. In the first reading, they will learn about Confucius, who has had a profound influence on society for over 2,500 years. Students will learn how to skim for the general idea and figure out words from structure clues. In Part 2, students will read about five heroes who are courageous enough to fight for the rights and dignity of the oppressed. Students will learn that heroes come from all continents and backgrounds. New vocabulary, reading strategies, and critical thinking will help students research, discuss, and organize their ideas.

Chapter Opener

❏ Direct students' attention to the photo and ask questions. *Who are these people? What are they doing?*

❏ Call on students to share their answers with the class.

❏ Put students in small groups to discuss the questions in the **Connecting to the Topic** section. (The photo is of an elderly volunteer tutoring a young girl in math.)

❏ Read the Russian proverb aloud and ask students what they think it means.

❝ A good reputation sits still; a bad one runs about. ❞

—Russian proverb

Chapter Overview

Reading Skills and Strategies

Skimming for the general idea

Identifying key terms

Previewing to determine organization

Identifying the voices in a reading

Critical Thinking Skills

Supporting or disproving a general statement
with facts

Expressing an opinion

Using a graphic organizer (a continuum) to rank leaders

Comparing ideas

Synthesizing Internet content: taking notes and
presenting results

Using a Venn diagram to compare and contrast two
topics in writing

Vocabulary Building

Figuring out meaning from structure clues: compound
words, prefixes, and suffixes

Forming new words from the same word family

Matching words to their definitions

Using expressive synonyms

Creating new words using noun suffixes

Focusing on words from the Academic Word List

Focus on Testing

Understanding sentence-insertion questions on tests
(Reading: The Most Dangerous Jobs in the U.S.)

Vocabulary

Nouns		Verbs	Adjectives
assistance*	innovator*	atone	benevolent
atrocities	investment*	conduct*	civil*
background	lament	eradicate	compelling
childhood	negotiations	founded*	Confucian
commitment*	notions*	modernize	depressed*
commoners	obstacles	monitors*	diligent
cornerstones	outlook	permeated	enduring
decisions	perception*	reared	governmental
defender	preparation	resigned	Influentlal
demilitarization	prestige	sacrifice	medical*
dynasty	principality	seized	overwhelming
eloquence	promotion*	strive	philosophical*
energy*	repression	suppress	political
etiquette	responsibility		
expression	role*	**Adverbs**	**Expression**
(the) Golden Rule	servitude	easily	take up the torch
holocaust	tyranny	primarily*	
	valor		
	violations*		

*These words are from the Academic Word List. For more information on this list,
see www.vuw.ac.nz/lals/research/awl.

Confucius, 551 B.C.E.–479 B.C.E

Before You Read

1 Skimming for the General Idea

- ❑ Go over the directions.

- ❑ Review the reading Strategy Box for skimming covered on page 58.

- ❑ Tell students to skim the reading and circle the best general idea of the reading.

- ❑ Take a vote, by show of hands, to see which statement students feel best expresses the overall idea of the reading.

- ❑ Have students state why they chose the statements they did.

ANSWER KEY

C

Strategy

Figuring Out Words from Structure Clues

- ■ Read the information in the Strategy Box, and explain as needed.

- ■ Review compound words and suffixes as needed.

- ■ Look at the examples provided in the box and ask students if they can think of any other examples of words like these. Provide a couple of examples, such as *headache*, *basketball*, and so on, to help them.

2 Figuring Out Words from Structure Clues

Best Practice

Activating Prior Knowledge

Activity 2 asks students to draw on the vocabulary they already know in order to figure out the meanings of compound words. By drawing on the vocabulary they already know, students are better able to figure out new words and read more fluently.

- ❑ Read the directions and do the first item as a class.

- ❑ Ask the students to complete the activity independently.

- ❑ Call on students to share their answers.

ANSWER KEY

Possible answers: 1. the shared condition of being children 2. a person's past, things someone has done in the past 3. land ruled by a prince 4. the main ideas that support a philosphy 5. someone who wishes to do good 6. someone who defends 7. view of things/the way someone sees things 8. one who starts new things 9. People who are common, not rich

Grammar Notes

Certain suffixes always make words the same part of speech. Refer to the Grammar Notes on noun suffixes in Chapter 6. Some suffixes are common adjective endings; **-able**, **-al**, **-en**, **-ful**, **-ic**, **-ive**, **-less**, **-ous**, and **-y**, all convert words into adjectives. The new words are in the same family but are different parts of speech.

- ■ **-able** changes verbs or nouns into adjectives: *like/likeable, pleasure/pleasurable*

- ■ **-al** changes nouns into adjectives: *finance/financial*

- ■ **-en** changes nouns into adjectives: *wood/wooden*

- ■ **-ful** changes nouns into adjectives: *beauty/beautiful*

- **-ic** changes nouns into adjectives: *scene/ scenic*

- **-ive** changes verbs into adjectives: *select/ selective*

- **-less** changes nouns into adjectives: *power/ powerless*

- **-ous** changes nouns into adjectives: *fame/ famous*

- **-y** changes nouns into adjectives: *rain/rainy*

Students should be made aware that sometimes other changes are made to the root word before the suffix is added. See the following vocabulary note.

Vocabulary Notes

Adding prefixes and suffixes can affect the spelling. Some common ideas to share with students include:

- Most prefixes do not alter the spelling of the word; the prefix can simply be added. Some exceptions are **ad-**, **com-**, and **in-**. For example, *legal* becomes *illegal* instead of *inlegal*. The last letter in the prefix changes to match the beginning consonant of the root.

- If a one-syllable root ends in a vowel and a consonant, double the final consonant before adding a suffix that begins with a vowel. For example, *run* becomes *running*.

Read

- Read the Introduction aloud or have a volunteer read it.

- Discuss the questions as a class.

- Have students read the passage silently within a time limit (10 minutes).

Content Notes

- Confucius's books have sold over 18 million copies in China.

- Shih Huang Ti was the first emperor in China. He founded the Chin dynasty from which China's name is taken. Although many good things happened during his reign (a network of roads was built, units of weights and coins were standardized), a lot of bad things also happened during his reign. For example, books that did not conform to Chin philosophy were burned and scholars who conformed to more traditional beliefs were buried alive. The dynasty collapsed four years after his death.

After You Read

3 Identifying Key Terms

- Model the activity by doing item 1, *The Analects* and ask students to choose the best match. Allow them to scan the reading to read the term in context.

- Have students complete the activity individually.

- Discuss the answers as a class. Check for comprehension by having students write sentences using the vocabulary.

ANSWER KEY:

1. c 2. g 3. d 4. b 5. f 6. e

Best Practice

Scaffolding Instruction

The following Expansion Activity, gets students to rely on their own experiences and use new vocabulary learned in this chapter in order to express their own philosophies. This activity and the discussion it promotes allows students to synthesize the material they have learned thus far in the chapter.

EXPANSION ACTIVITY

- The aim of this activity is to promote theme-based group discussions
- Copy and hand out Black Line Master, **Confucious Says, We Say** (BLM 17).
- Tell students they will have a chance to state their own philosophies.
- Put students into small groups of four. Encourage them to discuss what Confucius's philosophies (listed in the left column) mean to them.
- Then have the groups write their own philosophies in the right column and present them to the other groups.

4 **Forming New Words from the Same Word Family**

- ❑ Read the directions and discuss the answer for item 1.
- ❑ Have students complete the rest of the activity.
- ❑ Move around the classroom to ensure that students are following the instructions.
- ❑ Go over the answers.

ANSWER KEY

1. enduring 2. influential 3. easily 4. political
5. primarily 6. governmental 7. Confucian
8. philosophical 9. modernize

Best Practice

Organizing Information

Activities such as the following Expansion Activity will help students organize information they have learned in a visual way so they can better comprehend it. By having students write the information in a cluster diagram, students will not only be able to remember ideas from the reading but will also be able to apply their critical thinking skills as they categorize and organize information.

 EXPANSION ACTIVITY

- The aim of this activity is to provide practice with word families.
- Copy and hand out Black Line Master **Word Family Charts** (BLM 18).
- Explain that students should fill out a chart for root words and change the prefixes and suffixes to create several words from the same family.
- Go over the answers for the chart that is started for them on the worksheet.
- Challenge them to create two more charts on their own.
- Go over the answers and have students share their charts.

5 **Matching Words to Their Definitions**

Best Practice

Cultivating Critical Thinking

Vocabulary activities such as this one require students to apply their critical thinking skills in order to infer the meanings of vocabulary words they are not sure about. In this case, students need to scan the reading for the words they are not sure about and use the context to help infer their meanings. This activity teaches students to use a strategy that they can apply to a broad range of contexts, both inside and outside of the classroom.

- ❑ Read the directions and model the activity by doing the first item as a class.
- ❑ Have students complete the activity independently.
- ❑ Go over the answers.

ANSWER KEY

1. j 2. e 3. n 4. a 5. h 6. l 7. k 8. o 9. c 10. f
11. m 12. b 13. g 14. i 15. d

EXPANSION ACTIVITY

- The aim of this activity is to practice new vocabulary items.

- Tell students they will write a vocabulary quiz for the class.

- Have students choose three words from Activity 5 on page 158.

- For each word, ask them to write a sentence using the word in context. Tell them to make sure the context adequately conveys the word's meaning.

- Each student should write one of their sentences on the board and draw a blank line indicating where the vocabulary word should go.

- Have students copy the sentences from the board and fill in the blanks. They should be able to choose the correct vocabulary word based on the context of the sentence.

Strategy

Finding Facts to Support or Disprove General Statements

- Read the information in the Strategy Box, and explain as needed.

- Ask students to define "fact." Give the example *Earth is the third planet from the sun.*

- Ask the difference between "fact" and "opinion."

6 **Finding Facts to Support or Disprove General Statements**

- ❏ Put students in small groups and read the directions.

- ❏ Have them discuss the statements and decide whether or not they are true or false.

- ❏ When they have finished, have them compare their ideas with those of another group.

ANSWER KEY

1. T, He was reared in poverty and had no formal education.
2. F, Through diligent study, he educated himself and became a learned man.
3. T, For two thousand years his concept of government, and his ideas about personal conduct and morality permeated Chinese life and culture. Even today, his thoughts remain influential.
4. T, He was the first major philosopher to state the Golden Rule, "Do not do unto others that which you would not have them do unto you."

7 **Guided Academic Conversation**

- ❏ Put students into small groups to discuss the questions.

- ❏ Call on students to share their answers and drawings with the class.

ANSWER KEY

Answers will vary.

What Do You Think?

8 **Rating Leaders**

Best Practice

Making Use of Academic Content

Activities such as this help students develop and practice research skills. Learning how to do effective, accurate research is a valuable skill that students will find applicable in a variety of academic and professional contexts.

- ❏ Read the directions and prepare students for research.

❑ Schedule time in the school's computer lab for this activity or assign it as homework.

❑ Schedule time during the next class for students to share their information on the leaders they researched.

9 Rating Leaders Using a Continuum Graph

Best Practice

Organizing Information

Rating information on a continuum graph helps students grasp concepts and organize them in a format that will allow them to process and recall the information they have learned more easily.

❑ Read the directions, and explain as necessary.

❑ Compile a list of the leaders students researched for Activity 8.

❑ As a class, place the leaders on a continuum according to how much harm or good the class thinks they have done. Try to reach as much of a consensus as possible.

❑ Discuss the questions that follow the continuum graph.

Courage Begins with one Voice

Before You Read

1   Previewing to Determine Organization

- ❑ Direct students' attention to the information in the Reading Tip in the margin. Explain as needed.

- ❑ Read the directions and the three patterns of organization, and explain as needed.

- ❑ Give students time to skim the article and decide which pattern is used.

- ❑ Take a vote to see which pattern was chosen by the most students.

- ❑ Give them the right answer and discuss why this is the best choice.

ANSWER KEY

2

2   Using Expressive Synonyms

- ❑ Read the directions.

- ❑ Model the activity by completing the first item as a class.

- ❑ Have students complete the rest of the activity independently.

- ❑ Go over the answers.

ANSWER KEY

1. lament   2. eloquence   3. valor   4. overwhelming
5. take up the torch   6. atrocities   7. compelling
8. sacrifice   9. monitors   10. obstacles
11. conduct   12. atone

Read

- ❑ Read the Introduction aloud or have a volunteer read it.

- ❑ Discuss the questions as a class.

- ❑ Allow students 10 minutes to read the passage.

Content Note

- ■ Kerry Kennedy is a member of the famous American Kennedy family. Her uncle was President John F. Kennedy and her father was presidential hopeful Robert F. Kennedy. She was born September 8, 1959 and attended Brown University and Boston College Law School before marrying Andrew Cuomo, who is a member of another famous American political family. They have since separated and divorced. Kerry Kennedy founded The Robert F. Kennedy Memorial Center for Human Rights for which she led a delegation to Liberia in 1994. She currently serves on the Board of Directors for The Robert F. Kennedy Memorial.

After You Read

IDENTIFYING THE VOICES IN A READING

- ■ Read the information in the instruction note and explain as needed.

- ■ Tell students they can identify what words are direct quotes by the author's use of quotation marks.

- ■ Give students 1–2 minutes to skim the reading and find an example of a direct quote.

- ■ Call on a few students to read the quotations they found.

3   Identifying the Voices

- ❑ Read the directions, and explain as needed

- ❑ Have students complete the activity independently.

- ❑ Go over the answers.

ANSWER KEY

1. d 2. a 3. b 4. e 5. c

USING NOUN SUFFIXES TO CREATE NEW WORDS

- ■ Read the information in the instruction note and explain as needed.

- ■ Remind students that they should study their notes about suffixes from Chapter 6 and from Part 1 of Chapter 7.

- ■ Ask students to think of a new word for each of the suffixes listed. Answers will vary.

- ■ Compile a list on the board.

---

4 Using Noun Suffixes to Create New Words

- ❑ Read the directions and model the activity by completing the first item as a class.

- ❑ Have students complete the rest of the activity independently.

- ❑ Go over the answers.

ANSWER KEY

1. perception 2. expression 3. commitment
4. repression 5. responsibility 6. assistance
7. negotiations 8. preparations 9. demilitarization
10. investments 11. decisions 12. servitude

5 Focusing on Words from the Academic Word List

- ❑ Read the directions and direct students' attention to the words in the vocabulary box.

- ❑ Have students complete the activity independently.

- ❑ Review correct answers as a class.

- ❑ Check comprehension by asking students to use the vocabulary words in new sentences.

ANSWER KEY

1. assistance 2. medical 3. role 4. civil
5. monitors 6. violations 7. promotion
8. founded 9. depressed 10. energy

6 Guided Academic Conversation: How Do You Measure Courage?

Best Practice

Interacting with Others

The questions in Activity 6, Guided Academic Conversation, ask students how they measure courage. This activity gets students to engage in lively, authentic discussions, which require them to express their ideas clearly and comprehend those of other students. Interactive activities such as this help build students' confidence and fluency.

- ❑ Put students in small groups to discuss the questions.

- ❑ Once they have finished, tell them to join another group and compare their answers.

EXPANSION ACTIVITY

- ■ The aim of this activity is to practice writing interview questions based on the reading passage in Part 2.

- ■ Tell students to choose one of the human rights heroes mentioned in the reading passage.

- ■ Tell them to imagine they are going to interview that person on a news program.

- ■ Have them write 3-5 interview questions based on information they would like to find out about this person.

- ■ Tell them to try to use words they have learned in this chapter in their questions.

- Put students in pairs and have them explain to their partner why they chose the person they did and share their interview questions.
- Ask volunteers to share some of the questions they wrote that use words from the chapter.
- Make a list of the questions on the board.

1 Making Connections

- ❑ Go over the topics, and explain as needed

- ❑ Tell students to choose one of the topics and research it.

- ❑ If you have access to a computer lab, you can do this as a lab activity. If not, you can assign it for homework.

- ❑ Schedule time during the next class for students to report on their findings.

Responding in Writing

WRITING TIP: USING A VENN DIAGRAM TO COMPARE AND CONTRAST

- ◼ Read the Writing Tip.

- ◼ Model how to use a Venn diagram by drawing one on the board and asking students to compare and contrast two famous people.

- ◼ Brainstorm similarities and differences and write them in the Venn diagram on the board.

- ◼ Read the directions.

- ◼ Tell students to refer back to information in the chapter to review facts about the leaders they choose to compare.

- ◼ Encourage students to work independently as they follow the steps.

- ◼ Have students draw a Venn diagram describing two leaders and continue to use their diagram as they complete the writing steps.

Focus on Testing

Sentence-Insertion Questions on Tests

- ◼ Read the information in the Focus on Testing box, and explain as needed.

- ◼ Have students complete the Practice activity.

- ◼ Go over the answers.

ANSWER KEY
After square 3.

Self-Assessment Log

❑ Encourage students to maintain a self-assessment log.

❑ Allow class time so students can check the strategies and vocabulary they learned in the chapter.

❑ Tell students to find definitions in the chapter for any words they did not check.

8

Creativity

In this chapter, students will focus on creativity and creative people. They will read about creative people in two very different fields: architecture and music. At the end of the chapter, students will discuss the topic of male vs. female creativity. New vocabulary, reading strategies, and critical thinking skills will help students increase their reading and speaking fluency.

Chapter Opener

❏ Direct student's attention to the photo and ask questions: *Where do you think this photo was taken? Describe what you see.*

❏ Put students in small groups to discuss the questions in the **Connecting to the Topic** section. (The photo is of students at the National College of Art in Lahore, Pakistan sculpting with clay.)

❏ Read the quote aloud and ask students what they think it means.

❏ Lead the class in discussion and guide the conversation towards creativity.

❏ Ask students: *Who is a famous poet you are familiar with? What is it about poetry that you like/dislike? Are poems more creative than other types of writing?*

❝ Poetry arrived in search of me. I don't know, I don't know where it came from, from winter or a river. I don't know how or when...and it touched me. ❞

—Pablo Neruda, Noble Prize-winning poet from Chile (1904–1973)

Chapter Overview

Reading Skills and Strategies

Scanning for words

Making inferences about a person from reading about their words and actions

Finding the basis for inferences

Critical Thinking Skills

Expressing and comparing opinions and interpretations

Summarizing and reporting on group discussions and reporting them to the class

Identifying points of comparison

Synthesizing Internet content: taking notes and presenting results

Selecting and ordering descriptive details when writing about art

Vocabulary Building

Understanding the vocabulary of shapes and forms

Inferring the meaning of adjectives and adverbs from structure clues and context

Choosing synonyms or definitions for strong verbs

Matching words to their definitions

Focusing on words from the Academic Word List

Focus on Testing

Thinking twice about tricky test questions

Vocabulary

Nouns		Verbs	Adjectives	Adverbs
academy*	obstinacy	create*	circuitous	boldly
acoustic guitar	pioneer	dabbled	compulsory	continually
ambition	sex*	demonstrate*	contemporary*	remarkably
bass	show business	experiment	conventional*	stunningly
critical acclaim	small-scale	grappling	definitive*	
debut album	operations	launch	energetic*	
discrimination*	smuggled goods	murdered	high-profile	
fatigue	sources*	rapping	iconic	
funds*	spokesperson	shooting	indigenous	
guerrillas	violin	shuttling	individualistic*	
income*	weariness	smirk	pan-American	
issues*			proper	
label*			startling	

*These words are from the Academic Word List. For more information on this list, see www.vuw.ac.nz/lals/research/awl.

Guggenheim Museum, U.S.A.

Content Notes

- Born in 1904, Pablo Neruda is an artist of international fame. Neruda is a Chilean poet and writer who writes poetry on topics ranging from love to politics to nature.

- He had originally planned to be a teacher but when he moved to Santiago to study French at the Universidad de Chile, he decided to dedicate himself to poetry.

- In 1971, just two years before his death, he was awarded the Nobel Prize for Literature.

- His first two volumes of poetry were published within a year of each other. The second, "Twenty Poems of Love and a Song of Despair", was controversial because of its eroticism.

- During his life, Neruda maintained strong political beliefs in Communism.

Before You Read

Strategy

Understanding the Vocabulary of Shapes and Forms

- Read the information in the Strategy Box, and explain as needed.

- Ask students to think of items that have the geometric shapes that appear in the Strategy Box. Give them examples such as *The shape of our classroom is square. The shape of the chalkboard is rectangular. My ring is a circle.*

1 Understanding the Vocabulary of Shapes and Forms

- ❑ Read the directions and explain as needed.

- ❑ Have students complete the activity independently.

- ❑ Go over the answers.

ANSWER KEY

1. cube 2. triangle 3. square 4. polygon 5. cone
6. spiral (helix)

2 Guessing the Meaning of Adjectives and Adverbs

- ❑ Read the directions, and explain as needed.

- ❑ Review structure clues and do the first item as a class.

- ❑ Ask the students to complete the activity independently.

- ❑ Go over the answers.

ANSWER KEY

1. B 2. B 3. C 4. A 5. B 6. A 7. B 8. A 9. B 10. C

Read

- ❑ Read the Introduction aloud, or ask a volunteer to read.

- ❑ Discuss the questions as a class.

- ❑ Have students read the passage silently within a time limit (10 minutes).

Best Practice

Activating Prior Knowledge

The first column in a KWL chart such as the one used in the following Expansion Activity always requires students to draw on what they already know about a topic, in this case the Guggenheim Museum. By recalling what they already know, students are prepared to handle the reading selection.

 EXPANSION ACTIVITY

- The aim of this activity is to have students organize their ideas before, during, and after the reading.

- Before having students read the passage, copy and hand out Black Line Master **KWL Chart** (BLM 19).

- Explain that a KWL chart will help students remember and organize what they read. K stands for "What I KNOW". Students should write down information that they already know about the topic. Be sure they understand that there are no wrong answers. W stands for "What I WANT to Know" and students should fill this in with questions about the topic that they do not know the answer for but would like to learn about. L stands for "What I LEARNED" and is filled in after reading. Encourage use of this chart for textbook readings. Tell students to think about the questions in the Introduction box and to look at the title of the passage.

- Have students fill in the first two columns of the KWL chart based on the title and Introduction to the reading.

- Then have them read the article.

- Once they have finished, they should fill in the third column of the chart with notes from the reading.

- Have students compare their charts.

Content Notes

- Solomon Guggenheim was a philanthropist. He founded his not-for-profit foundation in 1937 with Hilla von Rebay, an artist. The foundation's primary success has been the construction of several internationally-renowned museums. The first was the

Solomon R. Guggenheim Museum. Others include: The Peggy Guggenheim in Venice, Italy; the Guggenheim Museum Bilbao in Bilbao, Spain; the Deutsche Guggenheim Berlin in Berlin, Germany; and the Guggenheim Las Vegas, in Las Vegas, Nevada, United States.

- The Guggenheim name is famous in the United States. The father, Meyer Guggenheim, was Swiss and emigrated to the United States in 1847. His family fortune came from mining and smelting. Of his ten children, seven were boys, five of whom followed Meyer in the family business; including Solomon before he ventured into the art world. One of the other brothers died in the Titanic disaster in 1912, while another brother became a senator for Colorado.

After You Read

Strategy

Making Inferences About a Person

- Read the information in the Strategy Box, and explain as needed.

- Ask students to think of an example similar to those provided. Guide them by saying, *For example, a person who has many friends and likes to lead groups is probably what kind of person?* Answers will vary.

3 **Making Inferences About a Person**

Best Practice

Cultivating Critical Thinking

Activities such as this require students to use critical thinking skills, for example, drawing conclusions from information they read. In this case, students are drawing conclusions about Frank Lloyd Wright and his relationships with people by inferring meaning from some of his statements and actions.

❑ Read the directions, and explain as necessary. Complete the first item as a class by reading the statement and discussing the answer. Ask students what words in the statement helped them determine their answers.

❑ Put students in pairs to complete the activity.

❑ When they finish, combine them in groups of four to compare answers.

❑ Discuss the answers as a class.

ANSWER KEY

Possible answers: 1. Wright had a lot of confidence in himself. He also believed he would be famous for his work. 2. Wright had assistants who were dedicated to working for him and who were very loyal to him. He was probably a good boss or a leader who inspired loyalty. 3. Wright thought he was too important to help the man with the roof, or he did not believe the problem was his fault. Perhaps he believed that practicality is not important. Wright believed architectural structures should expose people to their surroundings.

EXPANSION ACTIVITY

■ The aim of this activity is to practice making inferences.

■ Tell students they will have a chance to make inferences.

■ Ask students to bring in a quote they liked from a magazine, newspaper or book.

■ Put students in small groups to present their quotes and the meanings they infer from them. Have students infer the meanings of the other quotes presented by the members in their group.

■ Have each group select their favorite quote and ask a representative from each group to present the quote and what they think it means.

---

4 Scanning for Words

❑ Read the directions and model the activity by completing the first item as a class.

❑ Have students complete the activity independently. Encourage them to try it without looking back at the reading. If they need to refer back to the reading, however, the letter in parenthesis indicates the paragraph where it appears.

❑ Discuss the answers as a class.

ANSWER KEY

1. contemporary 2. pioneer 3. obstinacy
4. conventional 5. fatigue, weariness 6. smirk

5 Guided Academic Conversation

❑ Divide students into small groups to discuss the questions.

❑ Move around the classroom and make sure that all students are participating.

❑ Once the time limit is up, combine groups so students can compare answers.

❑ Discuss any questions or comments during a whole-class discussion.

Focus on Testing TOEFL® iBT

Thinking Twice about Tricky Questions

■ Read the Focus on Testing instruction note. Explain that test items generally follow the order of appearance in the text.

■ Direct students to the Practice section and have them complete the activity independently.

■ Remind students to apply the Making Inferences strategy that they learned on page 179.

- Have students complete the activity independently.

- Go over the answers as a class and discuss which questions were straightforward and which ones were tricky.

ANSWER KEY

1. A 2. B 3. C 4. C 5. A 6. B

6 Around the Globe

- ❑ Put students into small groups to read the article.

- ❑ Have them answer the questions that follow.

- ❑ Circulate around the room and help students as needed.

- ❑ Have students share and discuss their answers as a class.

Best Practice

Making Use of Academic Content

Incorporating math terms and utilizing tables, graphs, and charts will enable students to successfully handle the types of assignments they will encounter in a variety of academic courses.

REPRODUCIBLE   EXPANSION ACTIVITY

- The aim of this activity is to have students practice making bar graphs.

- Copy and hand out the two Black Line Masters **Bar Graphs**, and **The Tallest Buildings in the World** (BLMs 20 and 21).

- Take this opportunity to review the reading strategies on Reading Charts from Chapters 3 and 4. Explain that a bar graph is a good way to consolidate information in a chart and present information in a visual way.

- Tell students to use the information provided in **The Tallest Buildings in the World** chart to complete "Bar Graph A" at the top of the Black Line Master.

- Tell the students they will create their own bar graphs using Bar Graph B.

- Tell them to look at the information in **The Tallest Buildings in the World** chart and select five buildings to compare and write the names of each at the bottom of the chart as in "Bar Graph A".

- Tell them to choose the information they would like to compare (height in feet, height in meters, number of stories, etc.) and write it on the line above "Bar Graph B".

- Allow students 10-15 minutes to complete their bar graphs.

- Ask a few volunteers to present their bar graphs to the class.

Music Makes the World Go 'Round: Lila Downs, Nancy Ajram, and Don Popo

Before You Read

Strategy

Guessing the Meaning of Strong Verbs in Context

- Read the information in the Strategy Box, and explain as needed.

- Discuss the example provided—"grew up *shuttling* between Mexico and the U.S." Ask if they have heard the expression "shuttling between" before.

- Have students guess the meaning based on the context.

1   **Guessing the Meaning of Strong Verbs**

- ❑ Read the directions.

- ❑ Have students complete the activity independently.

- ❑ Go over the answers.

ANSWER KEY

1. B   2. B   3. C   4. A   5. C   6. C   7. C   8. A

2   **Finding the Basis for Inferences**

- ❑ Review the information on Making Inferences About a Person in the Strategy Box on page 179.

- ❑ Read the directions for Activity 2.

- ❑ Model the activity by going over the sample item as a class.

- ❑ Have students complete the rest of the activity independently.

- ❑ Go over the answers as a class.

ANSWER KEY

1. Her father was a professor from the United States and her mother, a singer, was a Mixteca Indian from Mexico

2. Her album, *Tree of Life*, includes songs in three of the indigenous languages of Mexico, Zapotec, Náhuatl, and Mixtec.

3. . . . Ajram began studying music under the supervision of some of the finest teachers in her country.

4. The 27-year-old rap artist sponsors workshops where poor kids can rap and break dance, create graffiti, or learn how to be a DJ . . . To inspire kids in his old Bogotá neighborhood, he gives away his own CDs which appeared on the Sony Music label . . . He encourages children to make their lives better by offering them workshops and giving away gifts.

5. Don Popo himself started making music at the age of 13, two years after his own father was murdered. It was the only way this silent young man could express his feelings.

Read

- ❑ Read the Introduction aloud or have a volunteer read it.

- ❑ Answer and discuss the questions as a class.

- ❑ Set an appropriate time limit for students to read the passage (10 minutes).

After You Read

3 Understanding the Reading: Comparison

Best Practice

Organizing Information

A comparison chart such as the one in this exercise can help students organize and process the information from the reading. Students who are visual learners will also benefit from having the information "illustrated." The concise format of this chart enables students to identify and recall details quickly and easily.

❑ Read the directions, and explain as needed.

❑ Model the activity by completing the first item as a class.

❑ Have students complete the chart independently.

❑ Go over the answers as a class.

ANSWER KEY

	Lila Downs	Nancy Ajram	Don Popo
1. Is a spokesperson for Coca-Cola.		✓	
2. Sings about the U.S./Mexico border.	✓		
3. Performs in a movie about Mexican artist Frida Kahlo.	✓		
4. Comes from Bogotá, Colombia.			✓
5. Won a prize for singing on a television program.		✓	
6. Works to create opportunities for young people in the community.			✓
7. Combines traditional Mexican forms with rap, jazz, and reggae.	✓		
8. Uses acoustic guitar, violin, and bass to do rap and hip-hop music.			✓
9. Did video clips of songs which led to popularity in the Arab world.		✓	
10. Heads a clothing company.			✓

4 Matching Words to Their Definitions

❑ Read the directions, and explain as needed.

❑ Have students complete the activity independently.

❑ Go over the answers as a class.

❑ Check comprehension by asking questions, such as: *What is an example of a high-profile job? What is one of your ambitions? What are some examples of smuggled goods? What is an example of discrimination?*

ANSWER KEY

1. l   2. d   3. h   4. a   5. o   6. n   7. b   8. j   9. f   10. e
11. c   12. k   13. i   14. g   15. m

5 Focusing on Words from the Academic Word List

❑ Read the directions, and explain as needed.

❑ Tell students to complete this activity independently.

❑ Review correct answers as a class.

❑ Check comprehension by asking students to use the new vocabulary in sentences.

ANSWER KEY
1. create 2. funds 3. demonstrate 4. label
5. academy 6. issues 7. sex 8. discrimination
9. sources 10. income

6 Guided Academic Conversation

Best Practice

Interacting with Others

This small group activity requires students to compile chain-of-events graphs together. It encourages cooperative learning since students need to agree on one right answer. By discussing the issues presented in the activity and preparing a report as a group, students will be prepared for the type of collaborative projects they will encounter in various academic settings.

- ❏ Read the directions, and explain as needed.
- ❏ Put students in small groups to discuss the questions.
- ❏ Tell students to take notes on the opinions of their groups.
- ❏ Have each group present one of their chain-of-events graphs.

ANSWER KEY
Answers will vary.

What Do You Think?

- ❏ Read the directions, and explain as needed.
- ❏ Read the Introduction aloud or ask a volunteer to read it.

- ❏ Tell students to read the passage silently.
- ❏ Put students into groups to discuss the questions.

EXPANSION ACTIVITY

- ■ The aim of this activity is to practice interaction through a topic-related debate.
- ■ Tell students they will participate in a friendly debate.
- ■ Divide the class into two teams: male and female.
- ■ Give them the topic: Who is more creative men or women?
- ■ Men present the argument that men are more creative. Give them five minutes.
- ■ Women then have five minutes to offer their arguments.
- ■ Consider having another teacher or a third group of students 'judge.'
- ■ For variation, you can have men argue that women are more creative while the women argue that men are more creative.
- ■ Other variations: have each team member present one argument, have mixed-gender teams, or change the topic slightly—Who is stronger?, Who is smarter?, or Who is the better parent?

1 Making Connections

- ❑ Read the directions and topics, and explain as needed.

- ❑ Tell students to choose one of the topics and research it.

- ❑ If you have access to a computer lab, you can do this as a lab activity. If not, you can assign it for homework.

- ❑ Schedule time during the next class for presentations.

Responding in Writing

Strategy

Writing Tip: Describing Art

- ■ Read the Writing Tip, and explain as needed.

- ■ Explain to students that when they prepare to write about a piece of art, they should think about how they want to describe it. If they describe a building, will they start outside and proceed inside? Will they start by describing colors or objects, etc.?

2 Writing About Art

Best Practice

Scaffolding Instruction

This writing activity uses the students' prior knowledge as a scaffold. This type of activity helps students draw on what they already know about a particular work of art or architecture as well as on the strategies they have learned in this chapter and in earlier chapters, such as organizing ideas in a cluster diagram, and using descriptive details. In this activity, students are being asked to write a well-organized description of a work of art.

- ❑ Tell students to bring in a picture of a piece of art or architecture they are interested in.

- ❑ Go over each of the steps, and explain as needed. For Step 1, you may want to draw a simple diagram on the board for review.

- ❑ Draw a sample cluster diagram on the board and have students copy it on a separate piece of paper. Remind them that this will be similar in structure to the cluster diagram they did in Chapter 6.

- ❑ Move about the room offering suggestions as students brainstorm and develop their paragraphs.

- ❑ Put students in groups of five. Have them put their pictures in the middle where everyone in their group can see them, and read their paragraphs. Other students in the group should be able to identify which picture goes with which paragraph.

Self-Assessment Log

- ❑ Encourage students to maintain a self-assessment log.

- ❑ Allow class time so students can check the strategies and vocabulary they learned in the chapter.

- ❑ Tell students to find definitions in the chapter for any words they did not check.

9

Human Behavior

In this chapter, students will focus on human behavior. In the first reading, they will learn about the ways people evaluate their own culture and other cultures. Students will learn about ethnocentrism and how it can be seen in many aspects of culture—including literature and language. In Part 2, students will read a short story about how people are influenced by their environments. New vocabulary, reading strategies, and critical thinking will be brought together as students create dialogues in Part 3.

Chapter Opener

❑ Direct student's attention to the photo and ask questions. *Who are these people? Where are they?*

❑ Put students in small groups to discuss the questions in the **Connecting to the Topic** section. (The photo is of a young couple sitting on a pier.)

❑ Call on groups to recount their discussions with the whole class.

❑ Read the Japanese proverb aloud and ask students what they think it means.

❝ Let a person so act by day that he or she may rest happily by night. **❞**

—Japanese proverb

Chapter Overview

Reading Skills and Strategies

Skimming for the main idea

Scanning for development of the main idea

Finding support for main ideas

Previewing for characters and plot

Expressing the theme

Critical Thinking Skills

Comparing opinions

Analyzing love poems (Readings: three poems)

Making inferences about characters

Synthesizing Internet content: taking notes and presenting results

Writing a dialogue

Vocabulary Building

Using prefixes to build new words

Scanning for words with clues

Focusing on words from the Academic Word List

Getting the meaning of words from context

Focus on Testing

Answering questions about the author's purpose or attitude

(Reading: *Gestural Ethnocentrism*)

Vocabulary

Nouns	Adjectives	Adverbs
aspect*	aware*	constantly*
barbarian	distasteful	objectively*
bias*	inconceivable*	
colleague*	inhuman	
culture*	irrational*	
despair	liberal*	
ethnocentrism	non-Western	
hue	open-minded	
insomnia	repugnant	
omission of syntax	repulsive	
outcome*	sexual*	
outlook	subarctic	
self-evaluation	unnatural	
subgroup		
world view		

*These words are from the Academic Word List. For more information on this list, see www.vuw.ac.nz/lals/research/awl.

Ethnocentrism

Before You Read

- ❏ Go over the information in the Reading Tip in the margin, and explain as needed.

- ❏ Ask students to guess the meaning of "ethnocentrism."

1 Skimming for the Main Idea

- ❏ Read the directions, and explain as needed.

- ❏ Ask students to write the author's explanation of ethnocentrism.

- ❏ Discuss the answers as a class.

ANSWER KEY

Possible answers: Ethnocentrism is the belief that one's own patterns of behavior are the best, the most natural, beautiful, right, or important. Therefore, other people who live differently live by standards that are inhuman, irrational, unnatural, or wrong. / Ethnocentrism is the view that one's own culture is better than all others; it is the way all people feel about themselves as compared to outsiders.

---

2 Scanning for the Development of the Main Idea

- ❏ Read the directions, and explain as needed.

- ❏ Have students complete the activity on their own.

- ❏ Discuss the answers as a class.

ANSWER KEY

1. 5
2. _____ choice of clothing
   _✓_ food preferences
   _✓_ language

_____ marriage ceremonies
_✓_ myths and folktales

---

3 Using Prefixes to Build New Words

- ❏ Read the directions, and explain as needed.

- ❏ Model the activity by doing item 1 as a class. Make sure students understand how the word was formed.

- ❏ Ask students to complete the activity.

- ❏ Discuss the answers as a class.

- ❏ Check comprehension by having students write sentences using the words.

ANSWER KEY

1. subartic 2. inconceivable 3. subgroups
4. inhuman 5. unnatural 6. irrational
7. distasteful 8. non-Western

Read

- ❏ Read the Introduction aloud, or ask a volunteer to read it.

- ❏ Discuss the questions as a class.

- ❏ Have students read the passage silently within a time limit (10 minutes).

Content Note

- ■ According to the U.S. Census Bureau, the state of Alaska has 626,932 Alaskan natives who comprise approximately 6% of the state's population.

After You Read

4 Using Clues to Scan for Words

❏ Model the activity by reading the first definition "the way one looks at the world" and asking students to scan the reading to find it in context.

❏ Make sure students understand why "outlook" is the correct answer.

❏ Have students complete the activity.

❏ Discuss the answers as a class.

ANSWER KEY

1. outlook, 2. liberal, open-minded
3. bias 4. self-evaluation 5. repulsive, repugnant
6. barbarian 7. hue 8. inconceivable

5 The Support Game: Finding Support for Main Ideas

❏ Put students in small teams of three to five.

❏ Read the directions and set a time limit of 10 minutes for students to complete the task.

❏ Have students report their findings.

❏ Have the class vote on which team is the winner.

ANSWER KEY

Possible answers:

1. In many languages, especially those of non-Western societies, the words used to refer to one's own tribe is "mankind" or "human".

The word *Eskimo* used by the Inuit means "eaters of raw flesh"

Inuit means "real people"

The word *barbarian* was used to describe tribes that lived around the edge of ancient Greek society.

2. An example of ethnocentrism can be found in the myths and folktales. For example, the creation myth of the Cherokee Indians.

3. In Southeast Asia, adults do not drink milk. To Americans, it is inconceivable that people in other parts of the world do not drink milk., In China, dog meat is a delicacy; but would make most Americans feel sick. Horse meat is also rejected by most Americans. The attitude of Indians toward eating beef is similar to the views of Americans' about eating dogs. The attitude of Chinese people towards eating dogs is similar to Americans' attitudes toward cows.

6 Focusing on Words from the Academic Word List

❏ Read the directions, and explain as necessary.

❏ Tell students to complete this activity on their own.

❏ Review the correct answers as a class.

❏ Check comprehension by asking students to use words in new sentences.

ANSWER KEY

1. culture 2. liberal 3. aspect 4. culture
5. sexual 6. outcome 7. constantly 8. aware
9. objectively 10. bias

7 Guided Academic Conversation

❏ Put students in small groups to discuss the topics.

❏ Move around the classroom to ensure that students are participating.

❏ Combine groups to share opinions.

Organizing Information

A Venn diagram is a visual tool that can help students make connections and see relationships between two things. It can also help them remember information through visual cues. Teachers can use Venn diagrams to assess students' understanding of the material and their ability to categorize information. The Venn diagram in the following Expansion Activity has students compare different types of gestures.

EXPANSION ACTIVITY

- The purpose of this activity is to research, compare, and contrast two different cultures.

- Tell students to reflect on some of the topics covered in the reading passage, *Ethnocentrism*, and their discussions in Activity 7 on pages 203–204. Ask them to choose a topic such as food, marriage customs, communication (gestures, greetings, language, etc.) and compare the attitudes and norms for that topic in two different cultures.

- Copy and hand out Black Line Master **Venn Diagram: Cultural Comparisons** (BLM 22).

- Model a Venn diagram on the board, and explain how it is helpful when comparing and contrasting two topics.

- Give students time to do research on the Internet or at the library. Tell them that they can also conduct their research by interviewing people from the cultures they are comparing.

- Have students complete the Venn diagrams and discuss the two questions on the BLM with a partner.

- Ask volunteers to present their findings to the entire class.

Focus on Testing | TOEFL® iBT

Questions about an Author's Purposes or Attitudes

- Read the information in the Focus on Testing box, and explain as needed.

- Have students complete the practice section.

- Discuss the answers as a class.

ANSWER KEY

1. D 2. C 3. A 4. B 5. A

8 **Around the Globe**

Making Use of Academic Content

In this activity, students are reading and analyzing short love poems from different cultures. Because poetry is an integral part of secondary and university literature and English courses as well as other humanities classes, this activity will provide practice with the type of material and tasks students may encounter in other courses.

Content Notes

- **Li Po** (701–762 CE) was a native of Sichuan China. As a teenager he went to live in the mountains with a religious leader named Tunyen-tzu. He later left and became a wandering poet. He wrote many poems during his lifetime, primarily about solitude, friendship, the passage of time, and nature. He is recognized as one of the greatest Tang poets.
  Source: www.humanisticletexts.org

- **Ono no Kamachi** lived during the mid-800s in Japan, was born into a literary family, and was perhaps an attendant to Emperor

Nimmei. Other than this, little else is known about her. Most of her poems are about love and the melancholy surrounding it.
Source: home.infoonline.net

- **Hafiz** lived sometime around 1310–1325 CE in south-central Iran. His real name was Shamseddin Mohammed, but his pen name was Hafiz or Hafez, which means one who has memorized the Koran. His poetry is written in Ghazal form, which is a strict Persian form of poetry comparable to English sonnets. Although there have been many attempts to translate his poetry into English, it is said that even the best translations are not fully successful.
Source: hafizonlove.com

❏ Put students in groups of three to five. Ask them to read the poems aloud in their groups and answer the questions that follow.

❏ Call on students to share their group's answers and opinions.

A Clean, Well-Lighted Place

Before You Read

1   Previewing for Characters and Plot

❑   Read the information about Ernest Hemingway.

❑   Read the instructions, and have students find the answer the questions.

❑   Go over the answers.

ANSWER KEY

1. three
2. dialogue
3. sad; Answers may include: The old man is lonely; The young waiter is unhappy about working late; The old man is in despair and lonely.

2   Getting the Meaning of Words from Context

❑   Read the directions, and model the activity by doing the first item as a class.

❑   Have students complete the activity independently.

❑   Go over the answers.

ANSWER KEY

1. B   2. C   3. A   4. B   5. A   6. C

Read

❑   Read or have a volunteer read the Introduction aloud.

❑   Discuss the questions as a class.

❑   Give students 10–15 minutes to read the story.

Content Note

■   In the year 2000, there were an estimated 35 million Americans aged 65 or older. Approximately 14% of those older American men had been widowed (their wives had died). Over 44% of women had lost their husbands. Those widows and widowers are more depressed and lonely than other age groups who still have their spouses.

Vocabulary Note

■   Often in English writing, authors use words from other languages. Hemingway uses some Spanish words, and their meanings are evident from the context. Sometimes words are *cognates*, which means they are spelled similarly in both languages and mean essentially the same thing. For example, *atender* in Spanish means *to attend to* in English. Students can often determine meanings from the spelling of foreign words. Explain that although foreign words might be frustrating, they can figure out the meanings with relatively little trouble.

After You Read

3   Making Inferences about Characters

Best Practice

Cultivating Critical Thinking

In this activity students must use the information from the dialogs to make inferences about the characters in the story. This activity requires students to draw conclusions based on the information provided by the author. Making inferences is a skill that students will need to use a variety of academic contexts.

❑ Read the directions, and discuss the words *maybe*, *perhaps*, *probably*, *must*.

❑ Have students complete the activity.

❑ Go over the answers.

ANSWER KEY

Possible answers: 1. The old man must be very sad about something. He has problems. He is probably lonely or worried about his life. 2. The waiter who spoke last probably has money problems of his own, so he might think everyone is worried about money. 3. The younger waiter is probably only saying this because he is tired and wants to go home. He thinks that if the man had killed himself, he would get to close the restaurant and go home early. 4. The older waiter probably doesn't mind staying late. Perhaps he doesn't have anyone waiting for him at home. Maybe he is as lonely as the old man. 5. The older waiter must substitute *nada* for other important words because he thinks that life for the old man and for himself is meaningless and offers them nothing, or *nada*.

Strategy

Expressing the Theme

■ Read the information in the Strategy Box, and explain as needed.

■ Remind students of the reading in Part 1 about human behavior (pages 199–201).

■ Ask students for synonyms for "theme." Answers may include *subject* or *topic*.

4 Expressing the Theme

❑ Read the directions, and have students choose which statement they feel best expresses the theme.

❑ Ask them to think about why their choice is better than the other two.

❑ Put students in pairs or small groups, and have them write their own themes.

❑ Call on students to share their themes with the class.

ANSWER KEY

2

EXPANSION ACTIVITY

■ The aim of this activity is to have students practice making story maps.

■ Copy and hand out Black Line Master **Story Map** (BLM 23).

■ Explain to students that "mapping" the story will help them remember characters, events, and themes from the short story.

■ Have students complete the story map for "A Clean, Well-Lighted Place" by Ernest Hemingway.

■ Have them compare their story map with a partner.

■ Go over the answers as a class.

5 Guided Academic Conversation

❑ Put students in small groups to discuss the topics.

❑ Have students share their opinions with the class.

6 What Do You Think?

Activating Prior Knowledge

By focusing on manners in the 21st century, students are able to bridge prior knowledge of the topic to material they read in the chapter. In this case, students are discussing their opinions of manners, culture, and society with which they are already familiar.

❑ Read the paragraph aloud, or ask a volunteer to read it.

❑ Put students into small groups to discuss the questions.

❑ Have one representative from each group share their answers.

1 Making Connections

> **Best Practice**
>
> **Scaffolding Instruction**
>
> Activities such as this will enable students to link knowledge recently acquired in this chapter with new information that they gather from their research. In this case, students are asked to research different attitudes toward either clothing styles or the importance of Hemingway.

- ❏ Read the directions and topics aloud, and explain as needed.
- ❏ Tell students to research the topic of their choice on the Internet.
- ❏ Have students present their findings to the class.

Responding in Writing

WRITING TIP: CREATING A DIALOGUE

- ■ Read the Writing Tip, and explain as needed.
- ■ Remind students about the short story in Part 2, which contains a lot of dialogue. If you haven't done so already, you may want to take this opportunity to teach students about quotation marks. See the following Grammar Notes.

> ### Grammar Notes
>
> - ■ Quotation marks are used to indicate a person's exact words. *He said, "I am going to the restaurant."*
> - ■ When a quote is broken, a comma is used before the second part of the quotation. *"I am going to the restaurant," he said, "but if you want to come too, that would be fine."*
> - ■ Punctuation that ends a quotation, such as commas, periods, question marks, or exclamation points, are placed inside the quotation marks. *She shouted, "No!"*
> - ■ For dialogues, every time the speaker changes, a new paragraph needs to be started. *He said, "Do you want to come with me?" "No, I have to go to school," she said.*

2 Writing a Dialogue

> **Best Practice**
>
> **Interacting with Others**
>
> Having students work with a partner to write a creative dialogue offers the chance for them to interact on two levels. First, they work together to discuss what their dialogues should be about. Second, they will read their dialogues in an attempt to make it as authentic as possible.

- ❏ Go over the directions and steps for the activity.
- ❏ Put students in pairs, and have them follow the steps.
- ❏ Move about the room and offer help to students as they write.
- ❏ Combine pairs so students can read their dialogues and get feedback.
- ❏ Collect dialogues after students have made their revisions.

Self-Assessment Log

- ❏ Encourage students to maintain a self-assessment log.
- ❏ Allow class time so students can check the strategies and vocabulary they learned in the chapter.
- ❏ Tell students to find definitions in the chapter for any words they did not check.

Crime and Punishment

In this chapter, students will explore what causes people to commit crimes, if criminals can be reformed, and discuss what the appropriate punishments for crimes should be. In Part 1, they will read a magazine article about criminals who try to overcome their crime addiction through meetings and spiritual help. In Part 2, students will read a fictional selection, a murder mystery, with a surprise ending. New vocabulary, reading strategies, and research will be brought together as students formulate their own viewpoints in Part 3.

Chapter Opener

- ❑ Direct students' attention to the photo and ask questions. *Who are the people in the photos? What's the situation?*

- ❑ Put students in small groups to discuss the questions in the **Connecting to the Topic** section. (The images show a woman being mugged by two men on a city walkway.)

- ❑ Call on groups to recount their discussions with the whole class. Compile a master list on the board.

- ❑ Read the Sanskrit proverb aloud and ask students what they think it means.

❝ The way of justice is mysterious. ❞

—Sanskrit proverb

Chapter Overview

Reading Skills and Strategies

Identifying the interviewees in an article

Understanding the setting

Identifying narrative elements

Scanning for specific terms

Reading and interpreting charts

Critical Thinking Skills

Reporting opinions

Using a graphic organizer (a storyboard) to summarize the plot

Interpreting a scene from the plot in a group skit

Synthesizing Internet content: taking notes and presenting results

Using a summary of an event to connect to a personal viewpoint in writing

Vocabulary Building

Getting the meanings of specialized terms from context

Inferring the meanings of adjectives from context and structure

Focusing on words from the Academic Word List

Identifying spelling variations

Matching descriptive adjectives to their contexts

Focus on Testing

Understanding prose summaries on tests

(Reading: *Privatized Prisons*)

Vocabulary

Nouns		Adjectives	Adverbs
accessory	tic	burly	abruptly
assault	tradition*	clean (in the sense	carefully
chapter* (of an	trafficking	of "free from drugs")	nervously
organization)	underlings	clean-cut	personally
cons		contentious	quickly
dependency	**Verbs**	hard-luck	suspiciously
extortion	addled	jailhouse hard	warily
fear	backslide	meaty	wearily
heroin	created*	modest	
homelessness	credits*	wrenching	**Idioms and Expressions**
principles*	deliberated		back when things were flush
robberies	draft*		I did my time (do time)
taxpayer	imposed*		making amends (make amends)
	responds*		the Old Man

*These words are from the Academic Word List. For more information on this list, see www.vuw.ac.nz/lals/research/awl.

Hooked on Crime

Before You Read

Strategy

Identifying the Interviewees in an Article

- Read the information in the Strategy Box, and explain as needed.

- Ask students to scan the article and find the name "Stan Mingo". Explain that he is an interviewee or main character in the reading.

1 Scanning: Identifying the Interviewees

- ❑ Read the directions to the class, and explain as needed.

- ❑ Ask students to find Stan Mingo's name again and the description provided.

- ❑ Have students complete the activity independently.

- ❑ Discuss the answers as a class.

ANSWER KEY

Possible answers: 1. Stan Mingo: a man with a "crime addiction" who is starting the meeting 2. Gary Johnson, executive director of Harbour Light, who believes crime is addictive 3. Rick A.: spokesman for AA who has asked that his surname not be used and who believes that spiritual principles of AA may be adopted by other addictions. 4. Benedikt Fischer: associate professor of criminology and public health at the University of Toronto; research scientist with the Toronto-based Centre for Addiction and Mental Health, who believes that the term addiction is not "terribly helpful". 5. George: has stolen money from family members. 6. Rick B.: a crime and drug addict, who is feeling shame and guilt for the first time in years.

EXPANSION ACTIVITY

- ■ The aim of this activity is to practice topic-related interviews.

- ■ Tell students to imagine that they are writing an article for a newspaper and have the opportunity to interview one of the interviewees summarized in Activity 1.

- ■ Ask students to think of good interviewing questions. Give some examples on the board such as *What is crime addiction? Do you believe a person can be addicted to crime? Why or why not? Why did you commit the crime?*

- ■ Tell students to pick one of the interviewees and create a list of three questions they would like to ask that person.

- ■ Consider expanding this activity by having students create a dialogue with answers from their interviewee. Answers can be developed from what students infer from the reading.

2 Getting the Meaning of Specialized Terms from Context

- ❑ Read the directions to the class.

- ❑ Model the activity by doing item 1 as a class.

- ❑ Ask students to complete the activity independently.

- ❑ Discuss the answers as a class.

- ❑ Check comprehension by having students write new sentences using the words.

ANSWER KEY

1. g 2. m 3. j 4. o 5. a 6. d 7. l 8. e 9. h 10. f 11. n 12. i 13. k 14. c 15. b

Vocabulary Note

■ Specialized crime and drug terms are used in academic courses such as sociology, health, criminology, and criminal justice. These words are also common in the everyday language of current events. Students will see this kind of terminology in journals, magazines, and newspapers.

Best Practice

Activating Prior Knowledge

Pre-reading questions, such as the ones in the Introduction to the article get students to draw upon the information they already know about the topic of crime addiction and share it with their classmates. By doing this, they will be better prepared to deal with the information presented in the article and throughout the chapter.

Read

❏ Read the Introduction, or ask a student to read it aloud.

❏ Discuss the questions as a class.

❏ Have students read the passage silently within a time limit (10-15 minutes).

Content Note

■ AA stands for Alcoholics Anonymous. It is an organization of people who all suffer from alcohol addiction and share their experiences, hope, and support with each other. AA is free and aims to help people stop drinking. AA has established 12 steps to overcoming an alcohol addiction. The 12 steps have been adopted by other groups formed to help people overcome other kinds of addictions, such as drug addiction and gambling addiction.

After You Read

Strategy

Understanding the Setting

■ Read the information in the Strategy Box, and explain as needed.

■ Ask students to tell something about the setting of the reading in Part 1.

3 **Understanding the Setting**

❏ Read the directions, and explain as needed.

❏ Have students complete the activity independently.

❏ Go over the answers.

ANSWER KEY

Possible answers: 1. alcohol, unknown not revealed 2. 12, crime, unknown not revealed 3. alibi, heroin 4. addiction, it guides people to safety, someone who has washed up on shore

4 **Guessing the Meaning of Adjectives from Context and Structure**

❏ Read the directions, and explain as needed.

❏ Have students complete the activity independently.

❏ Go over the answers.

ANSWER KEY

1. B 2. A 3. B 4. C 5. A 6. C

EXPANSION ACTIVITY

■ The aim of this activity is to provide additional practice with new vocabulary words.

- Tell students they will write a vocabulary quiz for the class.

- Have students choose three words from Activities 2 (page 222–223) and 4 (page 227–228).

- Ask them to write three sentences (one for each selected word) using the words in context. Ask them to make sure the context adequately conveys the word's meaning.

- Each student should write one of their sentences on the board and draw a line where the vocabulary word should go.

- Have students copy the sentences from the board and fill in the blanks. They should be able to choose the correct vocabulary word based on the context of the sentence.

5 Focusing on Words form the Academic Word List

- ❑ Read the directions, and explain as needed.

- ❑ Tell students to complete this activity on their own.

- ❑ Tell students to check their answers on page 225.

- ❑ Go over the answers as a class.

- ❑ Check comprehension by asking students to use words in new sentences.

ANSWER KEY

1. credits 2. draft 3. chapter 4. created
5. imposed 6. responds 7. principles 8. tradition
9. principles

IDENTIFYING SPELLING VARIATIONS

- Read the information in the instruction note, and explain as needed.

- Ask students to find examples of Canadian spelling in the reading.

- Compile a list on the board and write the American English spelling next to the Canadian spelling of the words.

6 Identifying Spelling Variations

- ❑ Read the directions.

- ❑ Have students complete the activity.

- ❑ Go over the answers.

ANSWER KEY

1. centre 2. Harbour 3. humour
4. neighbourhood

7 Guided Academic Conversation

Best Practice

Interacting with Others

Small-group discussions give students the chance to participate in authentic conversations about academic and general interest topics. Focused topics such as the questions in Activity 7 give students an opportunity to increase their fluency by expressing their ideas and opinions in conversations on a specific topic.

- ❑ Put students in small groups to read and discuss the questions.

- ❑ Ask them to discuss five of the six questions.

- ❑ Tell students that they should be prepared to report their group's opinions to the class.

What Do You Think?

8 Discussing the Death Penalty

Content Notes

- Murder is a crime that is punishable by the death penalty in some states in the U.S.

- The death penalty has been used in the United States since colonial times (the early 1800s).

- The United States is one of approximately 90 countries that enforces the death penalty.

- Although the electric chair and lethal injection are the methods used almost exclusively in the U.S., there are a few states that still maintain the firing squad, hanging, and the gas chamber as methods of execution in addition to lethal injections and/or the electric chair.

- The death penalty can be traced to Egypt in the 16th century B.C.E.

Sources: http://www.deathpenaltyinfo.org/article.php?scid=8&did=245

- ❏ Read or ask a volunteer to read the paragraph aloud.

- ❏ Put students into small groups to discuss the questions that follow.

- ❏ Have one representative from each group share answers.

Best Practice

Cultivating Critical Thinking

The following Expansion Activity will encourage critical thinking, decision making and group interaction. In this case, students must work together to develop a ranking system and support the reasons why they chose the punishments they did for each crime. By working in groups, they will need to listen to each other's ideas, be open to new opinions, and practice articulating their own ideas.

EXPANSION ACTIVITY

- The purpose of this activity is to have students practice ranking crimes on a continuum, and doing topic-related Internet research.

- Copy and hand out Black Line Master **Ranking the Crimes** (BLM 24).

- Have students brainstorm the names of crimes. You may want to have them brainstorm crimes according to certain categories, i.e. violent crimes, such as murder and assault, crimes that involve stealing, such as shoplifting, pick pocketing, etc.

- Write a list of the crimes on the board.

- Put students in small groups.

- Have students choose ten crimes from the list on the board or any other crimes they can think of. When they have their lists, have them rank them on the continuum from "most serious" to "least serious" and then think of an appropriate punishment or sentence for each crime.

- Give students time to do research on the Internet or in the school library if necessary.

- Have students complete the continuum.

- Call on students to present their work to the class.

Eye Witness

Before You Read

1 Identifying Narrative Elements

- ❑ Read the directions, and explain as needed.

- ❑ Remind students that the three elements of a story are setting, characters, and plot.

- ❑ Have students complete the activity independently.

- ❑ Go over the answers.

ANSWER KEY

Possible answers: 1. The title tells us that the main character witnessed a murder. His eyes are brown, he doesn't smile, his mouth is thin, and he has a tic over his left cheekbone. He is nervous. He is thin and has a moustache. He dresses neatly. His name is Mr. Struthers and he is important because he witnessed a crime. He only wants to speak to the lieutenant. 2. The narrator is the police officer who is interviewing Mr. Struthers. He is not an omniscient narrator. His name is Detective Cappeli. 3. Magruder is a police officer who had served on the force for a long time. 4. The victim is Lieutenant Anderson's wife. She was mugged and stabbed.

2 Scanning for Specific Terms

- ❑ Read the directions and explain as needed.

- ❑ Model the activity by doing the first item as a class.

- ❑ Have students complete the activity.

- ❑ Go over the answers.

- ❑ Check comprehension by having students use the words in new sentences.

ANSWER KEY

1. tic 2. underlings 3. taxpayer 4. Old Man
5. fear 6. accessory 7. deliberated

Read

- ❑ Read the Introduction aloud, or ask a volunteer to read it.

- ❑ Tell students to read the passage. Set a time limit (10–15minutes).

Content Notes

- ■ Edgar Allen Poe, an American author, is credited with writing the first mystery novel. Poe lived in the early 1800s. In 1841, he wrote *The Murders in the Rue Morgue*. The story's plot revolves around Chevalier C. Auguste Dupin who solves the crime and appears in several other Poe stories.

- ■ One of the more famous mystery detectives is Sherlock Holmes. His character was created by Sir Arthur Conan Doyle.

- ■ A real-life mystery is the story of the Boston Strangler. Albert Henry DeSalvo terrorized Boston from 1962–1964. He committed 13 murders before he was captured and sentenced to life in prison. He was murdered himself six years into his prison term. Even now, there are people who believe DeSalvo did not commit the crimes and the real Boston Strangler escaped punishment.

After You Read

 EXPANSION ACTIVITY

- The aim of this activity it to practice organizing the elements of the story "Eye Witness" using a chart.

- Copy and hand out Black Line Master **Story Elements Chart** ("Eye Witness") (BLM 25).

- Explain that this is a good way to organize details from the story.

- Ask students to fill in the story elements.

- Compare answers.

3 Finding Descriptive Adverbs

- ❏ Read the directions, and explain as needed. Remind students that adverbs are used to describe verbs.

- ❏ Have students complete the activity independently.

- ❏ Go over the answers.

ANSWER KEY

1. nervously 2. carefully 3. personally 4. warily
5. suspiciously 6. abruptly 7. quickly 8. wearily

Grammar Notes

- Most adverbs end with the suffix -ly. Some adverbs require no suffix: *least, worst, well, much,* and *little*. Adverbs can be categorized into four general groups:

- Adverbs of degree (describe the extent): Examples include *more, very, barely*.

- Adverbs of time (describe when): Examples include *then, soon, now*.

- Adverbs of place (describe where): Examples include *here, nowhere, there*.

- Adverbs of manner (describe how): Examples nclude *quickly, happily* and all of the examples from Activity 3.

Strategy

Understanding the Plot

- Read the information in the Strategy Box, and explain as needed.

- Walk students through the main events of the mystery, and have them identify which parts are significant to the plot.

 EXPANSION ACTIVITY

- The aim of this activity is to provide practice with sequencing the events of a story using a story sequencing map.

- Copy and hand out Black Line Master **Story Sequence Map** (BLM 26).

- Explain that a story sequence map is an excellent way to organize the details and plot from a story.

- Have them fill in the conflict, complications, climax, and ending of "Eye Witness" as defined in the Strategy Box.

- After they have completed their maps, put students in pairs or small groups to compare maps.

- Go over the answers.

4 **Making a Storyboard of *Eye Witness* for TV**

Best Practice

Organizing Information

A storyboard is a sequential, depiction of a story. A storyboard will help students recall the key parts of the narrative and pull the most important details from the story. The visual nature of this activity will help students remember the most important events of the story, and the order in which they occurred.

❑ Put students in pairs.

❑ Read the directions and steps, and explain as needed.

ANSWER KEY

Answers will vary.

5 **You Are on TV!**

❑ Put students in small groups and read the directions.

❑ Have students prepare to perform their storyboard.

❑ Tell each group to choose a director and actors for each character.

❑ Have each group act out their storyboard for the class.

EXPANSION ACTIVITY

■ The aim of this activity is to practice interactions through a fun theme-related group activity.

■ Consider a variation of Activity 5 (page 238).

■ Have all the groups act out their storyboards.

■ Have students vote for winners in Academy Awards categories such as Best Performance, Best Actor, Best Actress, Best Director, Best Supporting Actor.

■ Collect the votes and put the winning names into envelopes.

■ Stage an Academy Awards show and have student presenters read the nominees and pull the winning name from the envelope and announce the winners.

6 **Guided Academic Conversation**

❑ Put students in small groups to discuss the topics.

❑ Compare answers as a class.

Focus on Testing TOEFL® IBT

Prose Summaries on Tests

■ Read the information in the Focus on Testing box, and explain as needed.

■ Have students complete the practice.

■ Go over the answer.

ANSWER KEY

a, d, e

1 Interpreting Charts

- ❑ Go over the directions.
- ❑ Have students read the information in the box about the U.S. Prison Population.
- ❑ Put students in pairs to complete the activity.
- ❑ Go over the answers.
- ❑ Allow time for students to answer the discussion questions.
- ❑ Have pairs share their answers with the class.

ANSWER KEY

1. 23 2. Up 3. Federal

2 Making Connections

Best Practice

Scaffolding Instruction

Activities such as this will enable students to link knowledge recently acquired with new information they gather from their research.

- ❑ Read the directions and research topics aloud.
- ❑ Tell students to research the topic of their choice on the Internet.
- ❑ Have students report on their findings to the class.

Responding in Writing

WRITING TIP: DEVELOPING YOUR VIEWPOINT

- ■ Read the Writing Tip and explain as needed.
- ■ Ask students to share their viewpoint on a topic covered in the chapter. Answers will vary.

3 Writing about A Real Crime

Best Practice

Making Use of Academic Content

By reading an article and following the steps outlined in this activity, students will learn to how to write well-organized compositions about an article they have read. The skills they learn by doing this activity can be applied to the types of tasks they may be required to do in a broad range of academic settings.

- ❑ Read the directions and steps, and have students choose a topic.
- ❑ Have students work individually.
- ❑ Draw a sample cluster diagram on the board. Remind them to refer back to Chapter 6.
- ❑ Move about the room and offer suggestions as students write.
- ❑ Collect articles, cluster diagrams, outlines, and compositions after students have made their revisions.

Self-Assessment Log

- ❑ Encourage students to maintain a self-assessment log.
- ❑ Allow class time so students can check the strategies and vocabulary they learned in the chapter.
- ❑ Tell students to find definitions in the chapter for any words they did not check.

BLM 1

Name _____ Date _____

Compound Words

Directions: Match each of the words in column 1 with a word in column 2 to create a compound word. When you have finished matching all of the words, create new words using each part of the compound words and write them at the bottom of the page. When you finish, share your findings with the rest of the class.

Column 1:	Column 2:
1. bed	**A.** ship
2. black	**B.** chair
3. friend	**C.** room
4. sweet	**D.** light
5. basket	**E.** watch
6. mail	**F.** box
7. wild	**G.** life
8. wrist	**H.** ball
9. arm	**I.** berry
10. sun	**J.** heart

New Words

*bed*bug, bath*room*

_____

_____

_____

_____

_____

Name _____ Date _____

Canada / United States
Venn Diagram

Directions: Think about the questions below. Write the differences and similarities between Canada and the United States in the Venn diagram. Then compare your diagram with a partner's.

1. What things do Canada and the United States have in common?

2. What are some ways the two countries are different?

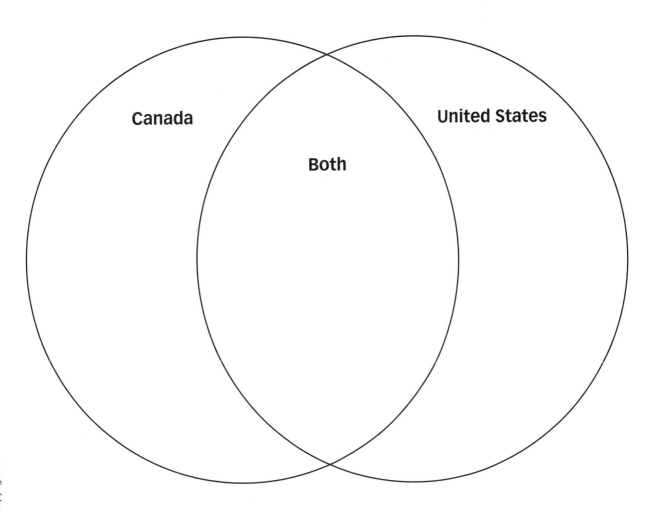

Name _____ Date _____

Idiom Puzzles

Idioms from "Beckham: An Autobiography"

took	a	knock	or	two		
in	a	comfort	zone			
whisked	off					
didn't	really	have	a	clue		
bracing	myself					
twist	in	the	pit	of	my	stomach
get	the	drift				
be	our	night				
feel	at	home				

Idioms related to baseball

get	to	first	base	
be	off	base		
strike	out			
play	ball			
throw	a	curve	ball	
play	hard	ball		
make	a	ballpark	estimate	
hit	the	home	stretch	
two	strikes	against	him	
step	up	to	the	plate

BLM 4

Name _____   Date _____

Chain of Events Diagram:
A Selection from My Autobiography

Directions: Think of a significant time in your life. For example when you got married, moved to a new country or city, etc. Think of four events that occurred during that time. Write them in the correct sequence in the diagram below. Then explain your diagram to your partner.

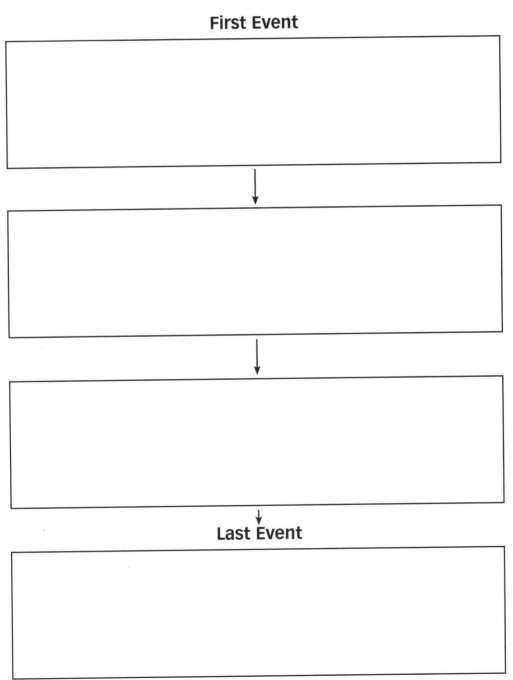

First Event

Last Event

 **BLM 5**

Name _____ Date _____

Topic: _____

Competition / Teamwork T-Chart

Directions: Complete the T-chart with your group. Write the reasons why you think competition or teamwork should be supported according to which topic you chose. Then write the reasons why the other concept should NOT be supported.

Competition	Teamwork

BLM 6

Name _____   Date _____

Information Gap: Population Charts

Student A

TITLE: Population of Children and Youths by Region

Directions: Look at the chart below. Ask your partner questions to help you fill in the missing information. Then discuss the information in the chart with your partner. Is there any information that surprises you?

	0–4 years	5–9 years	10–14 years	15–19 years
Africa	130,854			92,925
Near East		20,866	19,825	
Asia	328,062		347,096	
Latin America and the Caribbean			54,745	52,869
Europe and the New Independent States			55,184	58,301
North America	21,456	21,937		
Oceania	2,620	2,636		

- -

Student B

TITLE: Population of Children and Youths by Region

Directions: Look at the chart below. Ask your partner questions to help you fill in the missing information. Then discuss the information in the chart with your partner. Is there any information that surprises you?

	0–4 years	5–9 years	10–14 years	15–19 years
Africa		116,105	104,705	
Near East	22,474			18,830
Asia		332,255		332,546
Latin America and the Caribbean	55,193	55,747		
Europe and the New Independent States	55,193	55,184		
North America			23,260	22,537
Oceania			2,572	2,442

BLM 7

Name _____   Date _____

KWL Chart

Directions: Before you begin reading, fill in the first two columns. Fill in the last column after you complete the reading.

Remember KWL:

    K: What I KNOW

    W: What I WANT to know

    L: What I LEARNED

Reading Passage: *70 Brides for 7 Foreigners*

K	W	L

BLM 8

Name _____   Date _____

Prefix Categorizing

Directions: Form lists by placing each word from the box below under a prefix that can be used with it to make it mean the opposite.

agreeable	balanced (adj)	decisive	literate	responsible
allergic	believable	dressed	logical	robe
ambitious	clothed	dying	moral	sensitive
athletic	conclusive	establish (verb)	practical	skilled
available	convenient	honest	regular	steady
balance (noun)	decent	legal	relevant	swimmer

DIS   **IL**   **IM**   **IN**   **IR**   **NON**   **UN**

Name _____ Date _____

Fact and Opinion Organizer

Directions: Read your assigned paragraph and complete the Fact and Opinion Organizer. Compare your answers with the other students in your group.

Paragraph Letter _____

	Sentences from the reading Write specific sentences from the reading. Use exact wording.	**I know this is a Fact (or opinion) because...** Explain how you know that the sentence is a fact or opinion. Give signal words or other details.
FACTS Facts are statements that can be proven. You can usually find facts in other sources.		
OPINIONS Opinions are statements that express what a person thinks. They do not have evidence that you can find in another source.		

Name _____   Date _____

Venn Diagram: Comparing Travel Experiences

Directions: Discuss the following questions about the places you visited and make notes in the Venn diagram below.

1. Describe the place you visited.

2. Were there many tourists visiting? If so, describe them.

3. What was the general attitude of the locals toward the tourists?

4. How did the tourists treat the locals?

5. Do you feel the impact of tourism on that place was positive or negative? Explain.

Place I visited: _____   **Place my partner visited:** _____

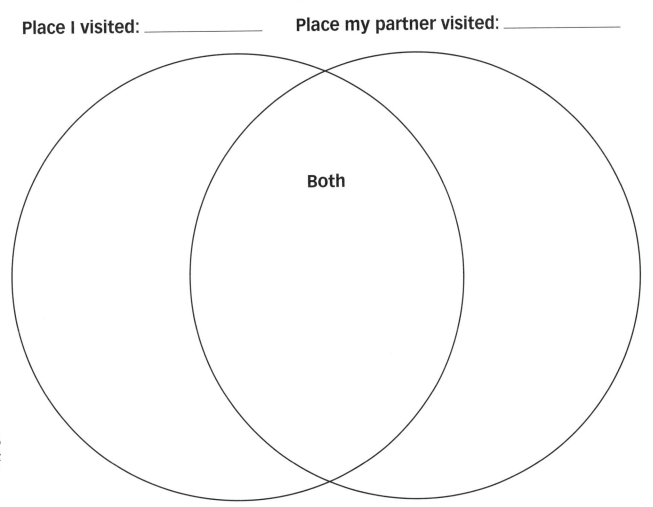

BLM 11

Name _____   Date _____

Fact and Opinion Chart

Directions: Study the reading on pages 108–110. Fill in the "Fact" column with specific, true ideas from the reading passage. Put your opinions about each fact in the "Opinion" column.

TITLE: _____

FACT	OPINION

Copyright © McGraw-Hill

BLM 12

Name _____ Date _____

Automobile Survey

Directions: Fill in the survey by interviewing five students in your class. Take notes and create your own comparison chart based on the data you collect from your interviews.

Question	Student 1	Student 2	Student 3	Student 4	Student 5
Do you have a car? If not, what method of transportation do you use?					
What kind of car do you have?					
How is it powered? *Example:* gas, electricity, hybrid					
Why did you choose your car? *Example:* cost, color, price, model, low maintenance, fuel efficiency?					
Do you like your car? Why? Why not?					

BLM 13

Name _____ Date _____

Blog Research Chart

Directions: Find a *blog* (*weblog*) on a topic that interests you. You can find listings of *blogs* by using a search engine and typing in the words *blogs*, *blog* listings, or *blog research*. Answer as many questions as you can in the chart below. Be prepared to present your findings to the class.

What is the name of the *blog*?	
Who created it? Why?	
What did you infer about the person who created the *blog*?	
What is the topic of the *blog*?	
What were some interesting facts you learned about the topic?	
Did the *blog* include any specialized terms related to the topic?	
Did the *blog* include links to any other sites or *blogs*? If so, what were they about?	
What is your opinion of this *blog*?	

Name _____ Date _____

Noun Suffix Clusters

Directions: Fill in each cluster diagram by putting a noun suffix in the middle and examples of nouns using the suffix in the smaller circles. Some noun suffixes to choose from: *-ist*, *-er/-or*, *-ance/-ence*, *-ness*, *-sion/-tion*, *-ment*, *-ity*

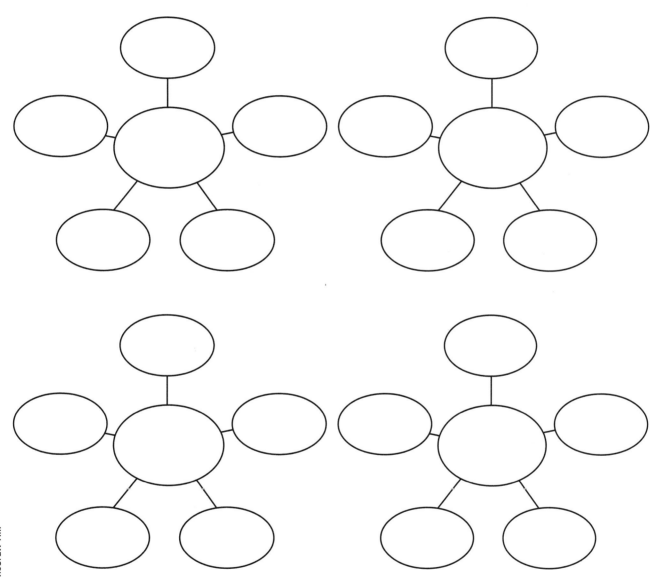

Name _____ Date _____

Pizzeria Marketing Plan Outline

Directions: Use the outline below to help you create a marketing plan for a pizzeria. Prepare to present your group's plan to the class.

1. Our Pizza Company's Name: _____

2. Our Market:

❑ Who are we marketing to (type of people, i.e. students, housewives, etc.)

_____

❑ Do we have an eat-in restaurant or delivery?

_____

❑ Where are we located?

_____

3. Our Competition:

❑ Who is our main competition?

_____

❑ How will we be different from our competition?

_____

4. Our Pizza:

❑ What is special about our pizza?

_____

❑ Do we sell any other products?

_____

5. Our strengths and weaknesses: _____

_____

6. Our Goals and Strategies:

❑ How will we tap a new market?

_____

❑ What is our pricing strategy? Do we offer specials such as "Buy 2, Get 1 Free?"
   What other specials do we offer?

_____

❑ How many outlets will we have?

_____

❑ Will we be a chain?

_____

7. Our Action Plan:

❑ Where will we advertise and how?

_____

_____

Name _____ Date _____

Futures

> **In one year, I will be...**
>
>
>
>
>
> **In 5 years, I will be...**
>
>
>
>
>
> **In 10 years, I will be...**

Name _____ Date _____

Confucius Says, We Say!

Directions: Work with your group. Look at the statements in the "Confucius Says!" column and decide what they mean. Then write some statements in the "We Say!" column based on your group's philosophies.

Confucius Says!	We Say!
Actions committed by a person build society.	
Attempts to obtain short-term pleasure are bad while long-term goals make life better.	
Do the proper thing at the proper time.	
Do the right thing for the right reason.	
Mourn your father and mother for three years after their death.	
Treat your inferiors as you would want your superiors to treat you.	

Name _____ Date _____

Word Family Charts

Directions: Complete the charts with the proper parts of speech. You can choose from the list below or choose your own words.

Root Words: commit, resign, endure, perceive, innovate, express, beauty, friend, select

Root Word	Noun	Adjective	Verb
select	selection	selective	select
commit	commitment		commit
friend			

Root Word	Noun	Adjective	Verb

Root Word	Noun	Adjective	Verb

BLM 19

Name _____ Date _____

KWL Chart

Directions: Before you begin reading, fill in the first two columns. Fill in the last column after you complete the reading.

Remember KWL stands for:

    K: What I KNOW

    W: What I WANT to know

    L: What I LEARNED

Reading Passage: *Guggenheim Museum, U.S.A.*

K	W	L

Name _____ Date _____

Bar Graphs

Directions: Use the information from the **Tallest Buildings in the World** chart (BLM 21) and complete the bar graph by filling in the bar above the building's name to the proper height.

Bar Graph A

Height in Feet:

Over 1500 feet					
1401-1500 feet					
1301-1400 feet					
1201-1300 feet					
1100-1200 feet					
Name of Building:	**Taipei 101**	**CITIC Plaza**	**Aon Centre**	**The Center**	**Jin Mao Building**

Directions: Create your own bar graph by using any information from the **Tallest Buildings in the World** chart (BLM 21). Write the information you will be comparing on the line above the chart (stories, height in feet, etc.) Put your column headings in the gray areas.

Bar Graph B

_____:

Name of Building:	___	___	___	___	___

Name _____   Date _____

Tallest Buildings in the World

Directions: Use the information in the chart below to help you complete Bar Graphs A and B (BLM 20).

Rank	Building	Location	Stories	Height in Feet	Height in Meters	Year Built
1	Taipei 101	Taipei, Taiwan	101	1,670	509	2004
2	Petronas Tower 1	Kuala Lumpur, Malaysia	88	1,483	452	1998
3	Petronas Tower 2	Kuala Lumpur, Malaysia	88	1,483	452	1998
4	Sears Tower	Chicago, Illinois, USA	110	1,450	442	1974
5	Jin Mao Building	Shanghai, China	88	1,380	421	1999
6	Two International Finance Centre	Hong Kong	88	1,362	415	2003
7	CITIC Plaza	Guangzhou, China	80	1,283	391	1996
8	Shun Hing Square	Shenzhen, China	69	1,260	384	1996
9	Empire State Building	New York City, New York, USA	102	1,250	381	1931
10	Central Plaza	Hong Kong	78	1,227	374	1992
11	Bank of China	Hong Kong	72	1,209	369	1989
12	Emirates Tower One	Dubai, UAE	54	1,165	355	1999
13	Tuntex Sky Tower	Kaohsiung, Taiwan	85	1,140	348	1997
14	Aon Centre	Chicago, Illinois, USA	80	1,136	346	1973
15	The Center	Hong Kong	73	1,135	346	1998

BLM 22

Name _____ Date _____

Venn Diagram: Cultural Comparisons

Directions: Write the cultural topic you chose on the line below. Then write the names of the two cultures you chose on the lines above the Venn diagram. Then, fill in the diagram with the differences and similarities you discovered through your research. When you have finished, discuss the two questions with a partner.

Topic: _____

Culture 1: _____ **Culture 2:** _____

1. What things do the two cultures have in common with regards to your topic?

2. What are some ways the two cultures are different with regards to your topic?

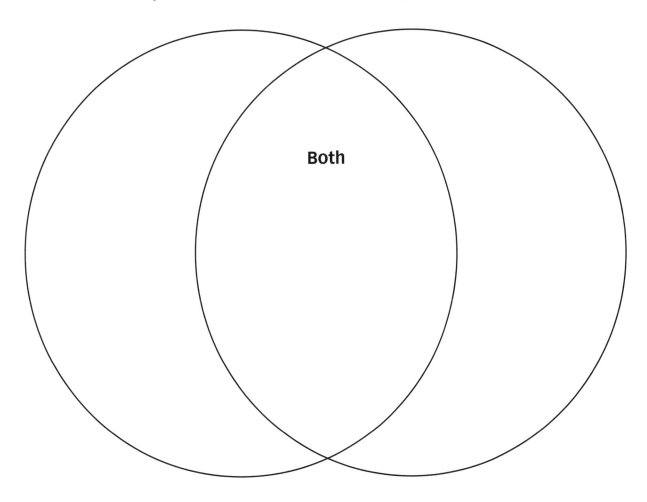

BLM 23

Name _____ Date _____

Story Map

Directions: Complete the story map with information from "A Clean Well-Lighted Place". Then compare your story map with your partner's.

TITLE:

AUTHOR:

SETTING/BRIEF DESCRIPTION:

CHARACTER/BRIEF DESCRIPTION:

CHARACTER/BRIEF DESCRIPTION:

EVENT: → EVENT: → EVENT: → EVENT:

PROBLEM:

RESOLUTION:

CONCLUSION:

GENERAL THEME:

REPRODUCIBLE

Name _____   Date _____

Ranking Crimes

Directions:

Step 1: Think of ten crimes and list them on the Crime List below.

Step 2: Decide which crime is the most serious and mark the corresponding letter (A, B, C, etc.) closest to "most serious" on the continuum. Rank all the letters in order from most serious to least serious.

Step 3: Copy the crimes in order from most serious to least serious into the "CRIME" column of the Crime Rank chart.

Step 4: Finally, write what you think is an appropriate punishment for each crime in the "PUNISHMENT" column.

Crime List

A. _____   F. _____

B. _____   G. _____

C. _____   H. _____

D. _____   I. _____

E. _____   J. _____

Continuum Scale

Most serious |——|——|——|——|——|——|——|——|——| Least serious

Crime Rank

CRIME	PUNISHMENT
1 (Most serious)	
2	
3	
4	
5	
6	
7	
8	
9	
10 (Least serious)	

Name _____   Date _____

Story Elements Chart

Directions: Fill in the organizer with at least three details from the story, "Eye Witnesss" for each section.

TITLE _____

Setting	
Main Characters	
Plot/Problems	
Solution	
Theme	

BLM 26

Name _____   Date _____

Story Sequence Map ("Eye Witness")

Directions: Fill in the story sequence map with key elements of the story's plot.

Setting:

↓

Conflict:

↓

Complications:

↓

Climax:

↓

Ending:

BLM 1 Answer Key

Idiom Puzzles

Idioms from the David Beckham autobiography

took	a	knock	or	two		
In	a	comfort	zone			
whisked	off					
didn't	really	have	a	clue		
bracing	myself					
twist	in	the	pit	of	my	stomach
get	the	drift				
be	our	night				
feel	at	home				

Idioms related to baseball

get	to	first	base	
be	off	base		
strike	out			
play	ball			
throw	a	curve	ball	
play	hard	ball		
make	a	ballpark	estimate	
hit	the	home	stretch	
two	strikes	against	him	
step	up	to	the	plate

BLM 6 Answer Key

Information Gap: Population Charts

TITLE: Population of Children and Youths by Region

	0–4 years	5–9 years	10–14 years	15–19 years
Africa	130,854	116,105	104,705	92,925
Near East	22,474	20,866	19,825	18,830
Asia	328,062	332,255	347,096	332,546
Latin America and the Caribbean	55,193	55,747	54,747	52,869
Europe and the New Independent States	44,479	46,577	55,184	58,301
North America	21,456	21,937	23,260	22,537
Oceania	2,620	2,636	2,572	2,442

BLM #8 Answer Key

Prefix Categorization

DIS	IL	IM	IN	IR	NON	UN
agreeable	legal	moral	conclusive	regular	allergic	ambitious
establish	logical	practical	convenient	responsible	athletic	available
honest			decent		swimmer	balanced
robe			decisive			believable
			sensitive			clothed
						dressed
						dying
						skilled
						steady

BLM #14 Answer Key

Possible answers: Cluster for **-tion/-sion** (in center circle): *globalization, emission, transmission, compensation, innovation.* Cluster for **-ment**: *management, requirement, environment, movement, settlement.* Cluster for **-ity**: *brevity, formality, humidity, nationality, prosperity.*

BLM 18 Answer Key

Word Family Chart

Possible answers:

Root Word	Noun	Adjective	Verb
select	selection	selective	select
commit	commitment	committed	commit
friend	friendship	friendly	befriend

Root Word	Noun	Adjective	Verb
beauty	beauty	beautiful	beautify
resign	resignation	resigned	resign
endure	endurance	endurable, enduring	endure

Root Word	Noun	Adjective	Verb
perceive	perception	perceptive	perceive
innovate	innovation	innovative	innovate
express	expression	expressive	express

BLM 20 Answer Key

Height in Feet:

	Taipei 101	CITIC Plaza	Aon Centre	The Center	Jin Mao Building
Over 1500 feet	▓				
1401-1500 feet	▓				
1301-1400 feet	▓				▓
1201-1300 feet	▓	▓			▓
1100-1200 feet	▓	▓	▓	▓	▓
Name of Building	Taipei 101	CITIC Plaza	Aon Centre	The Center	Jin Mao Building

BLM 23 Answer Key

Story Map

TITLE: "A Clean, Well-Lighted Place"

AUTHOR: Ernest Hemingway

SETTING/BRIEF DESCRIPTION: café, late at night, dark, shadowy

CHARACTER/BRIEF DESCRIPTION: old man—lonely, sitting alone, deaf, drinking, sometimes doesn't pay his bill

CHARACTER/BRIEF DESCRIPTION: waiter #1—young, talks a lot, married, unsympathetic

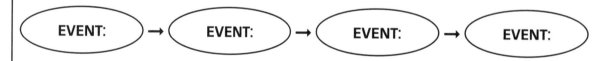

Possible answers:

PROBLEM: The young waiter does not sympathize with the old man and is in a hurry to go home. The old waiter sympathizes with the old man and is willing to let him stay as long as he wants in the café.

RESOLUTION: The old waiter explains his point of view to the young waiter.

CONCLUSION: All three characters leave the café.

GENERAL THEME: Some people have understanding and compassion for others and some don't.

BLM 25 Answer Key
Story Elements Charts ("Eye Witness")

Answers will vary. Possible answers:

Title: "Eye Witness"

Setting: the scene of the crime, the police station

Main characters: Struthers (the witness), Magruder, the narrator (Detective Cappeli), Lieutenant Anderson, Lieutenant Anderson's wife (the victim)

Plot/problems: Lieutenant Anderson's wife is mugged and murdered. The victim, Struthers, is afraid to talk about what he saw.

Solution: Struthers runs out of the police station when he sees Lieutenant Anderson. The reader must decide what happened.

Theme: This story is a murder mystery.

BLM 26 Answer Key

Answers may vary. Possible answers:

Title: "Eye Witness"

Conflict: Struthers is hesitant to talk about what he saw.

Complications: Struthers only wants to speak to lieutenant. He is afraid. The victim was married to the lieutenant.

Climax: Struthers agrees to help identify the murderer. The lieutenant enters the room and they look at each other.

Ending: Struthers runs out of the police station.

Name _____ Date _____ Score _____

Chapter 1 Test

The Challenges of Multiple Births

Section I Reading Comprehension Read the passage. Then answer the questions that follow.
(5 points each)

A   Although multiple births are still relatively rare, in vitro fertilization has brought about a sharp increase in the number of "multiples"—twins, triplets, and quadruplets. In the past, couples who were not able to have children could either remain childless or adopt a child. However, some were reluctant to adopt because they were not comfortable with the idea of taking in a "stranger's" child. Others had a very strong desire for their own biological offspring. With the development of in vitro fertilization, many of these couples are now able to have biological children of their own. Between 1980 and 2000, the number of twins born in the United States increased by 74%. At the same time, the number of higher order multiples—triplets or more—increased by 500%.
5

B   Multiple births can be very challenging for the mother-to-be. Imagine having several infants developing in a space designed for one. Although some of these women experience no problems, many have difficult pregnancies. Some mothers find themselves feeling extremely tired and short of breath. This is because the developing babies require a lot of iron and the mother begins to experience an iron deficiency. In order to carry the additional weight, her feet may grow as much as one shoe size. The shape of her body may also change permanently. As the babies develop, they push out the rib cage, expanding the size of her abdomen. To carry the additional weight, the thighs often become heavier. Despite a prescribed exercise program, these changes in body shape often remain after the pregnancy.
10

15

C   And it's not just the mothers who are affected. Many multiple-birth children face physical and other types of challenges as well. Many are premature babies and will spend months in the hospital before they can go home. If the respiratory system is underdeveloped, the baby may have trouble breathing. If the nervous system is not fully developed, the child may be born with cerebral palsy. Later in life, learning difficulties sometimes emerge. The good news is that medical science is constantly uncovering ways to help these tiny infants survive and thrive.
20

25

D   After the initial shock of having several children at once wears off, the parents-to-be are soon struck by the financial realities. "On, no! We can't afford five children!" they cry. However, most of these families make out just fine. People donate clothing, diapers, cribs, and baby food. Community groups raise money so the family can add living space to their house. Grocery stores come up with special discounts. Over time, these families somehow manage to survive. And with all the extra love in the house, money becomes less and less of an issue as time goes on.
30

1. What is the main idea of paragraph B?
- (A) Changes in body shape often remain after the pregnancy.
- (B) A woman's shoe size may increase during pregnancy.
- (C) Multiple births can cause problems for the mother.
- (D) Mothers of multiples should follow an exercise program after the pregnancy.

2. The number of twins born in the U.S. has increased by what percentage since 1980?
- (A) 200%
- (B) 500%
- (C) 20%
- (D) 74%

3. In paragraph C, the word *premature* probably means _____.
- (A) slow
- (B) early
- (C) healthy
- (D) difficult

4. In paragraph C, the word *emerge* probably means _____.
- (A) appear
- (B) get worse
- (C) survive
- (D) disappear

5. In paragraph D, which of the following is an example of an emotional reaction?
- (A) Money becomes less of an issue.
- (B) Community groups raise money for the family.
- (C) We can't afford five children!
- (D) Families somehow manage to survive.

Section II Strategy Choose the correct answer. (5 points each)

1. The main idea of paragraph A is not stated, it is implied. What is the implied main idea of paragraph A?
- (A) Childless couples used to have two choices.
- (B) The increase in multiple births is a result of in vitro fertilization.
- (C) Most couples want children.
- (D) Multiple births are becoming more common.

2. In paragraph B, which of the following is an example following up on the main idea?
- (A) Multiple births are challenging for the mother.
- (B) The mother's iron level often falls.
- (C) Some women experience no problems.
- (D) Several infants can develop in the space designed for one.

3. Which of the following statements can be inferred from the information in paragraph B?
- (A) Multiple births are easy for most mothers-to-be.
- (B) Developing babies don't require a lot of iron.
- (C) Multiple birth babies often have large rib cages
- (D) Women who have multiple births often can't wear the same clothes they wore before the births.

4. In paragraph D, the word *donate* probably means _____.

 Ⓐ buy

 Ⓑ give

 Ⓒ sell

 Ⓓ lend

5. What is the implied main idea of paragraph D?

 Ⓐ The financial problems are hard to overcome.

 Ⓑ People donate things to help these families.

 Ⓒ Stores often help these families.

 Ⓓ Money is not usually a terrible problem for these families.

Section III New Words Fill in the blanks with words from the box. **(3 points each)**

blunt	brevity	gardener	heritage	leisure
menial	outgoing	restless	symbol	vastness

1. Amos is too proud to do _____ chores around the house.

2. The eagle is the _____ of the United States of America.

3. Barbara isn't shy. She's very _____.

4. Carlos is really proud of his Spanish _____.

5. After I sit for two hours I start feeling _____.

6. It's impossible to imagine the _____ of outer space.

7. The best thing about his speech was its _____. Nobody got bored.

8. Her words weren't exactly impolite, but she was a little _____.

9. Ali works seven days a week. He has no _____ time.

10. The _____ is planting flowers in front of the house.

Section IV Building Vocabulary Circle the correct word in parentheses. **(2 points each)**

1. People who don't trust large corporations have (anti-business / non-business) feelings.

2. If you were not born in France, you are (anti-French / non-French).

3. Laws passed to prevent noise in a city are (anti-noise / non-noise) laws.

4. If you like music but you can't sing, you are (an anti-singing / a non-singing) person.

5. If you speak English that is not standard, you speak (anti-standard / nonstandard) English.

6. People who are (anti-city / non-city) people, don't like big cities.

7. If you are against pollution, you might join (an anti-pollution / a non-pollution) group.

8. People who talk all the time are (anti-stop / nonstop) talkers.

9. Drugs that attempt to destroy cancer are (anti-cancer / non-cancer) drugs.

10. (Anti-credit / Noncredit) courses do not give you academic credit.

TOTAL _____ /100 pts.

Chapter 2 Test
A Look at Teamwork and Competition

Section I Reading Comprehension Read the passage. Then answer the questions that follow. **(5 points each)**

A   Finding a balance between teamwork and competition is the key to success in a wide variety of fields. Medical research is one such area. Its discoveries have serious and wide-ranging effects. To do their best work, scientists are learning how to motivate themselves through competition with their colleagues, while at the same time doing a healthy amount of sharing information. The same principle holds true in business settings and in university classrooms. And research has recently uncovered another situation in which this balance is very important. It is a key element in helping twins develop as successful and independent individuals.   5

B   People who study the nature of business organizations have come up with the term "M-Form." It refers to the type of organization that is carefully constructed to maintain a balance between teamwork and competition. M-Form companies are made up of many different divisions that compete against each other for money and other resources. However, these same competing divisions must also work as a team— sharing laboratories, marketing staff, and production facilities. M-Form companies are not directed from the top down. Each division sets its own direction and makes its own decisions. Management's role is to put together an overall plan that is in the best interests of the whole company.   10   15

C   In terms of teamwork and competition, scientific researchers sometimes find themselves between a rock and a hard place (in a difficult situation without a simple solution). For example, scientists at several different universities and commercial laboratories may be researching ways to cure a particular type of cancer. They all describe some of what they are doing at conferences and in journals. This sharing helps all of them make advances in their research. In some ways, this puts them on the same team. On the other hand, there is sometimes fierce competition among colleagues to get credit for a discovery in order to increase their own prestige. In addition, commercial laboratories may have a lot of money tied up in their research. They may not want to share what they've spent millions of dollars to discover. In these cases, the agencies involved must do a lot of careful thinking about the proper balance between teamwork and competition.   20   25

D   Another fascinating example of ongoing teamwork and competition involves the lives of identical twins. Most twins are constantly compared to each other on everything from school grades to athletic ability. This competition has a special edge to it. It is not only about winning, but also about creating a separate identity. Most twins are able to work out what seems to be a highly productive balance. For Jake Adams, a member of his college tennis team, beating his twin, Jerry, is really important. However, if the two are playing doubles, they are a tough team to beat!   30   35

1. What is the main idea of paragraph A?

(A) Teamwork and competition improve classroom learning.

(B) Teamwork and competition among scientists yields good results.

(C) Teamwork and competition are important in a variety of situations.

(D) Businesses can use teamwork and competition to become more successful.

2. The word *principle* in paragraph A means _____.

(A) most important

(B) rule

(C) problem

(D) leader

3. What is the main idea of paragraph C?

(A) Universities and laboratories often compete with each other.

(B) Researchers can learn a lot from each other's discoveries.

(C) Researchers sometimes have a hard time balancing teamwork and competition.

(D) Commercial laboratories sometimes don't want to share their discoveries.

4. According to the reading, which resource do divisions in M-From companies NOT have to share?

(A) laboratories

(B) workspace

(C) marketing staff

(D) production facilities

5. The phrase *work out* in paragraph D means _____.

(A) solve

(B) do exercises

(C) disagree about

(D) create

Section II Strategy Choose the correct answer. (5 points each)

1. Which of the following does scanning NOT involve?

(A) reading word for word

(B) thinking of what you are looking for

(C) moving your eyes quickly through the text

(D) stopping to write down information

2. Which of the following sentences contains a metaphor?

(A) The company was made up of several divisions.

(B) They made advances in their research.

(C) They found themselves between a rock and a hard place.

(D) There is fierce competition among colleagues.

3. Which compound adjective CANNOT modify the noun *book*?

(A) low-price

(B) best-selling

(C) good-tasting

(D) well-known

4. In paragraph C, *fierce* probably means _____.
- Ⓐ mean
- Ⓑ easy
- Ⓒ strange
- Ⓓ difficult

5. In paragraph D, *beat* probably means _____.
- Ⓐ get
- Ⓑ reduce
- Ⓒ defeat
- Ⓓ research

Section III New Words Fill in the blanks with words from the box. **(3 points each)**

ascend	job	low-end	revenues	V.P.
global	leading-edge	nondescript	get the drift	vicious

1. The reporter was _____. She would not stop asking questions even though the interviewee was upset.

2. Many businessmen wear _____ suits to work. They never wear new styles or bright colors.

3. I know it doesn't pay a lot, but I really need this _____.

4. The company raised their prices in order to increase _____.

5. My boss is a _____. She hopes to become president someday.

6. I work for a _____ corporation with offices in 16 different countries.

7. Several Japanese companies are _____ producers of small cars.

8. I didn't buy a _____ TV. My new flat-screen TV cost over $3000.

9. It will take us over three hours to _____ this mountain.

10. Anne thought that by not returning John's calls that he would _____ that she didn't want to see him anymore, but he still kept calling her.

Section IV Building Vocabulary Mark each sentence with a *T* for *true* or an *F* for *false*. **(2 points each)**

_____ 1. *Earnings* is a synonym for *profit*.

_____ 2. *Cut* is a synonym for *slice*.

_____ 3. *Fail* is an antonym for *rally*.

_____ 4. *Interrupt* is a synonym for *cut in*.

_____ 5. *Office* is a synonym for *factory*.

_____ 6. *Cry* is a synonym for *chant*.

_____ 7. *Expensive* is an antonym for *low-cost*.

_____ 8. *Feel comfortable* is a synonym for *feel at home*.

_____ 9. *Don't like* is a synonym for *don't have a clue*.

_____ 10. *Dance around* is an antonym for *cavort*.

TOTAL _____ /100 pts.

Name _____ Date _____ Score _____

Chapter 3 Test
Building Strong Relationships

Section I Reading Comprehension Read the passage. Then answer the questions that follow.
(5 points each)

A   Like everything else in modern life, relationships have become the focus for extensive scientific study. This has resulted in the development of a plethora of organizations, self-surveys, magazine articles, books, and websites designed to help people learn how to have healthier, more enjoyable relationships.

B   The Washington, DC-based organization, Advocates for Youth, puts out information on how families can build stronger relationships among their members. After extensive study, this group came up with a list of the features that make for a happy, nurturing family life. The first trait on the list is commitment. When people put family first—before work or school activities or outside friendships—strong family relationships result. The second mark of a close family is appreciation. Family members who express affection for each other, and look for the positive not the negative, become much closer over time. A third important characteristic is simply time spent together as a family. Some busy parents make sure to spend small amounts of "quality time" with their children each week, but the research shows that the *quantity* of time also really matters a great deal. It takes time to develop and maintain strong, loving relationships. They don't grow out of spending half an hour together twice a week.

C   Psychologists who study marriage have found that one way to help guarantee a happy marriage is to use a prenuptial survey. One instrument that has received a lot of attention is the Premarital Personal Relationship Survey, nicknamed "Prepare." This questionnaire was created by University of Minnesota family psychology professor, David Olson. Originally it consisted of a few simple questions. The couple would then share their individual results with each other and discuss their similarities and differences. The test has since expanded to include 165 carefully-designed queries which clarify each person's attitudes toward money, sex, leisure time, children, and many other crucial areas. In some places, clergy won't marry a couple unless they complete the survey process together. Their aim is to create happier marital relationships and to help avoid marriages in which the couple has little chance for happiness together.

D   A website sponsored by the Contra Costa County school system in California provides guidance to teachers who want to help their students develop better interpersonal relationship with peers, school staff, and family members. The site shows teachers how to incorporate social skills training into language arts instruction. It demonstrates how to use stories, poems, and writing assignments in regular English textbooks to focus on such skills as showing respect, resolving conflict, and giving compliments. This focus on building relationships doesn't take time away from academic instruction, and it increases the chances for the students' personal success and happiness.

1. In paragraph A, the word *plethora* probably means _____.
   - (A) group
   - (B) few
   - (C) wide variety
   - (D) club

2. In paragraph B, how many traits of strong families are discussed?
   - (A) one
   - (B) two
   - (C) three
   - (D) four

3. What is the main idea of paragraph C?
   - (A) Prenuptial surveys help guarantee a happy marriage.
   - (B) Prenuptial surveys must be long to work well.
   - (C) Many clergy require that couples take a prenuptial survey before getting married.
   - (D) Couples who don't take a prenuptial survey have little chance for happiness.

4. What is the main idea of paragraph D?
   - (A) The website makes use of textbooks.
   - (B) Students do reading and writing assignments.
   - (C) Students learn to show respect and give compliments.
   - (D) The website helps teachers know how to help students learn social skills.

5. In paragraph D, the word *interpersonal* probably means _____.
   - (A) between two people
   - (B) impersonal
   - (C) large-group
   - (D) secret

Section II Strategy Choose the correct answer. **(5 points each)**

1. Which of the following does reading a chart for information NOT involve?
   - (A) Move your eyes quickly until you find the information you want.
   - (B) Write down all the important ideas you find.
   - (C) Ignore information that doesn't answer the question you're working on.
   - (D) Skim for the general idea.

2. Choose the most general statement below.
   - (A) Many websites help families learn how to build stronger relationships.
   - (B) Many websites contain surveys that help couples analyze their relationships.
   - (C) Many websites feature information about building relationships.
   - (D) Many websites describe ways that teachers can help students relate better.

3. Which of the following does skimming NOT involve?
   - (A) summarizing the idea in a single sentence
   - (B) looking at headings
   - (C) looking at photos
   - (D) noting the title

4. Choose the most specific statement below.
- (A) There are four men and twelve women in my "family living" class.
- (B) There are sixteen people in my "family living" class.
- (C) Most of the students in my "family living" class are women.
- (D) All of the students in my "family living" class have at least two children.

5. What does writing down the key points in a summary NEVER involve?
- (A) the author's opinion
- (B) main ideas
- (C) important facts
- (D) your opinion

Section III New Words Match each word with the correct definition. **(3 points each)**

_____ **1.** breadwinner   **a.** not true

_____ **2.** cottage   **b.** person who sends products to other countries

_____ **3.** valid   **c.** legal

_____ **4.** well-to-do   **d.** person who earns money

_____ **5.** exporter   **e.** large amount of flowing water

_____ **6.** palace   **f.** small amount of flowing water

_____ **7.** fictitious   **g.** small home

_____ **8.** nanny   **h.** rich

_____ **9.** trickle   **i.** very large home

_____ **10.** torrent   **j.** person who cares for children

Section IV Building Vocabulary Choose the correct antonym for each word. **(4 points each)**

1. flourish
- (A) get worse
- (B) move quickly
- (C) grow
- (D) forget

2. legal

    Ⓐ easy to understand

    Ⓑ unimportant

    Ⓒ against the law

    Ⓓ official

3. radical

    Ⓐ complete

    Ⓑ extreme

    Ⓒ major

    Ⓓ minor

4. blended

    Ⓐ pleasant

    Ⓑ separated

    Ⓒ strong

    Ⓓ interesting

5. advantageous

    Ⓐ inexpensive

    Ⓑ slow-moving

    Ⓒ harmful

    Ⓓ guaranteed

TOTAL ____ **/100 pts.**

Name _____ Date _____ Score _____

Chapter 4 Test

International Drug Research

Section I Reading Comprehension Read the passage. Then answer the questions that follow. **(5 points each)**

A   The 2005 film *The Constant Gardener*, directed by Fernando Meirelles and based
upon John le Carré's novel, brought popular attention to another problematic aspect
of globalization: international drug research. The film tells the story of Justin Quayle,
a low-level British diplomat stationed in Kenya, whose wife is suddenly killed. As
he looks for her murderers, he discovers the dangerous research a European drug   5
company is conducting on poor Africans. His wife had discovered the same research.
In order to create a safe tuberculosis drug to be sold in the West, a Dutch drug
manufacturer has forced a community of villagers to participate in their tests. The
villagers have been told that they would not receive any medical attention if they
refuse. With the help of British and Kenyan officials on their payroll, the company   10
covered up the many deaths caused by the research. When Justin's wife threatened to
reveal them, they killed her.

B   Although this is just a film, it presents some parallels with the real world. Western
drug researchers, whether corporate or nonprofit, conduct tests on people in
developing countries, such as Kenya in exchange for money or health care. Wealthier   15
nations protect their citizens by requiring evidence that new drugs work safely and
effectively before they allow them to be sold to the public. But the laws in these
affluent countries make it difficult for drug companies to conduct tests on citizens.
For example, the American drug company Pfizer went into Nigeria in 1996 when that
country was suffering from a widespread epidemic of bacterial meningitis. At the   20
time, Pfizer was trying to get approval from the US Food and Drug Administration
(FDA) for its new antibiotic, Trovan. In the US, the company needed proof that
Trovan, which was delivered in a pill form, would work as well as the standard
antibiotic that was delivered through an injection needle. In order to receive this
proof, Pfizer gave equal numbers of children the pill and the injection. At the end of   25
the trial, both groups suffered the same number of deaths. Based on the high numbers
of children in these test groups, the FDA gave the company approval to market oral
Trovan to children with meningitis. Yet some critics claim that it was unethical to test
an unproven drug in the middle of an epidemic. Others are disturbed by the fact that
the injected drug was given in smaller quantities than usual.   30

C   The ethical dilemma of this and similar cases is compounded by the fact that while
new drugs are often tested in poor countries, their results are rarely applied or
available there. Also, drug researchers seldom seek to prevent diseases like malaria,
polio, and other common threats to good health in the developing world.

1. Western drug researchers work in the developing world in order to _____

   Ⓐ   prevent diseases like malaria and polio.

   Ⓑ   produce thrilling movies everybody will enjoy.

   Ⓒ   save Nigerian children from dying of meningitis.

   Ⓓ   prove that new drugs will safely and effectively cure sicknesses.

2. Critics of the American company Pfizer claim they received FDA approval for the new meningitis antibiotic Trovan by _____

   Ⓐ   testing it against an inadequate dosage of the standard meningitis antibiotic.

   Ⓑ   delivering it to patients in a pill form.

   Ⓒ   delivering it to patients through an injection needle.

   Ⓓ   making it difficult to conduct tests on their own citizens.

3. The word "corporate" in paragraph B probably means _____

   Ⓐ   rich.

   Ⓑ   poor.

   Ⓒ   relating to business.

   Ⓓ   not profitable.

4. Justin Quayle is _____

   Ⓐ   a drug researcher.

   Ⓑ   a current low-level Kenyan diplomat.

   Ⓒ   a character in a movie.

   Ⓓ   a tuberculosis patient.

5. The writer of the above passage _____

   Ⓐ   is neutral toward the subject of international drug research.

   Ⓑ   believes that international drug research will create a healthier world.

   Ⓒ   is critical of international drug research.

   Ⓓ   believes that all international drug research must stop now.

Section II Strategy Each question refers directly to certain words in the passage. Look back at them before you decide on your answers. **(5 points each)**

1. A different way to say that the film "brought popular attention to another problematic aspect of globalization" is: _____

   Ⓐ   The film made people think critically about globalization

   Ⓑ   The film made globalization even more popular than it already is.

   Ⓒ   The film has many different aspects.

   Ⓓ   The film is very popular.

2. Another way to say the film has "some parallels with the real world" is: _____

   Ⓐ   The film reflects something that is real.

   Ⓑ   The film is not real at all.

   Ⓒ   The film is made in the real world.

   Ⓓ   The film is a documentary.

3. The word *affluent* is used in Paragraph B. What is a synonym for *affluent*?

- (A) poor
- (B) rich
- (C) large
- (D) small

4. Another way to say "The ethical dilemma of this and similar cases thickens" is: _____

- (A) International drug research has proven to be more concerned with profits than with saving lives.
- (B) International drug research continues to raise more and more questions on right and wrong.
- (C) International drug research has proven to bring good health to the whole world.
- (D) All of the above

5. Another way to say "Drug researchers seldom seek to prevent diseases like malaria, polio, and other common threats to good health in the developing world" is: _____

- (A) Drug researchers are more concerned with diseases that are common in wealthy countries.
- (B) Malaria and polio are easy to cure.
- (C) Drug researchers are more concerned with diseases that are common in poor countries.
- (D) People in wealthy countries suffer from malaria and polio.

Section III New Words Fill in the blanks with words from the box. **(3 points each)**

acquiring	affluent	benefits	communities	compensation
found	hence	physical	prevent	virtually

It is difficult to judge the _____ of international drug research because there is
                                        1
so much controversy surrounding the issue.

There are many _____ all over the world that do not have access to adequate
                            2
health care.

What do you think would be fair _____ for participating in a clinical test of a
                                              3
new drug?

_____ all nations stand to gain from more research into world health issues.
          4
Our sense of _____ well-being is essential to leading productive lives.
                      5

The need to _____ unethical research practices is very strong.
                    6

People in _____ countries tend to take many things for granted. Since they
                  7
have everything they want, they have _____ little need to question where things
                                                    8

come from.

_____ information about the business practices of large corporations is often
₉

very difficult and time-consuming, _____ it is important to keep abreast of
₁₀

current events and the daily news.

Section IV Building Vocabulary Match the words on the left with the synonyms on the right.
(4 points each)

_____ **1.** looks for   **a.** searches

_____ **2.** goes on the trail   **b.** contagious disease

_____ **3.** manufacturer   **c.** proof

_____ **4.** evidence   **d.** is assigned to

_____ **5.** epidemic   **e.** maker

TOTAL _____ /100 pts.

Chapter 5 Test
Fiber Optic Technology

Section I Reading Comprehension Read the passage. Then answer the questions that follow. **(5 points each)**

A   Fiber optic cables have many advantages over copper wire, which used to be the material of choice for transmitting telephone and other communication signals such as television from one point to another. To begin with, fiber optic cable is cheaper to manufacture than copper wire. Secondly, it is lighter and thinner, so it takes up less space. In addition, fiber optic cables distort the signals much less than copper wires do, and low-power transmitters can be used with fiber optics instead of the high-voltage transmitters needed for copper wires. That saves a lot of money. New fiber optic cables offer so many advantages that copper wire connections for telephones, television, the Internet, and other communication services may soon be a thing of the past.   5
10

B   The main characteristics of fiber optic cables are that they are very flexible and deliver an extremely clear picture. This makes them invaluable in situations where very clear images are needed and space is severely limited. For this reason, many medical devices used inside the human body, including some that are used for surgery, feature fiber optic technology. Today, gall bladder operations can be performed using a laparoscope which contains a camera and tiny surgical tools connected to a viewing screen by fiber optic cables. There is no need for a large incision; the surgeon inserts the laparoscope containing a fiber optic cable through the belly button and takes out the gall bladder in tiny pieces.   15

C   The part of the fiber optic cable that light travels though is called the *core*. It is the flexible glass center of the cable. Wrapped around the core is a layer called the *cladding*. It's purpose is to reflect all the light in the core back into the core without letting any escape. Wrapped around the cladding is yet another layer called the *buffer coating*. It protects the inside of each strand from damage and moisture. The cables you see running to your television set or connecting computers in an office are actually bundles of many separate fiber optic strands. What you see on the outside is called the *jacket*, the final covering that holds all the strands together.   20
25

D   But just how does a fiber optic cable work? Imagine what it looks like to shine a flashlight down a long straight hall, lighting up the space. Then imagine that the hall suddenly has hundreds of twists and turns. How are you going to get that light to travel around corners? You can do it by lining the hall with mirrors. The cladding in a fiber optic cable is actually a mirrored surface that produces that same effect. *Optical generators* every half mile or so boost the power of the light signals. This combination delivers crystal clear images over distances of hundreds of miles.   30

1. What is the main idea of paragraph A?
- (A) Most communications signals used to be carried by copper wires.
- (B) Fiber optic cables are lighter and cheaper than copper wires.
- (C) Fiber optic cables have many advantages.
- (D) Copper wires may soon be a thing of the past.

2. What is the meaning of the word *invaluable* in paragraph B?
- (A) very useful
- (B) awkward
- (C) useless
- (D) expensive

3. The outer layer of a fiber optic cable is called the _____.
- (A) cladding
- (B) core
- (C) buffer coating
- (D) jacket

4. Which paragraph in the reading passage is organized from general to specific?
- (A) A
- (B) B
- (C) C
- (D) D

5. What is the meaning of *crystal clear* in paragraph D?
- (A) shiny
- (B) like a mirror
- (C) extremely accurate
- (D) moving

Section II Strategy Choose the correct answer. **(5 points each.)**

1. New fiber optic cables offer so many advantages that copper wire connections for telephones, television, the Internet, and other communication services may soon be a thing of the past. What does *a thing of the past* mean?
- (A) no longer used
- (B) a better way of doing things
- (C) an important part of the history of communications
- (D) very useful

2. The hurricane was so strong it blew the car over onto its roof. Which compound word means the same as *blew the car over onto its roof*?
- (A) overcame the car
- (B) upended the car
- (C) downloaded the car
- (D) undertook the car

3. What is the first step in creating an informal study outline?
- (A) Making a list of examples
- (B) Making a list of points with regular numbers
- (C) Writing a brief summary
- (D) Making a list of points with roman numerals

4. Which compound adjective best describes fiber optic cables?
- (A) low-tech
- (B) little-known
- (C) light-weight
- (D) high-priced

5. If you find a word you don't understand near the beginning of an article, what should you do?
- (A) Skim the whole article for general information and then return to the word.
- (B) Read the article two or three times and then return to the word.
- (C) Change the word to another part of speech.
- (D) Scan the article for a definition of the word.

Section III New Words Match each word with the correct definition. **(3 points each)**

_____ **1.** braking   **a.** form of transportation

_____ **2.** efficient   **b.** accept an electronic file

_____ **3.** data   **c.** add electricity to something

_____ **4.** scenario   **d.** plan

_____ **5.** charge   **e.** stopping

_____ **6.** handmade   **f.** side by side

_____ **7.** interwoven   **g.** well-organized

_____ **8.** download   **h.** closely connected

_____ **9.** vehicle   **i.** information

_____ **10.** parallel   **j.** not manufactured

Section IV Building Vocabulary Complete each sentence with the correct compound word from the box. **(2 points each)**

handmade	machine-washable	small-scale	timepiece	well-read
home-based	newlywed	speedway	top hat	worn out

1. Two hundred years ago, clothes were all _____.

2. All of our furniture is very old and _____.

3. Today most people buy only _____ clothes because dry cleaning is expensive.

4. Professor Franklin knows a lot. She's a _____ person.

5. It's a _____ restaurant. There are only seats for ten people.

6. Linda just got married. She's a _____.

7. My grandfather's watch is my favorite _____.

8. My aunt makes birthday cakes in her house and sells them. She has a _____ business.

9. At formal weddings the groom wears a tuxedo and a _____.

10. My brother likes to race his car at a nearby _____.

TOTAL _____ /100 pts.

Chapter 6 Test

The History of Money

Section I Reading Comprehension Read the passage. Then answer the questions that follow.
(5 points each)

A   The *Yen*, the *Dollar*, the *Quetzal*, or the *Peso*—no matter what the currency is
called, money is an important part of life in nearly every culture today and has been
throughout history. The concept of money dates back thousands of years. Originally,
money did not consist of metal coins or paper bills. Rather, people paid for things
with objects that were useful and therefore considered valuable. We sometimes   5
call this *commodity money*. Some examples of commodity money used throughout
history are iron nails, rare seashells, bread, and livestock, such as pigs or cattle.

B   Salt and other spices were also once used as money. In fact, the word *salary* (the
money that employees are paid weekly or monthly by their employers) is derived
from the Latin word *salarium* meaning a payment made in salt. The expression *He's*   10
(not) worth his salt is probably derived from this, because it was used to mean that
someone's work was (or wasn't) worth the amount of money (or salt) he or she was
being paid. There is also evidence that, during the Middle Ages, pepper was used as a
form of money, hence the old French saying *As dear as pepper*. In England, one could
actually pay one's rent in pepper! Even in more modern times commodity money has   15
been used in cases where there was no access to actual currency. An example of this
was during and after World War II in Europe, where tobacco was often used in place
of money.

C   Certain metals, such as gold, silver, and copper have been used as commodity money
for thousands of years. Metals were exchanged in the form of jewelry and nuggets   20
(small lumps) and eventually appeared in the form of coins around 560 B.C.E. The use
of metals coins as money became widespread after the use of the touchstone was
discovered. The touchstone enabled people to find how much of a certain type of
metal was contained in a nugget and therefore determine its value. Eventually, the
system of representative money emerged in the form of paper bills. This system is   25
called *representative money*, because the paper itself is of very little intrinsic value,
but is based on its correlation to a valued commodity, such as gold.

D   Currencies and methods of transaction seem to be constantly evolving. An example
of this is the use of *electronic money*, money that is transferred electronically. Thanks
to modern technology and electronic money, people are now able to pay their bills,   30
transfer funds from one account to another, and receive their paychecks from their
employers without ever stepping into a bank. It looks like the concept of money is
here to stay, but we are probably still in for more surprising changes in the future.

(source: http://en.wikipedia.org/wiki/History_of_money)

1. What is the main idea of the reading passage?

(A) Commodity money was used before coins and paper money.

(B) Money has always been an important part of life.

(C) Salt is a very valuable substance.

(D) Money will soon be a thing of the past.

2. According to the reading passage, when was pepper used as a form of commodity money in Europe?

(A) during World War II

(B) present day

(C) thousands of years ago

(D) during the Middle Ages

3. According to the reading passage, which item was often used in place of money in Europe after World War II?

(A) rare shells

(B) bread

(C) tobacco

(D) iron nails

4. In paragraph C, *determine* probably means _____.

(A) weigh

(B) decide

(C) increase

(D) test

5. Which of the following does the article NOT mention as something people can now do without going to a bank?

(A) pay their bills

(B) deposit their paychecks

(C) transfer funds

(D) buy food and clothing

Section II Strategies Choose the best answer. **(5 points each)**

1. In paragraph A, *considered* probably means _____.

(A) thought of

(B) traded

(C) valued

(D) represented

2. In paragraph B, the Latin word *salarium* means _____.

(A) salty

(B) valuable

(C) a payment in salt

(D) a touchstone

3. In paragraph B, *derived from* probably means _____.

(A) traded

(B) came from

(C) changed

(D) discovered

4. In paragraph B, *dear* probably means _____.

    (A) small

    (B) delicious

    (C) valuable

    (D) worthless

5. In paragraph C, *intrinsic* probably means _____.

    (A) metallic

    (B) expensive

    (C) rare

    (D) natural

Section III New Words Complete the sentences with the words below. **(4 points each)**

affordable	anticipated	enormous	mentality	succulent
amicable	convenience	inclined	specialities	transform

1. The new movie theater in downtown Los Angeles has 28 screens, making it the biggest movie theater in California. It's _____!

2. I was _____ to tell Marta that her outfit didn't match, but decided not to because she's very self-conscious as it is.

3. Many people consider shopping online to be a real _____, as it saves them from having to spend a lot of time in their cars and in shopping malls.

4. Karen has a very positive _____ and always sees the bright side of every situation. That's probably why she's always so happy.

5. The company's Chief Financial Officer increased our department's budget last year, because she _____ our sales would go up 10% over the previous year.

6. These strawberries are perfectly ripe. They are delicious and so _____!

7. James found that living in New York City was too expensive, so he decided to move somewhere where housing was more _____.

8. Even though Ana and Peter are divorced, their relationship is _____ and they still call each other on their birthdays.

9. It's amazing how new furniture can _____ a room. Our living room looks completely different!

10. That shop sells some delicious Italian _____, such as olives, fresh pasta, and many different kinds of cheese.

Section IV Building Vocabulary Match the word on the left with the suffix on the right that changes its part of speech. **(2 points each)**

1. danger	**a.** -ity
2. afford	**b.** -ion
3. protect	**c.** -able
4. power	**d.** -ous
5. technical	**e.** -ful

TOTAL _____ **/100 pts.**

Name _____ Date _____ Score _____

Chapter 7 Test
The Life of Thurgood Marshall

Section I Reading Comprehension Read the passage. Then answer the questions that follow.
(4 points each)

A   Thurgood Marshall, born in Baltimore, Maryland in 1908, was the first African
American to become a Justice of the United States Supreme Court. His grandfather
had been a slave and he was raised by parents who were not yet themselves totally
free of the limitations that race imposed upon blacks in American society. His father
was a steward at an all-white country club and his mother taught in a segregated   5
school. But his family saw his abilities and did everything possible to ensure his
success in life.

B   After graduating from Lincoln University in 1930, Marshall applied to the University
of Maryland School of Law. At this time, however, the university still had a strict
policy of racial segregation—only whites were allowed to attend. He next applied to   10
Howard University, a well-respected, historically black university in Washington, D.C.
Howard was not associated with any religious institution and was open to people of
both sexes and of any race. He excelled in his studies there and after graduating in
1933 opened his own law practice in Baltimore. The next year he was involved in a
lawsuit against the University of Maryland, the institution that had refused to allow   15
him to attend their law school. He proved that the other universities that blacks were
free to attend either did not have law schools or were in other ways unequal to the
University of Maryland. Because of Marshall's hard work, the state courts ruled that
the university must admit people of all races.

C   Marshall continued to fight for racial equality all his life. As chief counsel for the   20
National Association for the Advancement of Colored People (NAACP), he won many
important cases that helped bring about the end of segregated educational systems
in the U.S. On June 13, 1967, President Lyndon B. Johnson appointed Marshall to the
Supreme Court. Although there were many objections, Johnson said that it was, "the
right thing to do, the right time to do it, the right man and the right place." Marshall   25
served on the court for twenty-four years compiling an impressive record that
included strong support for constitutional protection of individual and civil rights.

D   The good work that Marshall did during his life will not soon be forgotten. Several
middle schools also bear his name, including those in St. Petersburgh, Florida and
Marion, Indiana. His name was also given to the law schools at the University of   30
Maryland and the University of California, San Diego. The Washington, D.C., airport
is now called The Baltimore-Washington International Thurgood Marshall Airport.
The Columbia Pike, a highway in Virginia, has been renamed the Thurgood Marshall
Memorial Highway. And in 2006, the Episcopal Church even nominated him for
sainthood.   35

1. In what year did the University of Maryland Law School begin admitting black students?

- (A) 1930
- (B) 1933
- (C) 1934
- (D) 1940

2. In paragraph B, the word *segregation* probably means _____.

- (A) separation
- (B) punishment
- (C) equality
- (D) awareness

3. Which quote from paragraph B <u>disproves</u> the following statement: *African Americans could attend any college they chose*.

- (A) . . . Howard University, a well-respected, historically black university . . . .
- (B) . . . the university still had a strict policy of racial segregation.
- (C) Howard . . . was open to people of both sexes and of any race.
- (D) . . . the other universities that blacks were free to attend . . . did not have law schools . .

4. Which quote from paragraph C <u>proves</u> the following statement: *President Johnson totally supported the appointment of Marshall as a Supreme Court Justice*.

- (A) . . . there were many objections . . .
- (B) Marshall served on the court for twenty-four years . . .
- (C) . . . President Lyndon B. Johnson appointed Marshall to the Supreme Court.
- (D) . . . Johnson said that it was, "the right thing to do, the right time to do it, the right man and the right place."

5. What is the main idea of paragraph D?

- (A) Marshall's memory has been honored in many different ways.
- (B) Many schools have been named in Marshall's honor.
- (C) Thurgood Marshall may become a saint.
- (D) An airport and a highway have been named for Marshall.

Strategy II Strategy Read the sentences below. Choose the correct expressive word or phrase to replace the common words in italics. **(4 points each)**

1. Jonas Salk invented a vaccine that helped _____ (end) polio in children.

- (A) conclude
- (B) destroy
- (C) eradicate
- (D) finish off

2. Good food and enough sleep are _____ (sources) of good health.

- (A) realizations
- (B) promotions
- (C) backgrounds
- (D) cornerstones

3. The early death of a mother can _____ (upset) a young child.
- Ⓐ be bothersome for
- Ⓑ confuse
- Ⓒ annoy
- Ⓓ overwhelm

4. If you want to get good grades, you must be a _____ (serious) student.
- Ⓐ nervous
- Ⓑ diligent
- Ⓒ perfect
- Ⓓ knowledgeable

5. The Kennedys have become a famous political _____ (family).
- Ⓐ dynasty
- Ⓑ force
- Ⓒ federation
- Ⓓ component

Section III New Words Fill in the blanks with words from the box. **(3 points each)**

atone	compelling	influential	resigned	seized
commoners	founded	permeated	role	suppress

1. I spent a lot of time in my grandparent's home. They were very _____ in my life.

2. Although I was very nervous, I tried to _____ any outward signs of it.

3. After three years as president of the company, Mr. Harold _____ last week.

4. It was a _____ story. I finished the whole book in one sitting.

5. Mary George _____ the first museum in our community.

6. The king never talked with the _____.

7. The invading army _____ the property of wealthy landowners.

8. The _____ of a tutor is to help a student learn.

9. Danny wanted to _____ for the harm he had caused his family.

10. The cigarette smoke _____ the entire house.

Section IV Building Vocabulary Read the sentences below. In each blank, write a compound word, a word with a prefix, or a word with a suffix that means the same as the words in parentheses. **(3 points each)**

1. You can usually buy camera film in a (store that sells drugs) _____.

2. The house looks as if it is (not finished) _____.

3. The book was so good I (read it a second time) _____ it.

4. Most children enjoy playing (not indoors) _____.

5. They usually play in the (yard that isn't the front yard) _____.

6. Thurgood Marshall was a (person who defends) _____ of the rights of

   all people.

7. At $50.00 each, these shirts are really (the opposite of underpriced) _____!

8. Carla has to make an important (thing she has to decide) _____ by Friday.

9. Where is the (clothes you wear when you're doing sports) _____ department?

10. The local newspaper took a(n) (against the war) _____ stand.

TOTAL ____ /100 pts.

Chapter 8 Test

Kala Ramnath

Section I Reading Comprehension Read the passage. Then answer the questions that follow. **(5 points each)**

A   Although the modern-day violin was originally made in Italy in the 1700s, some say the first violin can be traced to an ancient Indian instrument called the Ravan Hatta. With such a rich musical history in India, it is not surprising that perhaps one of the most accomplished violin musicians in the world is India's remarkably talented Kala Ramnath. Born into a family of critically-acclaimed Indian musicians including violin legend Professor T.N. Krishnan, Kala demonstrated musical talent from childhood. She began playing when she was only three. At that time, she started her music education by studying under her grandfather, Vidwan Shri Narayan Lyer. Under his guidance, there was no room for laziness or excuses for not practicing, nor were there any breaks or trips outside of the home for leisure or fun. Kala's second teacher was her aunt, also a well-known violinist. Later, she moved on to study under high-profile musician Sangeet Martand Pandit Jasraj. With the help her three teachers, she mastered the techniques and the creative artistry that has set her apart from others.

B   Although she learned the classical techniques with her teachers, Kala has since developed her own individual style. She uses unique bow and finger techniques to create notes that sound more like a human voice singing than a violin. These techniques have earned her violin the nickname of "The Singing Violin." She and her singing violin have toured the world extensively. Kala has performed in the United States, Greece, Australia, Canada, the United Arab Emirates, and Bangladesh.

C   In addition to having toured in various parts of the world, she has also experimented with incorporating different types of sounds into her music. She has played with Ray Manzarek who played keyboards for the American rock band, The Doors, and with Eduardo Niebla, a Flamenco guitarist. She has also played alongside South Africa's Lucas Khumalo and Kúnlé Odutayo to create music with an African-Indian fusion.

D   Kala has expanded her career beyond music into the areas of theater and radio broadcasting, where she has also excelled. She has gone beyond being thought of only as a musician to being a well-known personality in the worlds of TV and radio broadcasting. Although a pioneer in mixing her music with that of other cultures and genres, Kala is still, and always will be, considered an icon of North Indian classical music.

Source: http://www.kalaramnath.com/

1. The main idea of this article is that _____
- (A) classical violin music is very popular in India.
- (B) Kala's violin sounds like voices singing.
- (C) Kala Ramnath is very talented.
- (D) Kala is a famous radio and TV star.

2. The first modern-day violin was made in _____
- (A) India.
- (B) Italy.
- (C) Bangladesh.
- (D) South Africa.

3. How many violinists did Kala study under?
- (A) 5
- (B) 4
- (C) 3
- (D) 2

4. Why has Kala's violin been nicknamed "The Singing Violin"?
- (A) She can make the violin sound like a voice singing.
- (B) The violin sings.
- (C) Kala sings while she plays.
- (D) People sing to her music.

5. Kala has not worked with an artist from _____
- (A) South Africa.
- (B) Spain.
- (C) United States.
- (D) Bangladesh.

Section II Strategy This section refers directly to certain words in the passage. Look back at them before you decide on your answers. **(5 points each)**

1. In paragraph A, the word *remarkably* could be replaced with the word _____.
- (A) curiously
- (B) ordinarily
- (C) noticcably
- (D) interestingly

2. In paragraph A, what inference can be made about Kala?
- (A) She enjoys traveling around the world.
- (B) She works hard.
- (C) She can play many musical instruments.
- (D) She dislikes practicing the violin.

3. In paragraph B, what word could be used in place of *conventional*?
- (A) unique
- (B) traditional
- (C) modern
- (D) strict

4. Use the structure clues and context to guess the meaning of the word *fusion* in Paragraph D.

  Ⓐ a blend
  Ⓑ an ingredient
  Ⓒ a song
  Ⓓ a band

5. What inference can be made about Kala's grandfather?

  Ⓐ He was strict.
  Ⓑ He was lazy.
  Ⓒ He liked to play the violin.
  Ⓓ He didn't like music.

Section III New Words Complete each sentence with the correct word. **(4 points each)**

ambition	circuitous	compulsory	continually	critical acclaim
dabbled	demonstrate	experiment	funds	pioneer

1. The taxi driver took a _____ route back to the hotel. The ride took half an hour

    and cost twenty dollars!

2. There was no discussion about the rules; the president of the company made them

    _____ and the employees were required to follow them.

3. Michael's career was dentistry, but for fun he _____ in oil painting. On his days off,

    he painted landscapes and portraits of his friends.

4. The weather during our vacation was horrible. It rained _____ for eight days. We

    didn't see the sun once!

5. My _____ drove me to find a better job with higher pay and more status.

6. When Bill Gates first started his career, people thought his ideas were crazy; now he is considered a

    _____ in the world of computers.

7. The high school had an event to help raise _____ for a new athletic center.

8. Tom Cruise is an actor who has received _____; he has received good reviews from

    audiences all over the world.

9. In his next movie, Cruise will _____ and play a different kind of role. Usually he

plays the hero; in his new movie he plays the villain.

10. Before having the students complete the activity, the teacher has to _____ how to

use a Venn diagram.

Section IV Building Vocabulary Match the adjectives on the right with their definitions on the left.
(2 points each)

1. startling   **a.** correct

2. energetic   **b.** active

3. definitive   **c.** surprising

4. contemporary   **d.** modern

5. proper   **e.** conclusive

TOTAL _____/100 pts.

Chapter 9 Test
Culture Shock

Section I Reading Comprehension Read the passage. Then answer the questions that follow.
(5 points each)

A Anyone who has spent time in another country has probably experienced some
degree of *culture shock*. What is culture shock? The term was coined in 1958
to describe the feelings of anxiety, discomfort, and disorientation that people
experience when moving to a new country and culture. Culture shock is said to
have a few different stages, which set in after a person has spent a few weeks in the   5
new environment. The first stage of culture shock is sometimes referred to as the
"honeymoon" stage, because everything in the new culture is new and exciting. There
are different foods to try, interesting places to visit and possibly a very different
climate to experience. All of these things may seem exotic and thrilling for a little
while, but this excitement eventually wears off.   10

B The second stage of culture shock occurs when the differences of the new
environment start to seep in and are suddenly perceived as more irritating
and disorienting than interesting and exciting. At this stage, many people tend
to feel a sense of disconnectedness due to language problems and cultural
miscommunications that they experience by doing everyday activities, such as taking   15
public transportation and buying groceries. This stage is often characterized by the
newcomer feeling angry and impatient and rejecting the new culture and its strange
way of doing things.

C When people enter into the third stage of culture shock, they still experiences
difficulties, but tend to deal with them with more patience and a sense of humor.   20
Perhaps because they have had more of a chance to understand the culture they are
in, they are more easily able to accept and appreciate its differences. At this stage,
people also start to feel a sense of wanting to belong. In the fourth stage, people tend
to truly feel a sense of belonging within the new culture and are able to accept the
good and bad aspects of it. In addition to these four stages of culture shock, there is a   25
fifth, which people may experience upon reentry to their native culture. This occurs
when people discover that things changed while they were away. This is sometimes
called *re-entry shock*.

D Although it is nearly impossible to avoid culture shock, there are things people can do
in order to ease the stress they experience as a result of it. Here are a few suggestions   30
that may help. Be patient. It's important to remember that adjusting to a new culture
is a process that takes time. Maintain contact with the new culture by learning the
language and getting involved in the community. Set some simple goals for yourself
to help you see your progress. Remember that although living in a new culture can be
very difficult, it can also be very rewarding!   35

Source:http://edweb.sdsu.edu/people/CGuanipa/cultshok.htm

1. What is the main idea of the reading passage?
- Ⓐ Culture shock caused anxiety.
- Ⓑ New places and cultures are very exciting at first.
- Ⓒ Culture shock cannot be avoided.
- Ⓓ There are different stages of culture shock.

2. The first stage of culture shock is sometimes referred to as the "honeymoon stage" because _____
- Ⓐ people often spend their honeymoons in other countries.
- Ⓑ everything is exciting and new.
- Ⓒ there are lots of exotic flowers.
- Ⓓ there are lots of everyday miscommunications.

3. According to the reading passage, people generally start feeling a sense of disconnectedness during the _____ stage of culture shock.
- Ⓐ first
- Ⓑ second
- Ⓒ third
- Ⓓ fourth

4. According to the reading passage, what do people often discover during the fifth stage of culture shock?
- Ⓐ Things about their native culture changed while they were away.
- Ⓑ They can no longer communicate in their native language.
- Ⓒ They preferred the food in the "new" culture.
- Ⓓ Their native culture seems boring and unfriendly.

5. Which of the items below does the reading passage NOT give as a suggestion for easing the stress of culture shock?
- Ⓐ be patient
- Ⓑ maintain contact with the new culture
- Ⓒ set simple goals for yourself
- Ⓓ avoid taking public transportation

Section II Strategies Use the context and your knowledge of word forms to choose the best meanings for the words in italics. **(5 points each)**

1. In paragraph A, the word *coined* probably means _____.
- Ⓐ bought
- Ⓑ changed
- Ⓒ invented
- Ⓓ described

2. In paragraph A, the word *thrilling* probably means _____.
- Ⓐ very exciting
- Ⓑ difficult
- Ⓒ strange
- Ⓓ humorous

3. In paragraph B, the word *irritating* probably means _____.

   (A) new

   (B) disorienting

   (C) calming

   (D) annoying

4. In paragraph D, the word *goals* means _____.

   (A) points

   (B) objectives

   (C) customs

   (D) ideas

5. In paragraph D, the word *rewarding* means _____.

   (A) hopeless

   (B) shocking

   (C) exciting

   (D) satisfying

Section III New Words Match the words on the left with their synonyms in the right column.
(4 points each)

_____ **1.** colleague   **a.** end result

_____ **2.** despair   **b.** always, continually

_____ **3.** outcome   **c.** unbelievable

_____ **4.** inconceivable   **d.** opinion

_____ **5.** irrational   **e.** alert

_____ **6.** bias   **f.** receptive to new ideas

_____ **7.** open-minded   **g.** the beliefs and ways of life of a group of people

_____ **8.** culture   **h.** a feeling of being without hope

_____ **9.** aware   **i.** without reason or logic

_____ **10.** constantly   **j.** someone you work with

Section IV Building Vocabulary Add a negating prefix to the following words to change their meanings. **(2 points each)**

1. happy: _____

2. decisive: _____

3. aware: _____

4. honest: _____

5. accurate: _____

TOTAL _____/100 pts.

Chapter 10 Test

Frank W. Abagnale

Section I Reading Comprehension Read the passage. Then answer the questions that follow. **(5 points each)**

A   Frank W. Abagnale has been affiliated with the FBI (Federal Bureau of Investigation) and is one of the world's most renowned authorities on money-related crimes. For over thirty years, he has acted as a consultant and has given numerous lectures on how to prevent money-related crimes to businesses and government agencies around the world.

5

B   How did Abagnale become such an authority on these subjects? Strangely enough, he gained his keen insight into these topics by committing numerous money-related crimes himself. When he was 16, his parents got divorced. Shortly afterwards, he left home and went to New York on his own where he managed to get a job and open a bank account. Soon after, he committed his first crime, which involved writing bad checks against his own account. He made out several checks for more money than he had in his checking account. Because he knew that it was only a matter of time before his bank demanded that he pay the amount he owed, he opened new accounts at several other banks under different identities.

10

C   As time went on, he came up with various clever ways to defraud banks. For example, he printed his own checks and convinced banks to cash them. He also took deposit slips from the bank, wrote his name on blank deposit slips and placed them back in the stack of blank ones, so when customers filled out deposit slips to deposit money into their accounts, the money went into his account instead of theirs. It is said that during a mere five year period, he managed to cash approximately 2.5 million dollars in forged checks. He supposedly cashed checks in every state in the United States and in 26 other countries!

15

20

D   Eventually, Abagnale's luck ran out and he was arrested in France at the age of 21. He was sent to Perpignan's House of Arrest where he spent six months in squalid conditions and became very ill. Eventually, he ended up back in the United States to serve a 12-year prison sentence. However, halfway through his sentence he was released on the terms that he would use his "special talents" to assist the federal government and law enforcement agencies free of charge. He assisted these agencies by lecturing and teaching their employees how to prevent money-related crimes.

25

E   Now over 30 years later, he is still associated with the FBI. In the meantime, he founded Abagnale & Associates, an organization that advises banks and various other businesses on fraud. He has written several popular books including *Catch Me If You Can*, which was made into a movie starring Leonardo DiCaprio and Tom Hanks. Frank W. Abagnale is now a multimillionaire from the money he has earned from his books and consulting business.

30

35

Sources: http://www.abagnale.com/aboutfrank.htm
http://en.wikipedia.org/wiki/Frank_Abagnale

1. What is the main idea of the reading passage?

    (A) Frank W. Abagnale wrote fraudulent checks all over the world.

    (B) Frank W. Abagnale has used his personal experience to help government agencies and businesses prevent fraud.

    (C) Frank W. Abagnale has written several best-selling books, including *Catch Me If You Can*.

    (D) Frank W. Abagnale was very good at defrauding people.

2. According to the reading, which of the choices describes something that Abagnale did NOT do in order to defraud banks?

    (A) He printed his own checks and cashed them.

    (B) He opened several accounts at different banks.

    (C) He withdrew real money and photocopied it.

    (D) He wrote his account number on deposit slips.

3. Abagnale cashed bad checks in how many countries outside the United States?

    (A) 16

    (B) 26

    (C) 30

    (D) 12

4. Why was Abagnale released from prison early?

    (A) Because he had to serve another prison sentence in France.

    (B) So he could write books and make movies about his crimes.

    (C) Because he convinced authorities that he did not commit the crimes.

    (D) So that he could help government and law enforcement agencies.

5. How long has Abagnale been assisting the FBI?

    (A) over 30 years

    (B) 12 years

    (C) 26 years

    (D) Since he was 16

Section II Strategies Use the context and your knowledge of word forms to choose the best meanings for the words in italics. **(5 points each)**

1. In paragraph A, *renowned* probably means _____.

    (A) well-known

    (B) intelligent

    (C) wealthy

    (D) helpful.

2. In paragraph B, *keen* probably means _____.

    (A) fast

    (B) evil

    (C) very good

    (D) criminal

3. In paragraph C, *clever* probably means _____.

    Ⓐ inexpensive

    Ⓑ famous

    Ⓒ quick

    Ⓓ skillful

4. In paragraph C, *mere* probably means _____.

    Ⓐ long

    Ⓑ short

    Ⓒ difficult

    Ⓓ approximate

5. In paragraph D, *squalid* probably means _____.

    Ⓐ dangerous

    Ⓑ strange

    Ⓒ very dirty

    Ⓓ comfortable

Section III New Words Fill in the blanks with the correct word. **(4 points each)**

accessory	backslide	clean-cut	deliberated	responds
addled	burly	credits	draft	warily

1. Whenever the teacher asks a question, Seth does two things before he _____.

He thinks about his answer and he raises his hand.

2. Although Monique did not commit the crime, she was arrested for being an _____

to the crime, because she let the thief stay in her home after the robbery and did not call the police.

3. Nobody could believe that Thomas was the murderer based on his _____

appearance. He had short hair and no facial hair, and he dressed very conservatively.

4. The jury _____ for three days before all twelve members agreed that the accused

man was innocent.

5. Although she studied a lot for the test, she _____ her tutor for teaching her some

helpful ways of remembering new vocabulary words. Without her tutor, she might not have done as

well on the exam.

6. Sue helped me _____ an outline for my paper. Now I will be able to do the

research and write a complete essay.

7. Once they are released from prison, many criminals _____ because they are

unable change their criminal tendencies and end up back in prison.

8. The fact that their car had been stolen _____ their minds so much, that they were

unable to fill out the police report properly.

9. The movie star was accompanied by three _____ body guards, so nobody dared

approach her for her autograph or to take photos.

10. When Carla heard the knock at her door, she opened it _____ as it was late at night

and she wasn't expecting anyone.

Part IV Building vocabulary Match the descriptive adverbs with their definitions. **(2 points each)**

_____ **1.** abruptly   **a.** directly

_____ **2.** nervously   **b.** fast

_____ **3.** personally   **c.** unexpectedly

_____ **4.** quickly   **d.** cautiously

_____ **5.** suspiciously   **e.** anxiously

TOTAL _____ /100 pts.

Chapter 1 Test Answer Key

Section I

1. C 2. D 3. B 4. A 5. C

Section II

1. D 2. B 3. D 4. B 5. D

Section III

1. menial 2. symbol 3. outgoing 4. heritage
5. restless 6. vastness 7. brevity 8. blunt 9. leisure
10. gardener

Section IV

1. anti-business 2. non-French 3. anti-noise 4. a non-singing 5. nonstandard 6. anti-city 7. anti-pollution
8. nonstop 9. anti-cancer 10. Noncredit

Chapter 2 Test Answer Key

Section I

1. C 2. B 3. C 4. B 5. D

Section II

1. A 2. C 3. C 4. D 5. C

Section III

1. vicious 2. nondescript 3. job 4. revenues 5. V.P.
6. global 7. leading-edge 8. low-end 9. ascend
10. get the drift

Section IV

1. T 2. T 3. T 4. T 5. F 6. F 7. T 8. T 9. F 10. F

Chapter 3 Test Answer Key

Section I

1. C 2. C 3. A 4. D 5. A

Section II

1. B 2. C 3. A 4. A 5. D

Section III

1. d 2. g 3. c 4. h 5. b 6. i 7. a 8. j 9. f 10. e

Section IV

1. A 2. C 3. D 4. B 5. C

Chapter 4 Test Answer Key

Section I

1. D 2. A 3. C 4. C 5. C

Section II

1. A 2. A 3. B 4. B 5. A

Section III

1. benefits 2. communities 3. compensation
4. virtually 5. physical 6. prevent 7. affluent
8. found 9. acquiring 10. hence

Section IV

1. a 2. d 3. e 4. c 5. b

Chapter 5 Test Answer Key

Section I

1. C 2. A 3. D 4. B 5. C

Section II

1. A 2. B 3. D 4. C 5. D

Section III

1. e 2. g 3. i 4. d 5. c 6. j 7. h 8. b 9. a 10. f

Section IV

1. handmade 2. worn out 3. machine-washable
4. well-read 5. small-scale 6. newlywed 7. timepiece
8. home-based 9. top hat 10. speedway

Chapter 6 Test Answer Key

Section I

1. B 2. D 3. C 4. B 5. D

Section II

1. A 2. C 3. B 4. C 5. D

Section III

1. enormous 2. inclined 3. convenience 4. mentality
5. anticipated 6. succulent 7. affordable 8. amicable
9. transform 10. specialties

Section IV

1. d 2. c 3. b 4. e 5. a

Chapter 7 Test Answer Key

Section I

1. C 2. A 3. B 4. D 5. A

Section II

1. C 2. D 3. D 4. B 5. A

Section III

1. influential 2. suppress 3. resigned 4. compelling
5. founded 6. commoners 7. seized 8. role 9. atone
10. permeated

Section IV

1. drugstore 2. unfinished 3. reread 4. outdoors
5. backyard 6. defender 7. overpriced 8. decision
9. sportswear 10. anti-war

Chapter 8 Test Answer Key

Section I

1. C 2. B 3. C 4. A 5. D

Section II

1. C 2. B 3. B 4. A 5. A

Section III

1. circuitous 2. compulsory 3. dabbled 4. continually
5. ambition 6. pioneer 7. funds 8. critical acclaim
9. experiment 10. demonstrate

Section IV

1. c 2. b 3. e 4. d 5. a

Chapter 9 Test Answer Key

Section 1

1. D 2. B 3. B 4. A 5. D

Section 2

1. C 2. A 3. D 4. B 5. D

Section 3

1. j 2. h 3. a 4. c 5. i 6. d 7. f 8. g 9. e 10. b

Section IV

1. unhappy

2. indecisive

3. unaware

4. dishonest

5. inaccurate

Chapter 10 Test Answer Key

Section I

1. B 2. C 3. B 4. D 5. A

Section II

1. A 2. C 3. D 4. B 5. C

Section III

1. responds 2. accessory 3. clean-cut 4. deliberated
5. credits 6. draft 7. backslide 8. addled 9. burly
10. warily

Section IV

1. c 2. e 3. a 4. b 5. d

Reading Strand Placement Test
Vocabulary Section

Vocabulary I Choose the best word to complete each sentence. (**2 points each**)

Example: Brazil and Argentina are the largest _____ in South America.
- (A) categories
- (B) cities
- (C) countries
- (D) neighborhoods

1. No one lives with Rosa in her apartment. She lives _____.
- (A) alone
- (B) lonely
- (C) only
- (D) together

2. Tom's family has 3 children, Amy's family has 3 children, Reina's family has 2 children, and Ben's family has 2 children. The _____ number of children in these families is 2.5.
- (A) small
- (B) average
- (C) equal
- (D) total

3. When teachers speak too softly and rapidly, it is _____ for their students to understand them.
- (A) easy
- (B) little
- (C) different
- (D) difficult

4. In many cultures, women do most of the _____. For example, they clean the floors and wash the clothes for their families.
- (A) farming
- (B) homework
- (C) housework
- (D) cooking

5. Mr. Lee's restaurant is successful because he always waits on his _____ politely and serves them wonderful meals.
- (A) customs
- (B) customers
- (C) consumers
- (D) users

6. In a basketball game, two teams _____ against each other to score points by throwing a ball into a basket.
- Ⓐ compete
- Ⓑ cooperate
- Ⓒ complete
- Ⓓ exercise

7. In this country doctors usually have high _____, or position in the society.
- Ⓐ profession
- Ⓑ situation
- Ⓒ state
- Ⓓ status

8. Many companies in the computer industry were started by very young people. For example, Bill Gates was only twenty years old when he and Paul Allen _____ the Microsoft Corporation in 1975.
- Ⓐ based
- Ⓑ discovered
- Ⓒ located
- Ⓓ founded

9. _____ up to 20% is customary in U.S. restaurants. Some places even add 15% to the bill for all parties of six or more.
- Ⓐ Waiting
- Ⓑ Tipping
- Ⓒ Buying
- Ⓓ Eating

10. I wouldn't go to the new mall just yet. If you can _____ another week or two, until the Grand Opening is over, the crowds will be much more manageable.
- Ⓐ hold out
- Ⓑ hold up
- Ⓒ wait on
- Ⓓ hold onto

Vocabulary II Read each item and then answer the vocabulary question below it. **(2 points each)**

Example: The city government recently announced plans to build a new road through Mountain Dale, a beautiful neighborhood on the south side of the city. The residents of Mountain Dale are angry about the road. Yesterday a group of them went to a meeting at City Hall to express their *views* on the city's plans.

Which of the following is closest in meaning to *views* as it is used above?
- Ⓐ pictures
- **Ⓑ opinions**
- Ⓒ sights
- Ⓓ beautiful scenery

1. The brain is divided into many parts. Each part serves specific and important functions. The cerebrum is the largest and most complex *area* of the brain. It controls thought, learning, and many other activities.
   Which of the following is closest in meaning to *area* as it is used above?
   - (A) the size of a surface, calculated by multiplying the length by the width
   - (B) a particular subject or group of related subjects
   - (C) a particular part or section
   - (D) a part of an activity or a thought

2. By studying the pyramids of Egypt, researchers have learned a great deal about ancient Egyptian *culture*. They have discovered, for example, that different social classes existed even in the earliest cities.
   Which of the following is closest in meaning to *culture* as it is used above?
   - (A) activities that are related to art, music, and literature
   - (B) a society that existed at a particular time in history
   - (C) a scientific experiment of people from a particular country
   - (D) education of people in a certain social group

3. Timothy is going to ride his bike around the world. In order to see all the countries and sights he wants to, before he begins his adventure, he will *map* his route.
   Which of the following is the closest in meaning to *map* as used above?
   - (A) to pack bags for a trip
   - (B) to plan the path of a trip
   - (C) to prepare a bicycle for a trip
   - (D) to talk about something

4. With today's computer networks, the *transmission* of data from one place in the world to another can happen instantly.
   Which of the following is closest in meaning to *transmission* as it is used above?
   - (A) the process of working together on the same computer network
   - (B) a job that involves traveling from one place to another
   - (C) the set of parts of a vehicle that take power from the engine to the wheels
   - (D) the process of sending information using electronic equipment

5. Roger has some annoying tendencies. For one thing, he's *inclined* to talk about himself and his achievements.
   Which of the following is closest in meaning to *inclined* as it is used above?
   - (A) bending forward to say something
   - (B) likely to do something or behave in a particular way
   - (C) holding a particular opinion
   - (D) talking a lot about the same thing

6. At medical centers throughout the United States, researchers are *conducting* investigations into the causes of heart disease.
   Which of the following is closest in meaning to *conducting* as it is used above?
   - (A) carrying out an activity or process in order to get information or prove facts
   - (B) directing the playing of an orchestra, band, etc.
   - (C) carrying something like electricity or heat to cure heart disease
   - (D) guiding or leading someone somewhere

7. In recent years, it seems that headlines and articles about war and violence have *occupied* the front pages of newspapers everywhere.

Which of the following is closest in meaning to *occupied* as it is used above?

- (A) taken up time
- (B) lived in a place
- (C) controlled a place by military force
- (D) filled a particular amount of space

8. Studies in public schools have shown that *exposure* to art and music has many benefits for children. It improves their literacy, critical thinking, and math skills.

Which of the following is closest in meaning to *exposure* as it is used above?

- (A) a situation in which someone is not protected from risk or danger
- (B) attention that someone gets from newspapers, television, etc.
- (C) the chance to experience something
- (D) the act of showing something that is usually hidden

9. Ronald and James are roommates in a university dormitory. They have frequent arguments because Ronald prefers to go to sleep early and James always stays up late. Also, Ronald likes quiet while he studies, but James insists that loud music helps him concentrate. How can James and Ronald *resolve* these conflicts?

Which of the following is closest in meaning to *resolve* as it is used above?

- (A) make a definite decision to do something
- (B) solve again using new techniques
- (C) gradually change into something else
- (D) find a satisfactory way of dealing with a problem or difficulty

10. It is important that students learn to read and write before they go to college. In particular, they need to practice reading on their own and learn how to write a *succinct* and logical argument.

Which of the following is the closest in meaning to *succinct* as used above?

- (A) taking a long time to explain
- (B) correct
- (C) original
- (D) clearly and concisely expressed

Reading Section

Directions: Read each passage and answer the questions below it. **(2 points each)**

Reading Passage I

A How do you react to the taste of different foods, like coffee or lemon? Do they have a flavor that you like? Or do they taste very strong to you? Why do people react differently to different flavors?

B We all know that different people have different food preferences. Researchers have discovered some reasons for these differences. Your culture and your life experience are partly responsible for your preferences for certain foods. Your food preferences are also partly genetic. (Your genetic preferences are the ones that you were born with.) In order to discover people's genetic preferences, researchers use a chemical called PROP. People taste it and respond to the taste. To some people, PROP has no flavor. The researchers classify these people as "nontasters." To other people, the flavor of PROP is a little bitter, or sharp. These people are "tasters." Then there are the people who can't stand the flavor of PROP. They find it to be unbearably bitter. These people are the "supertasters." Tasters have more taste buds on their tongues than nontasters do, and supertasters have many more taste buds than tasters do. This explains why supertasters are more sensitive to PROP and to the flavors in certain foods. So if you think the flavors in coffee, grapefruit juice, and broccoli are very strong, you may be a "supertaster."

Example: The topic of the reading passage is _____.
- Ⓐ the flavor of coffee
- Ⓑ becoming a supertaster
- **Ⓒ differences in people's taste sensitivity**
- Ⓓ research in the flavor of different foods

1. The main idea of the reading is that _____.
- Ⓐ there are people who like different foods
- Ⓑ there are cultural and genetic reasons for the differences in people's food preferences
- Ⓒ some foods have a very strong flavor
- Ⓓ PROPs can be used to identify different types of tastes

2. The meaning of *genetic* preferences is _____.
- Ⓐ preferences for certain foods
- Ⓑ preferences researchers have discovered
- Ⓒ the preferences of some people
- Ⓓ the preferences that people are born with

3. What is PROP?
- Ⓐ a chemical
- Ⓑ something that people are born with
- Ⓒ a discovery
- Ⓓ a researcher

4. Why do researchers use PROP?
   - (A) because it has no flavor
   - (B) to find out the responses to foods people were born with
   - (C) to discover the flavors in certain foods
   - (D) because people like its flavor

5. A food that is bitter has _____.
   - (A) no flavor
   - (B) little flavor
   - (C) a coffee flavor
   - (D) a sharp flavor

6. People who _____ are classified as *supertasters*.
   - (A) can't stand the flavor of PROP
   - (B) think that PROP has no flavor
   - (C) think that PROP tastes a little bitter
   - (D) like bitter flavors

7. Taste buds are probably _____.
   - (A) tiny pieces of food
   - (B) the small bumps on the surface of people's tongues
   - (C) chemicals in food that give it its flavor
   - (D) something in broccoli, grapefruit juice, and coffee

Reading Passage 2

A   After a cold, snowy winter, many people look forward to the long hot days of summer. The normal heat of summer can be pleasant. However, it's important to be aware that excessive—that is, too much—heat can be dangerous. There are other summer weather dangers, for example, tornadoes, lightning, and floods, but excessive heat kills more people each year than any of these. According to meteorologists (weather scientists), a heat wave is a period of excessive heat that lasts two days or more. A heat wave stresses people and can cause illnesses. These illnesses include heat cramps, heat exhaustion, and heat stroke. The people who are at the greatest risk during heat waves are the elderly, babies, and those with serious diseases.

B   High humidity (moisture in the air) can make the effects of heat even more harmful. As humidity increases, the air seems warmer than it actually is because it's more difficult for the body to cool itself through the evaporation of perspiration. During heat waves, meteorologists use the heat index to determine the level of danger. The heat index measures how hot it really feels when high humidity is added to the actual air temperature. As an example, if the air temperature is 95° F (Fahrenheit) and the humidity is 35%, the heat index is 98° F. But if the air temperature is 95° F and the humidity is 70%, the heat index is 124° F. Doctors say that even young, healthy people can die of heat stroke if they exercise outside when the heat index is high. During a heat wave, it's best to take it easy, drink plenty of water, and stay out of the heat as much as possible.

1. The main idea of Paragraph A is that _____.
   - (A) people look forward to the long hot days of summer
   - (B) too much heat can have dangerous effects
   - (C) tornadoes, lightning, and floods are dangerous
   - (D) meteorologists can define heat waves

2. The main idea of Paragraph B is that _____.
   - (A) humidity is moisture in the air
   - (B) meteorologists use the heat index during heat waves
   - (C) high humidity increases the danger of high air temperatures
   - (D) it's important to stay inside during a heat wave

3. The word *excessive* means _____.
   - (A) too much
   - (B) important
   - (C) long
   - (D) coming in waves

4. In the passage, lightning is mentioned as an example of _____.
   - (A) excessive heat
   - (B) a storm
   - (C) a stress on people
   - (D) a summer weather danger

5. A meteorologist is _____.
   - (A) a doctor
   - (B) a weather scientist
   - (C) a space scientist
   - (D) a dangerous weather condition

6. The heat index measures _____.
   - (A) the amount of moisture in the air
   - (B) air temperature
   - (C) a person's body temperature
   - (D) the temperature the body feels when heat and humidity are combined

7. Based on the information in the passage, which statement is true?
   - (A) Young, healthy people are more likely to die from excessive heat than elderly people are.
   - (B) The elderly, babies, and people with serious diseases are most likely to die from excessive heat, but it can kill young, healthy people, too.
   - (C) Perspiration is a dangerous effect of excessive heat.
   - (D) All heat waves include high humidity.

8. Why did the author write this passage?
   - (A) To warn people about the dangers of excessive heat and give suggestions about avoiding them.
   - (B) To give people useful information about the weather in the summer.
   - (C) To describe the work of meteorologists and their use of the heat index.
   - (D) To let people know how the body can cool itself naturally.

Reading Passage 3

A Even though education is compulsory (required by law) for children in the United States, it is not compulsory for them to go to a conventional school to get that education. In every one of the 50 states, it is legal for parents to educate their children at home, or to "home school" their children. Although no state requires parents to have special training to home school their children, the regulations parents must follow vary widely from state to state. New Jersey, for example, imposes virtually no requirements. In contrast, New York requires home schoolers to notify their school districts, file instructional plans and frequent reports, and submit the results of tests or other forms of assessment for each child.

B Increasing numbers of American families have been opting for home schooling. According to the National Center for Educational Statistics, about 1.1 million children were being home schooled in the spring of 2003. This represents an increase from the 850,000 who were being home schooled in the spring of 1999. In addition, the home-schooling rate—the percentage of the school-age population that was being home schooled—increased from 1.7 percent in 1999 to 2.2 percent in 2003.

C A survey conducted in 2003 asked parents to give their most important reasons for home schooling their children. Thirty-one percent cited concerns about the environment in conventional schools, including safety, drugs, or negative peer pressure. Thirty percent said that the most important reason was to provide religious or moral instruction. Sixteen percent said that the most important reason was dissatisfaction with academic instruction at conventional schools. Parents gave other reasons, too; for instance, many said that they wanted to strengthen family bonds or allow their children more freedom.

D It is difficult to show whether conventional schooling or home schooling works better. Home-schooled children tend to score significantly higher than the national average on college entrance tests. But educators say that it isn't easy to determine how meaningful the figures are, given the complexities of making direct comparisons. In the debate about home schooling, socialization is more of an issue than achievement. Advocates of conventional education believe that home-schooled children are at a disadvantage because they miss out on the kinds of social interaction and relationships with peers that are an essential part of a total education. Advocates of home schooling say that home-schooled children are not socially isolated; they think that home-schooled children have a larger social structure because they can be out in the world, in contact with people of different ages, and having experiences that they could never have in conventional schools.

Directions: For each question, choose the best answer based on the reading passage.

1. The word *conventional* means _____.
   - (A) relating to a meeting
   - (B) following what is normal or usual
   - (C) following a religion
   - (D) educational

2. According to the passage, increasing numbers of American families are choosing home schooling. What information does the author give to support this statement?
   - (A) In every one of the 50 states, it is legal for parents to educate their children at home.
   - (B) Thirty-one percent of parents say that the most important reason for home schooling is concerns about the environment in conventional schools.
   - (C) The number of children who were being home schooled increased from 850,000 in 1999 to about 1.1 million in 2003.
   - (D) A survey was conducted in 2003.

3. Scan (look quickly through) the passage to find the answer to this question: How many of the parents surveyed in 2003 said that the most important reason for home schooling their children was dissatisfaction with academic instruction at conventional schools?
   - (A) 1.1 million
   - (B) 30 percent
   - (C) 16 percent
   - (D) 2.2 percent

4. Three of the following statements give facts, and one gives an opinion. Based on the reading passage, which one is the opinion?
   - (A) Home-schooled children are at a disadvantage because they miss out on some kinds of social interaction and relationships.
   - (B) Thirty percent of parents who home school their children said that the most important reason was to provide religious or moral instruction.
   - (C) The home-schooling rate increased from 1.7 percent in 1999 to 2.2 percent in 2003.
   - (D) The regulations that parents of home schoolers must follow vary widely from state to state.

5. Which paragraph gives information about the number of home-schooled children who attend college?
   - (A) Paragraph B
   - (B) Paragraph C
   - (C) Paragraph D
   - (D) That information is not given in the passage.

6. In Paragraph D, the author implies, but does not state directly, that _____.
   - (A) home-schooled children tend to score significantly higher than the national average on college entrance tests
   - (B) it should be easy to make direct comparisons between conventional and home schooling
   - (C) parents are not academically qualified to teach their children
   - (D) there is controversy about the benefits of home schooling

7. Based on Paragraph D, we can conclude that advocates of conventional education object to home schooling mainly because home-schooled children _____.
   - (A) cannot achieve academically
   - (B) cannot be compared to conventionally educated children
   - (C) are not well socialized
   - (D) have too much freedom

Reading Passage 4

A   In recent years, the game of golf and golf tourism have grown in popularity in many places in the world. Golf, which traces its roots back to 15th century Scotland, is often viewed as a pleasant and harmless way to relax in a natural setting. But golf courses are not natural developments. They are artificial constructions that have a big environmental impact. As a result, there is often controversy about the building of golf courses.

B   Opponents of the use of land for golf courses bring up a number of environmental concerns. One is that a golf course covers a great deal of land, typically up to 200 acres, and in the process of developing this land into a golf course, it is common for fragile native ecosystems such as wetlands, rainforests, or coastal dunes to be destroyed. Indigenous grasses, shrubs, and trees are removed and replaced by foreign vegetation. The construction process causes soil erosion and results in the loss of biodiversity and habitat for wildlife. Another concern is the amount of chemical pesticides, herbicides, and fertilizers used to maintain the grass on a golf course once it is established. These chemicals can result in toxic contamination of the air, the soil, the surface water, and the underground water, and this in turn leads to health problems for people who live near the course or downstream from it, for people who work at the course, and even for the golfers. Yet another concern is that golf courses require an enormous amount of water every day. Their water consumption can lead to depletion of scarce fresh water resources. These and other concerns about golf courses have provoked protests, most recently in east and southeast Asia, against planned golf projects.

C   Designers, developers, and operators of golf courses have become increasingly aware of the environmental issues and of the protests. Consequently, they have sponsored research into more environmentally sensitive ways of constructing and maintaining courses. They believe that it is possible to build golf courses which protect and preserve the natural features of the landscape and natural habitats for wildlife. Their suggested practices include using native trees and shrubs, planting types of grass that require less water and are best adapted to the local climate, and using reclaimed water. Proponents of golf courses believe that these "green" golf courses can actually provide environmental benefits to their sites.

D   However, even a "green" golf course is likely to result in some environmental degradation and loss of habitat. Therefore, many biologists and wildlife ecologists, such as Lawrence Woolbright, a professor at Siena College in Albany, New York, contend that the best places to construct new golf courses are places that are already degraded, such as former landfills (garbage dumps) and old industrial sites, rather than on undeveloped land. A golf course that transforms a degraded site into a scenic landscape with wetlands and woodlands and habitat for wildlife could actually be a benefit to the environment.

1. Which of the following is the best statement of the main idea of the reading passage?
   - (A) Golf courses are artificial constructions, and are often built with no regard for the environment.
   - (B) Controversies about golf courses affect the tourist trade.
   - (C) Golf courses have significant effects on the environment, and these effects lead to controversy.
   - (D) Golf and golf tourism are growing in popularity internationally, leading to a more negative effect on the environment.

2. What word is opposite in meaning to the word *indigenous*?
- Ⓐ native
- Ⓑ foreign
- Ⓒ natural
- Ⓓ vegetation

3. Which of the following is *not* mentioned in the passage as a negative environmental impact of a golf course?
- Ⓐ the destruction of fragile native ecosystems
- Ⓑ soil erosion caused by cutting down trees
- Ⓒ pollution caused by traffic and maintenance equipment
- Ⓓ depletion of scarce fresh water resources

4. Which of the following best summarizes the environmental concerns of opponents of the use of land for golf courses?
- Ⓐ They are concerned about the amount of land that a golf course covers.
- Ⓑ They are concerned about the impact of the process of constructing new golf courses.
- Ⓒ They are concerned about the impact of the maintenance of established golf courses.
- Ⓓ All of the above.

5. Based on Paragraphs C and D, we can infer that a "green" golf course is one that _____.
- Ⓐ consumes a great deal of water
- Ⓑ is environmentally sensitive
- Ⓒ is new and not degraded
- Ⓓ has grass, shrubs, and trees

6. Based on the information in Paragraph C, we can conclude that _____.
- Ⓐ it is certain that "green" golf courses have already been built
- Ⓑ it is certain that "green" golf courses will be built in the future
- Ⓒ it is not certain that any "green" golf courses have already been built or will be built in the future
- Ⓓ opponents of golf courses accept the idea that "green" golf courses can actually provide environmental benefits to their sites

7. Based on Paragraph D, we can infer that the author of the passage _____.
- Ⓐ agrees with Lawrence Woolbright
- Ⓑ disagrees with Lawrence Woolbright
- Ⓒ is willing to accept some environmental degradation and loss of habitat
- Ⓓ is opposed to all golf courses

8. What would be an appropriate title for this reading passage?
- Ⓐ A Brief History of Golf
- Ⓑ Golf's Dirty Side
- Ⓒ Why Make Golf Green?
- Ⓓ The Beauty of Golf

Answer Key for Reading Strand Placement Test

Vocabulary I

1. A 2. B 3. D 4. C 5. B 6. A 7. D 8. D 9. B 10. A

Vocabulary II

1. C 2. B 3. B 4. D 5. B 6. A 7. D 8. C 9. D 10. D

Reading Passage 1

1. B 2. D 3. A 4. B 5. D 6. A 7. B

Reading Passage 2

1. B 2. C 3. A 4. D 5. B 6. D 7. B 8. B

Reading Passage 3

1. B 2. C 3. C 4. A 5. D 6. D 7. C

Reading Passage 4

1. C 2. B 3. C 4. D 5. B 6. C 7. A 8. C

SCORING FOR INTERACTIONS/MOSAIC READING PLACEMENT TEST	
Score	**Placement**
0–40	Interactions Access
41–55	Interactions 1
56–70	Interactions 2
71–85	Mosaic 1
86–100	Mosaic 2

This is a rough guide. Teachers should use their judgment in placing students and selecting texts.